THE STANDING BEAR CONTROVERSY

THE STANDING BEAR CONTROVERSY

Prelude to Indian Reform

VALERIE SHERER MATHES
AND RICHARD LOWITT

UNIVERSITY OF ILLINOIS PRESS

Urbana and Chicago

© 2003 by the Board of Trustees
of the University of Illinois
All rights reserved
Manufactured in the United States of America
C 5 4 3 2 1

∞ This book is printed on acid-free paper.

Library of Congress Cataloging-in-Publication Data
Mathes, Valerie Sherer, 1941–
The Standing Bear controversy : prelude to Indian reform /
Valerie Sherer Mathes and Richard Lowitt.
    p.   cm.
Includes bibliographical references and index.
ISBN 0-252-02852-X (cloth : alk. paper)
1. Ponca Indians—Relocation. 2. Standing Bear, Ponca chief.
3. Indians of North America—Government relations.
4. Indians of North America—Legal status, laws, etc.
I. Lowitt, Richard, 1922– II. Title.
E99.P7M17   2003
978'.004975—dc21   2002155077

To Pamela Herr
and
Gene M. Gressley

CONTENTS

Illustrations follow page 62

ACKNOWLEDGMENTS

In the course of our research, we have incurred numerous debts. Our heart-felt thanks to the staff members at the Nebraska State Historical Society and to the librarians at the Sonoma Valley Regional Library, the Rosenberg Library at City College of San Francisco, the University of Nebraska, the University of Oklahoma, and the law schools at the latter two institutions. Also thanks must go to lawyers in the Clerk's Office at the Federal District Court in Omaha and the archivist at the Federal Records Center in Kansas City who provided us with documents to a Dundy decision not found in any case book. We also examined materials from other repositories: the Library of Congress, the National Archives, and the United States Military Academy.

We owe a particular debt of gratitude to Robert L. Olson in Niobrara, Nebraska. At the end of the day as he was about to close his municipal office, he took the time to answer our questions, photocopy relevant material, and provide us with a map and other materials that guided us to Ponca sites in the surrounding area.

Richard Lowitt thanks his colleague William T. Hagan of the University of Oklahoma and John Lovett in the Western History Collection at the university. Lovett responded to numerous requests for obscure items with alacrity. Many of these requests were suggested by Hagan, who graciously answered questions and provided numerous bibliographical sources. Thanks are also extended to Paul Glad, a colleague, and to John Wunder of the University of Nebraska and Blue Clark of Oklahoma City University, both of whom explained the complexities involved in the question of Indian citizenship. Howard Meredith and Lee Hester, of the Indian Studies Program at the University of Science and Arts of Oklahoma, greatly expanded his knowledge of and sensitivity to things Indian. Finally a special debt of gratitude is extended to Barbara Perry, who transcribed an illegible scrawl into legible English.

Valerie Sherer Mathes's debt of gratitude extends over many years, beginning with her initial research on Helen Hunt Jackson's Indian reform in 1979. Through much of this research, Pamela Herr of Palo Alto has cheerfully guided her work on Jackson. Special thanks go to Margaret Szasz at the University of New Mexico, who made numerous suggestions that greatly improved the manuscript. In addition Charles Robinson III shared his extensive knowledge on General George Crook, and Nan Card, curator of manuscripts at the Rutherford B. Hayes Presidential Center, provided a better understanding of the president's role in the Ponca controversy. Others deserving of thanks include fellow Western Writers of America member Lou Rodenberg; Sonoma county author Mary Woodward Priest; and City College of San Francisco colleague Tim Killikelly. Finally, thanks must be extended to the American Philosophical Society for a grant from the Phillips Fund for Native American Research. This stipend made travel to distant research facilities possible.

Both authors want to thank the manuscript's readers for the University of Illinois Press, Blue Clark, Albert Hurtado, and Howard Meredith. A special note of appreciation is due our editor, Carol Bolton Betts, whose endeavors considerably improved our manuscript.

THE STANDING BEAR CONTROVERSY

PROLOGUE

In the spring of 1877, members of the Ponca tribe were arbitrarily removed to the Indian Territory by government officials. One of the chiefs, Standing Bear, attempted to lead a small group home to their reservation between the Missouri and Niobrara Rivers in present-day Nebraska, only to be arrested and detained at Fort Omaha. The ensuing courtroom drama and a subsequent lecture tour of eastern cities brought to American audiences the plight of this tribe as well as the problems facing other Indians.

Standing Bear had a pivotal role in the late nineteenth-century Indian reform movement. The outlines of his ordeal are known to scholars and readers of western history, but larger numbers of people from the Dakotas to Oklahoma are aware of him thanks to geographical features that bear his name—a bridge across the Missouri River near Niobrara, Nebraska, where his people made their home, and a small lake in the Papillon Creek project south of Omaha. There is a bust of him in the Oklahoma state capitol and a massive statue of him in Ponca City, Oklahoma, where the government forcibly relocated his people, even though the Ponca chief, having no desire to reside in the Indian Territory, walked back to his homeland. Through his resolve, he also walked into history. A man of few words, yet often eloquent, Standing Bear sparked a controversy that started with a fateful decision in a Nebraska courtroom, extended eastward to the nation's capital, and accelerated into a legal battle for Indian citizenship. In short, his actions led to the rise of a western-based reform movement that spread to the East and culminated several years later in the passage of the General Allotment Act, or Dawes Act, the most devastating piece of legislation affecting Indians in the history of the American republic.

The controversy launched by Standing Bear occurred as developments on the national scene prompted many Americans to reexamine the Indian question. Unfortunately the needs and desires of the Indians were lost in this process of reexamination. Nomadic Plains tribes wanted to continue to hunt the buffalo and practice the religious beliefs of their ancestors. White Americans wanted their land. The Red River War of 1874–75 had effectively forced Southern Plains tribes onto reservations while their northern brethren, the Lakotas and Northern Cheyennes, met the same fate following the Bighorn, Yellowstone, and Powder River expeditions of 1876. The defeat of these tribes prompted Lieutenant General Philip Sheridan, commander of the Division of the Missouri, which included the entire Plains region, to report in 1879 to the secretary of war that "there has been no general combination of hostile Indians in this military division during the past year, and I doubt that such combinations can ever exist again."[1] Peace now paved the way for government officials to encourage nomadic tribes to follow the sedentary, agricultural way of the Poncas and other village Plains tribes living on the eastern fringe.

In the post–Civil War period, the military frontier was rapidly being replaced by a farmers' frontier thanks to advancing railroads bringing in hordes of white settlers. But these same railroads could easily be employed to shift military units efficiently from one frontier post to another, enabling the army to amass large concentrations of troops either to remove various tribespeople to unwanted reservations and force them to remain there, or to pursue them if they fled. And flee they did, driven by hunger, disease, or a desire simply to return to former homelands or to secure new ones. The most notable examples were the Nez Perces, who in 1877 unsuccessfully fled toward Canada, and the Northern Cheyennes (1878) and the small party of Poncas (1879), who fled the Indian Territory and headed north.

Significantly, Standing Bear's long walk occurred just as the Civil War amendments to the federal Constitution accorded former slaves the rights and privileges of citizens. If the Indians of the Great Plains could find a place, as freedmen in the South had, as agrarian producers in this rapidly expanding economy, development in the West could proceed at an even quicker pace. Allotment of Indian lands in severalty would not only end the Indian practice of holding lands communally;[2] it would also allow investors, speculators, and other land grabbers to further the cause of an expanding capitalist economy under the umbrella of what many Americans at the time considered a fundamental reform of Indian policy. Senator Henry Laurens Dawes of Massachusetts, who came to public attention as a critic of the harsh treatment the Poncas received at the hands of officials of the Department of the Interior during the administration of Rutherford B. Hayes, became a leading supporter of allotment. Thanks to his role in a Senate investigation, Dawes assumed the reformer's mantle without losing support of the Boston Associates and other Massachusetts venture capitalists seeking further opportunities to assist big cattle outfits, mining syndicates, lumber combines, and others in developing western lands.

Thus, the decision of Judge Elmer Scipio Dundy in May 1879 to release Standing Bear appealed to a moral-reform sentiment that had been abating since Appomattox. Critics such as Henry Adams and the young Theodore Roosevelt attacked these reformers—many of them women and clergymen—as "sentimentalists." But the reform impulse cast a wide net, spreading into the highest realms of government and culminating in 1887 with the lone piece of legislation through which Senator Dawes is remembered today.

The first history of the Ponca removal was *The Ponca Chiefs: An Indian's Attempt to Appeal from the Tomahawks to the Courts,* written in 1880 by Zylyff, a pseudonym for the Omaha, Nebraska, journalist Thomas Henry Tibbles. A year later the New England–born poet and essayist Helen Hunt Jackson wrote an article on the Poncas in *A Century of Dishonor.* Thereafter little if anything was written about them until the 1930s; but from then on, articles on the tribe appeared in the *North Dakota Historical Quarterly, Mississippi Valley Historical Review, Nebraska History, Chronicles of Oklahoma, Journalist History, South Dakota History,* and *Montana, The Magazine of Western History* in almost every decade. In addition, authors of scholarly studies of the late nineteenth-century Indian reform movement, such as Loring Benson Priest (1942), Henry E. Fritz (1963), Francis Paul Prucha (1976), Robert H. Keller (1983), and Frederick E. Hoxie (1984), have made some mention of Standing Bear and the Poncas, while Robert Winston Mardock (1971) and John N. Coward (1999) included a full chapter on this subject in their books. Other books on the history of Nebraska and Indian Territory also include references, some lengthy, to the Ponca removal.

Therefore, we recognize that the tragedy of Ponca removal is well known to scholars and to readers of accounts of Indian-white relations. Our study probes more fully into the removal of the Poncas, the district court case of *Standing Bear v. Crook* (1879), and the lecture tour that publicized their tragedy to eastern audiences. But more important, in the second half of this study, we cover the role of the Boston Indian Citizenship Committee, the Senate committee hearings, the role of President Rutherford B. Hayes's commission, and finally the public conflict that erupted between Secretary Carl Schurz and Massachusetts Senator Henry Laurens Dawes.

While the Ponca controversy besmirched Schurz's reputation, which the secretary had gained largely as a leading proponent of good government and civil service reform, it advanced that of the Massachusetts senators. Dawes, who succeeded Charles Sumner, played the major role in the Senate hearings, while George Frisbie Hoar emerged as an early advocate of Indian citizenship and enjoyed a long career as a champion of good government and a critic of American expansion. At one point President Hayes considered calling for the resignation of Schurz. Instead, he appointed a commission to resolve the controversy, only to see its recommendation subverted by both the interior secretary and the Senate.

Our research leads us to suggest that Judge Dundy and the lawyers who defended Standing Bear, Andrew Jackson Poppleton and John Lee Webster, merit further attention, although we have not attempted to ascertain what impact their participation in Standing Bear's case had on their careers. All were prominent westerners. Poppleton, a former mayor of Omaha, at the time of the trial was the chief counsel of the Union Pacific Railroad. Webster, a promising young lawyer, along with Poppleton later argued for Indian citizenship in another important case.

We also argue that Indian reform had strong western roots, belying the conventional wisdom that it was generated by former abolitionists and other eastern humanitarians. The westerners who prompted the eastern reformers were led by Thomas Henry Tibbles and Susette La Flesche, or "Bright Eyes," the daughter of an Omaha chief. Accompanied by Standing Bear, Tibbles and La Flesche toured eastern cities to raise funds to bring the case before the Supreme Court. We portray Tibbles, who put his entire career on hold to aid the Poncas, in a much more sympathetic way than have previous authors.

Although Helen Hunt Jackson shared these reformers' outrage, we have relegated her to a minor role because her Indian reform activities have been well documented. It must be clearly understood, however, that once she had been introduced to Standing Bear, she changed the focus of her writing from travel pieces, poetry, and novels to what could be described as investigative reporting that alerted the reading public to the Indians' situation. Through her two Indian books, *A Century of Dishonor* and *Ramona*, still in print after more than a century, Jackson delineated the travesty apparent in the government's dealing with Indians and thus influenced others to join her cause.

The misfortune of the Poncas cast a long shadow. It colored the outlook of two venerable military leaders who pursued careers fighting Indians. Generals George Crook and Nelson A. Miles leveled criticism at the government's Indian policy largely as a result of their official contacts with Standing Bear and his people. Although we acknowledge their voices, we leave discussion of their roles as reformers to others more qualified.

The issues raised by *Standing Bear v. Crook* would reverberate across Indian country and the nation, leading to a dramatic change in federal Indian policy. The Ponca controversy, which began in the West with the local Omaha Ponca Relief Committee (also known as the Ponca Relief Committee), expanded eastward to become a public crusade leading most notably to the formation of the Boston Indian Citizenship Committee. Once westerners alerted eastern humanitarians to the condition of the Poncas, rising public awareness of federal treatment of Indians led to further reform organizations—the Women's National Indian Association, the Indian Rights Association, and the annual gathering known as the Lake Mohonk Conference.

In this manner the Ponca controversy, serving as a catalyst to nineteenth-century Indian reform, culminated in the passage in 1887 of the General Allotment Act sponsored by the Indians' champion in the United States Senate, Henry Laurens Dawes. The Dawes Act was viewed by reformers as espousing sound Gilded Age doctrine. It proclaimed virtues and values held dear by most Americans—laissez-faire, private property, and U.S. citizenship—and offered Indians assimilation to mainstream American life. In reality, the Dawes Act spelled disaster. Once allotments were made, the remaining reservation lands were thrown open to public sale resulting in the loss of more than ninety million acres. But more important, these new policies were initiated by government officials and reform organizations intent on remolding the Indian into a small independent husbandman. The Indians were never a part of the process; Indians were silent because they were not citizens and could not vote. Thus this legislation did not liberate them from dependence on the government, but instead pauperized them.

Notes

1. Hutton, *Phil Sheridan and His Army,* 331.
2. Severalty, or the possession of land individually, became a major component of this late nineteenth-century Indian reform movement.

PART ONE

In late December 1878, a sixteen-year-old Ponca boy died in the Indian Territory. His last wish was that his bones be buried in the land of his birth. His father, Chief Standing Bear, known to his people as *Ma-chu-nah-zha,* promised he would do so. "I could not refuse the dying request of my boy," the chief later remarked. "I have attempted to keep my word."[1] By honoring his promise to his son on January 2, 1879, Chief Standing Bear set in motion a sequence of events that influenced the lives of numerous prominent Americans, including two United States senators, a secretary of the interior, a western journalist, and a New England–born poet and author, and changed the lives of thousands of Indians whose future would be determined in part by the dramatic shifts in federal Indian policy that resulted.

By the end of the 1860s, endemic corruption in the Indian Office had been reinforced by a spoils system that encouraged the appointment of new Indian agents with each incoming administration. White settlers moving west seldom doubted their right to Indian lands and encroached upon them relentlessly. The removal of the regular army from western posts during the Civil War was the final invitation to encourage tribal aggression. These conditions, according to the historian Francis Paul Prucha, "fostered a restlessness among the western tribesmen" and consequently "furnished fertile soil for the seeds of reform to sprout."[2] The Indians' resistance, reflecting increasing concern for the vulnerability of their homelands, served as a magnet for federal reaction.

In January 1865 James R. Doolittle of Wisconsin, a member of the Senate Committee on Indian Affairs, initiated a national reform movement when he introduced a resolution calling for a committee to investigate the condition of western Indians. Until November 1864 the senator had viewed Indians as "inferior" people who could be saved only by the civilization process. Then the massacre that month of Southern Cheyenne and Southern Arapaho men, women, and children by Colorado volunteers at Sand Creek brought him into the ranks of the reformers. The Senate authorized a Joint Special Committee of three senators and four representatives. Doolittle would serve as chair. The committee's report, based on comprehensive questionnaires filled out by agents, military commanders, and others, along with interviews of frontier officials, was submitted on January 26, 1867. It concluded that Indian numbers were declining because of disease, intemperance, "loss of their hunting grounds and . . . the destruction of that game upon which [they] subsist." Further reduction was due to wars that "in a large majority of cases . . . [were] to be traced to the aggressions of lawless white men, always to be found upon the frontier."[3]

In addressing the often contentious issue of whether the Indian Office should belong to the civil or military arm of the government, committee members recommended that the Department of the Interior's control should not be returned to the Department of War. Rather, they advised that boards of inspection should be created to "save the country from many useless wars with the Indians, and secure in all branches of the Indian service greater efficiency and fidelity."[4]

As the Doolittle committee labored over its report, Indian resistance against military posts and encroaching settlers continued. When a presidential commission of military officers and civilians, appointed in early 1867, concluded that western tribes desired peace, Congress created the Peace Commission, a body to be chaired by the Indian commissioner and composed of three army officers and three civilians, including the chairman of the Senate Committee on Indian Affairs. Commission members were directed to establish peace with hostile tribes, settle them on reservations, provide for the safety of frontier settlements and transcontinental railroads, and institute a plan for "civilizing" the Indians. These directives, commonly referred to as "Grant's peace policy," reached a zenith in 1869 with the inauguration of Ulysses S. Grant, who worked closely with the nation's churches to create a Christian approach to Indian affairs.[5]

To implement the "peace policy," the commission was authorized to negotiate treaties with western tribes in hopes of preventing future military resistance. It was this policy that set in motion events that led to the death of Standing Bear's son. The Fort Laramie Treaty of 1868, negotiated with various bands of Lakotas (Sioux), recognized their hunting grounds in the Powder River area; closed the infamous Bozeman Trail, which had sparked Red Cloud's War of 1866; and removed the three forts guarding it. In addition, the treaty designated southern Dakota Territory (present-day South Dakota)

west of the Missouri River as the Great Sioux Reservation. By the stroke of
a pen, officials had mistakenly included much of the Ponca Reservation as
part of the newly organized Sioux domain. The Poncas' land, which spanned
some ninety-six thousand acres north of the Niobrara River and which was
guaranteed by a federal treaty of March 1865, was, by the stipulations of the
Fort Laramie Treaty, no longer theirs. At best, relations between the Lakotas
and Poncas had been unfriendly in the past. Now that Ponca land was part
of their reservation, Lakota warriors could justify an increase in raiding.[6]

In the spring of 1880, during extensive hearings before a Senate Select
Committee investigating the removal of the Ponca tribe, the acting Indian
commissioner, Edwin J. Brooks, testified that in the view of the Supreme
Court decision in the Cherokee Tobacco Case of December 1870, "a subsequent treaty repealed a former one, . . . and the lands which had formerly
been occupied by the Poncas, under their treaties, were now in reality the
lands of the Sioux, the Ponca treaties having been repealed." The Interior
Department thus recognized the Lakota claim and argued that removal of
the Poncas "was considered to be an absolute necessity."[7]

Their subsequent arbitrary removal initially to the Quapaw Reservation
in the northeastern corner of the Indian Territory led to many deaths, including that of Standing Bear's son. Intent on burying the boy in his ancestral home, the grieving father and a few followers fled the Indian Territory
only to be arrested and confined at Fort Omaha, Nebraska. They were subsequently freed by a federal district court decision in *United States ex rel.
Standing Bear v. Crook.* Meanwhile prominent citizens of Omaha had
formed the Omaha Ponca Relief Committee and laid plans for an eastern
lecture tour. Its immediate success prompted proper Bostonians to establish
the Boston Indian Citizenship Committee.

Thus Indian resistance to white encroachment, coupled with the ineffec-
tive and fraudulent practices of the Indian Office, led western humanitarians to seek relief for the Poncas by initiating a campaign that would ex-
pand into a reform movement addressing federal policy toward all Indians.
This then is the story of the removal of the Poncas, their struggle to regain
their ancestral lands, and the widespread ramifications of these events.[8]

Notes

1. Tibbles, *The Ponca Chiefs,* 25 (quote); see also idem, *Buckskin and Blanket
Days,* 197.

2. Prucha, *American Indian Policy in Crisis,* 4. Indian reform had actually begun
tentatively during the Lincoln presidency but "the change . . . was intellectual rather

than practical," according to Nichols in *Lincoln and the Indians,* 210. Nichols graphically detailed the misuse of Indian funds and the constant fraud in the Indian Office during Lincoln's administration.

3. Prucha, ed., *Documents of United States Indian Policy,* 103. For information on Doolittle's change in attitude see Nichols, *Lincoln and the Indians,* 156, 171–72. One of the most comprehensive studies of Sand Creek is Hoig, *The Sand Creek Massacre.*

4. Prucha, ed., *Documents of United States Indian Policy,* 105.

5. Books and articles on the "peace policy" include: Prucha, *The Great Father,* 1:479–606; idem, *American Indian Policy in Crisis,* 30–102; Utley, "The Celebrated Peace Policy of General Grant," 183–99; Mardock, *The Reformers and the American Indian,* 47–228; Priest, *Uncle Sam's Stepchildren;* Fritz, *The Movement for Indian Assimilation;* and Keller, *American Protestantism and the United States Indian Policy.* In Hoxie, *A Final Promise,* 3–81, the goals of the peace policy, and its successes and failures, are detailed; the Ponca controversy is discussed on pages 4–10. For Quaker implementation of the policy see Milner, *With Good Intentions.*

6. Lake ("Standing Bear! Who?" 457–58) assumes the mistake "resulted from a lapse of memory" on the part of the commissioners, who were prominent military leaders, thus making it awkward to question their decision. In turn, the Senate did not notice the mistake. Lake notes that at the time of the Fort Laramie Treaty, the Niobrara River was Nebraska's northern boundary.

7. U.S. Senate, *Testimony Relating to the Removal of the Ponca Indians* (hereinafter cited as *Testimony Relating to Removal*), 285.

8. The literature on Ponca removal is fairly extensive. See for example Jackson, *A Century of Dishonor,* 186–217; idem, *The Indian Reform Letters,* 6–21, 22–199; Wishart, *An Unspeakable Sadness,* 202–216; Coward, *The Newspaper Indian,* 196–223; Mathes, *Helen Hunt Jackson and Her Indian Reform Legacy,* 21–37; and Mardock, *The Reformers and the American Indian,* 168–91. See also Jacobs, "A History of the Ponca Indians," 117–52, specifically, for the actual removal.

Articles include: Mathes, "Ponca Chief Standing Bear"; idem, "Helen Hunt Jackson and the Campaign for Ponca Restitution"; idem, "Helen Hunt Jackson and the Ponca Controversy"; Coward, "Creating the Ideal Indian"; Mardock, "Standing Bear and the Reformers"; King, "'A Better Way'"; J. Clark, "Ponca Publicity"; and Hayter, "The Ponca Removal."

CHAPTER ONE

THE PONCA CHIEF'S JOURNEY
TO THE INDIAN TERRITORY

The Poncas, Omahas, Kansas, Osages, and Quapaws comprised the Dhegiha division of the Siouan linguistic family, and, according to tradition, they had once lived in the Southeast.[1] By about 1500 the five tribes were located at the junction of the Ohio and Wabash rivers. They subsequently separated, fanning out toward the north and the west. By the early 1700s the Poncas were living in the drainage area of the Niobrara River, and at its junction with the Missouri River they built earthen lodges protected by stockades of cottonwood logs. Their extensive territory was bounded on the north by the White River, on the east by the Missouri River, on the south by the Platte River, and on the west by the Black Hills. Here they hunted buffalo during the summer and winter, fished in the rivers and streams, harvested their fields of corn, beans, squash, and pumpkins, and traded with the Omahas (their closest kinsmen) and later with Europeans and Americans. Male Poncas' traditional roles included hunting, defending the villages, engaging in warfare when necessary, manufacturing needed weapons, and making ceremonial and political decisions. Their wives, sisters, and daughters engaged in domestic chores, which included the building and repairing of lodges. Women also collected wild plants, sowed and harvested domesticated food crops, reared the children, and dressed animal skins.

The treaties of peace and friendship negotiated with the federal government in 1817 and again in 1825 did not bring the Poncas peace with their more aggressive neighbor, the Lakotas, primarily the Brulé, who numbered almost four thousand, eight hundred of whom were warriors who frequently raided Ponca villages. The Brulé movement down from the White River cut off the Poncas' access to their traditional hunting grounds, which at the same time were being depleted of buffalo. The Poncas were pushed ever closer to starvation. The final straw was the Omaha sale of land between Aoyway

Creek and the Niobrara that the Poncas claimed as theirs. Within three years settlers had taken up some of this ceded land, moving onto the Poncas' cornfields and forcing them at one point to winter at the town of Niobrara. Thus in March 1858—in return for thirty years of annuities; houses; one or more manual-labor schools that stressed agriculture, mechanic arts, and housewifery; mechanic shops; a sawmill and gristmill; as well as the services of a miller, a mill engineer, a farmer, and an interpreter—the Poncas ceded all lands to the government, retaining only a small reservation in the southeastern corner of Dakota Territory along the Missouri River north of the Niobrara—rugged land with scant timber resources and scarce fertile soil. The decade of the 1860s was difficult, with only two good harvests due to either grasshopper infestations or drought conditions and only three successful buffalo hunts.[2]

In a treaty negotiated in 1865, the Poncas relinquished an additional thirty thousand acres in return for their old burial grounds, some cornfields south of the Niobrara River, near the mouth of Ponca Creek in modern-day Nebraska, and islands in the river. The treaty stipulated that the Poncas, not the government, had to reimburse any settlers claiming rights to these newly ceded lands. This reservation, consisting of ninety-six thousand acres, was now located to the east and south of the previous one, closer to the Missouri River.[3]

Following treaty negotiations, the nine Ponca bands settled in the eastern part of their reservation in three scattered villages. During 1865 and 1866 they enjoyed good crop yields, built log houses or the more traditional earthen lodges, sent their children to the reservation schools, and attended church in the Episcopal chapel. The Reverend J. Owen Dorsey, a resident missionary between 1871 and 1873, described the men as sober, honest in character, and "very eager to learn." He personally conducted afternoon adult classes to meet their needs. Despite their persistence, the Poncas lived on "the verge of starvation." Further loss of life was temporarily averted when William Welsh of the Board of Indian Commissioners intervened and purchased supplies for them.[4]

Working to overcome adversity, by the mid-1870s the Poncas earned a favorable assessment as "peaceable, agriculturally disposed . . . , not utterly averse and unaccustomed to work."[5] Standing Bear and his family lived in a twenty-by-forty-foot house, which he had built out of sawed lumber. The two-room structure had windows, two stoves for heating, two beds, a table and four chairs, three lamps, and a closet full of dishes. In addition, Standing Bear had built a stable and a hog pen. He dressed in modern western clothing, raised various crops on his two-hundred-steps-long field, and herded his horses, hogs, and cattle. Clearly he could be viewed by "peace policy" reformers as being well on the road to "civilization."[6]

Beneath the surface of this prosperity, the condition of the tribe remained "wretched," or so said Edward C. Kemble, who was later appointed to remove the Poncas to the Indian Territory. Kemble's initial visit to their reservation occurred in 1862 when he was in the army. He returned a decade later as the secretary of an Episcopal church commission and found little improvement. Although the Indians actively hunted, gathered native crops, and farmed, their efforts were never enough to ward off starvation. They received additional food and clothing from the church when inadequate government annuities failed to alleviate their situation. Kemble claimed that Principal Chief White Eagle and his followers, who represented most of the full-bloods at the settlement on the Niobrara, wished to move from the reservation. Kemble's assessments were, of course, self-serving; he was testifying in defense of his actions before a Senate Select Committee, which, in early February 1880, began investigating Ponca removal.[7]

The tribe's survival, which was threatened by frequent Lakota raids, required the support of United States soldiers at the Ponca Agency beginning in 1870. If outside attacks were not of enough concern, there was the occasional flood, like the one in 1873 that ruined one village and destroyed cornfields. Two years later the Poncas lost their crops again, this time by a plague of grasshoppers. John E. Cox, a soldier from nearby Fort Randall who was stationed at the Ponca Agency, wrote that the grasshoppers "began to fall like snow" and soon covered the ground. "By night all vegetation was gone . . . even the . . . leaves from the trees." The Indians had lost everything. The grasshoppers, Cox recalled, remained until winter and returned again in the spring.[8]

The mistaken inclusion of Ponca lands in the Great Sioux Reservation in 1868 proved to be the final blow to the tribe's peace and security. Shortly thereafter Lakota raids increased, prompting William H. Hare, Episcopal bishop of Nebraska and supervisor of the Ponca mission, to report in 1872 that "the wild frenzy of rage into which the periodical incursions of the Sioux have plunged the Poncas, and their expectation momentarily of attack, have been great obstacles to their progress."[9] During the next two years, Charles P. Birkett, the Ponca agent, repeatedly wrote to Indian Commissioner Edward Parmelee Smith and the commander of Fort Randall requesting guns, ammunition, and military protection. On May 17, 1873, sixty mounted Lakota warriors attacked a Ponca settlement but were driven off. The following March over thirty warriors killed work oxen and forced Ponca herders to flee. Agent Birkett informed Commissioner Smith that he was training a small company of Poncas for police duty.[10] Despite all efforts, the raids continued unabated.

By the summer of 1875, a newly appointed agent, Arthur J. Carrier, expressed grave concern over Lakota raiders' "warlike and murderous visits," which were hampering his "civilization" efforts. He predicted that if their activity continued, the government stood to lose "not less than fifty thousand dollars in property destroyed." He requested increased military support.[11] Carrier's replacement, James Lawrence, noted in a letter dated June 20, 1876, that a Ponca had been killed and thirty horses stolen when a raiding party of thirty or forty Lakotas had recently attacked the lower camp.[12] Although army orders generally prohibited the lending of weapons to Indian agencies, on August 1, 1876, Lieutenant General Philip H. Sheridan, commanding the Division of the Missouri, authorized the shipment of twenty rifles and ammunition to the Ponca agent.[13]

For years the Poncas had been suffering due to hostile raids and near starvation, often forced to survive on wild potatoes and government rations. Finally in the early 1870s, government officials and some tribal leaders concluded that removal to a safer location was imperative. Commissioner Smith instructed Barclay White, superintendent of Indian Affairs for the northern superintendency, to hold a council with Ponca and Omaha chiefs and headmen to discuss removal of the Poncas to the Omahas' reservation. At the Omaha council house on November 6, 1873, fifteen Ponca chiefs, including Principal Chief White Eagle, and the second-ranking chief, Standing Bear, agreed to move, provided the government would compensate them and the Omahas would sell them land at a fair price. Superintendent White later testified that "the Omaha were unanimous in their willingness to receive the Poncas," and both sides agreed to two and a half dollars per acre.[14] However no action was taken. Although White could offer no reason for the inactivity, Carrier later testified that the Indian commissioner had confided to him that Nebraska senators objected to the removal; the state already had enough resident Indians.[15]

Although some elected officials did not view the Omaha Reservation as a viable home for the Poncas, Standing Bear did. On September 30, 1875, Carrier reported to Commissioner Smith that the Ponca leader had "been on a visit to the Omahas since last winter," allegedly "prompted to leave his own reservation by reason of the jealousy then existing among the chiefs here, and for fear of the Sioux." Carrier, who on September 11 had reinstated Standing Bear as a tribal chief, described the Ponca leader as a good man who "would make an excellent, even an exemplary, farmer if fair opportunities were offered, where there was no common enemy such as the Sioux to be dreaded."[16]

The Poncas, however, would not be moving to the Omaha Reservation. During an informal meeting with the chiefs in February 1875, Carrier asked if they wanted to move to the Indian Territory. Before they committed themselves, the chiefs asked if "two or three of their number could first visit" and make sure the land would be good for farming.[17] Believing he had their best interest at heart, in June Carrier traveled to Washington to confer with government officials. When Commissioner Smith proved noncommittal, the agent met for almost two hours with President Grant at his vacation residence in Long Branch, New Jersey. Grant informed Carrier that if the Indians were willing to remove, he would need to have them sign a document, which he would then forward to the White House.[18]

On September 23, 1875, over fifty Ponca chiefs, headmen, and tribal members, including White Eagle and Standing Bear, signed a paper that had been drawn up by Agent Carrier and translated by an interpreter, Charles P. Morgan, an Iowa Indian who lived with the Omahas.[19] In this document, the Poncas expressed "their strong desire to be removed from [their] present reservation in Dakota Territory to the Indian Territory . . . to live in peace and prosperity."[20] Continual Lakota raids made it difficult for them to work their land, as Standing Bear so graphically pointed out to Carrier. "I tell you, when I go to my field, I have got to go with my rifle on my back; and when I work, I must keep one eye on my plow and one eye on those hills yonder."[21] Sometime later, however, after conferring with Joseph La Flesche, the Omaha chief, the Poncas held another council and decided against leaving their Niobrara lands.[22]

When Standing Bear was shown this September 1875 document during Senate hearings in 1880, he informed Senator John T. Morgan of Alabama that the words they had signed "were entirely different from the words on this paper."[23] Carrier remarked that Standing Bear could not be expected to "understand the idioms and phraseology of the English language, and its full purport and meaning."[24] But he was not the only chief to discredit this document. White Eagle informed the senators that the Poncas had never signed any paper agreeing to remove to the Indian Territory; "we did not know at that time that there was any such place . . . ; we only talked about going to the Omahas." White Eagle's claim was substantiated by Standing Buffalo.[25]

The misunderstanding over this document was due in part to the language barrier. The interpreters were often unable to communicate proficiently in either language. The Reverend Samuel Dutton Hinman, an Episcopal missionary, observed that "hardly one interpreter in a hundred [was] competent to interpret such languages as you must necessarily use in a treaty or negotiation."[26] Susette La Flesche, daughter of the Omaha chief, a graduate of the Elizabeth Institute for Young Ladies in New Jersey, and Standing Bear's interpreter, observed that Charles Morgan was not a "very good interpreter." The young Omaha had first-hand knowledge of Morgan's ability; he had lived for a time with her family.[27] La Flesche also explained that there was no word comparable to "territory" in the Ponca language. The closest word that Morgan could have used would be "country," or to be more exact, "the native people's land." Therefore the Poncas had committed themselves to move to "the country of the Omaha Indians," not the Indian Territory.[28]

While the Indian signatories understood the document "to be a preliminary to a negotiation to remove to the Omaha Reservation," Carrier informed President Rutherford B. Hayes in a letter dated October 6, 1877, that the intent of the document was "to secure the sanction of the government for a delegation of their chiefs going to see the Indian country." Upon learning from Standing Bear that removal had been "unreasonable and intolerant . . . leaving no doubt in their minds that . . . [it] was a foregone conclusion," Carrier expressed regret that the document had ever been signed or forwarded to the Indian Office, while insisting the Poncas' removal "would never be carried out against their will."[29]

Removal to the Omaha Reservation would have been the most logical solution. The Indian Bureau initially chose this course, requesting Congress to approve its decision. Instead, without explanation, on August 15, 1876, Congress appropriated twenty-five thousand dollars to remove the tribe to the Indian Territory, claiming the Poncas' exposure to Lakota raids imposed "a serious obstacle in the way of progress in civilized life which they seem disposed to make." This decision was made despite the efforts of James Lawrence to convince Commissioner John Quincy Smith, successor to Edward Parmelee Smith, that many tribal members strongly opposed this action.[30] More important, at this particular time the Poncas probably had little to fear from Lakota raids. The Battle of the Little Bighorn had occurred in late June 1876, and by August combined forces under Generals George Crook and Alfred H. Terry were engaged in mop-up operations against widely scattered Lakota and Northern Cheyenne bands. Furthermore, Agent Carrier had engineered a peace treaty between the Brulé and the Poncas in January 1876 at the Ponca Agency. And in his Senate testimony, Carrier explained that the peace had been strictly observed. Nevertheless, Congress appropriated an additional fifteen thousand dollars in 1877 to enforce the removal.[31]

Ignoring the growing opposition and the recent treaty with the Brulé, in January 1877 Commissioner Smith directed Indian Inspector Edward C. Kemble to proceed to the Ponca Agency and hold a council on the subject of removal. Kemble was selected to "take charge of th[is] delicate and difficult task" because he was experienced and in the past had carried out his duty with "industry, intelligence, and fidelity." Above all, Smith believed Kemble "a just, humane, and honest man."[32]

If Kemble found "the feelings of the tribe generally to be in favor of the proposed removal," he was, with the help of the principal men, to select a delegation of ten and visit the Indian Territory.[33] Because Commissioner Smith believed that it was in the best interest of the Poncas to incorporate with the Osage, he ordered Kemble to visit their reservation and confer with the agent. If the tribes refused to merge, the inspector was to encourage the Osage to sell the Poncas a tract of some fifty thousand acres at fifty cents an acre. Smith concluded that expenses for the trip should not exceed twenty-five hundred dollars.[34]

Kemble arrived on January 24 and subsequently scheduled three councils. The Poncas "expressed great unwillingness to listen—to even listen—to any proposition for removal," noted Kemble, who tried hard to convince them that there was good land in the Indian Territory. During later testimony he informed the chair of the special Senate committee that he "would sooner put [his] right hand in the fire and burn it off than to lead the [Poncas] into a country where there were swamps and disease, and where the climate was bad."[35]

The presence of Kemble and his associates on the Ponca Reservation took the Indians by surprise. "We did not have any knowledge of what they had come there to say," Standing Bear later testified. The tribe received orders to "pack up [because] the President" said they had to move. When Standing Bear informed the inspector that his people had resided on this land for generations and hoped to grow old and die there, the response was: "hurry up; settle it among yourselves, quick"; then Kemble added, "talk like men; be brave." After the Poncas questioned the inspector about the president's orders, Kemble finally agreed to send a delegation to the Indian Territory and then to Washington to inform President Hayes of the decision. Standing Bear saw no harm in viewing the land; "if we do not like it[,] we won't take it," he informed the senators.[36]

Kemble's recollections were quite different. He believed that in negotiations with the Indians, allowances had to be made for "peculiarities, such as childishness and indifference to their own welfare." He testified that officials "may have to decide . . . what is best for them," much like one does when dealing with a child. He wrote Commissioner Smith that the Poncas agreed to surrender their lands and look for a new home in the Indian Territory and that they would then travel to Washington to visit the president.[37]

On February 2, 1877, Kemble, Agent Lawrence, and the agency interpreter, Charles Le Claire, set out from the Ponca Reservation with ten Ponca leaders—White Eagle, Standing Bear, Standing Buffalo, Smoke Maker,
Frank La Flesche, Little Chief, Big Elk, Gahega, Michel Cerre (Cera, Le
Claire's brother), and Antoine (Lone Chief, Le Claire's uncle). Reverend
Hinman, authorized to accompany them, was detained at the Santee Mission and followed a day later. The small party traveled by wagon to Yankton
where Kemble purchased "civilized clothing" for the Indians. They boarded
a train for Independence City, Kansas, then transferred to wagons and jolted
over rough roads through inhospitable terrain plagued by wind and rain.
Arriving at the Osage Agency in the north-central part of the territory on
February 9, they learned that the agent and the principal men of the tribe
were in Washington, D.C. No preparations had been made for their visit.
Kemble immediately informed Commissioner Smith that he would show the
Ponca delegation land in the Kaw country to the north instead.[38]

Although Smith preferred the Osage Reservation, he agreed that the neighboring Kaw Reservation was a viable alternative. If the Poncas disliked either one, then the next choice was Quapaw land in the extreme northeastern part of the Indian Territory. Smith recommended that the Indians be
given ample time to visit these three sites "so that they may be enabled to
understandingly represent their opinions and feelings in regard to a matter
of so great importance to them and their people."[39]

The selection process did not go smoothly. Only two Osage leaders were
available to confer with the visitors; then White Eagle, Smoke Maker, and
several others became ill during a sleet and rain storm that was so severe it
forced the entire party to remain in camp for five or six days. Moreover the
chiefs were unimpressed with the country, which they described as "stony
and broken," nor with its shirtless residents, with burnt skin, and hair that
"stood up as if it had not been combed since they were little children. We
did not wish to sink as low as they seemed to be," remarked eight of the
chiefs in a letter later written for them and published in the *Sioux City Daily
Journal*.[40]

Homesick and despondent, they refused to make any selection. Kemble
subsequently wrote that "like children, Indians are easily depressed away
from home, amid strange and uncongenial surroundings, and our Poncas
were dispirited almost from the hour they set foot on Indian Territory soil."[41]
On February 15 the party left the Osage Reservation and spent a day at the
Kaw Station, where they enjoyed better weather and some entertainment provided by the local chiefs. Standing Buffalo described the terrain between the
Osage and Kaw reservations as very rocky with minimal timber resources,

small creeks, and no large rivers.[42] White Eagle later testified that not only were the Osages and Kaws poverty stricken and sick but their lands were poor. They "were not able to do much for themselves," he concluded.[43] All members of the delegation agreed; they disliked all the lands they had seen.

When the Ponca delegation refused to make a selection, Kemble led the way to Arkansas City, Kansas, on February 17. The group visited lands along the Arkansas River that he described as "rich and fertile." The Indians remained unimpressed. At Arkansas City, Kemble, Lawrence, and Hinman held another council with the Indians, who again demanded to be taken home. On February 19, while the Poncas remained in the hotel, the three government officials visited an area along the Chikaskia River, southwest of Arkansas City, which they described as rich in soil and possessing good water and timber.[44]

When a telegram to the commissioner requesting additional instructions brought no response, Kemble and the others assumed "that as no orders were sent us to take the delegation back to their homes we could not yield to their wishes in this respect." The Indians were informed that they would all proceed to Independence, Kansas, where another telegram would be sent. "We left them to deliberate upon this," Kemble noted, "but in less than an hour afterwards eight of the delegation, comprising all the full-bloods, set out from the hotel and started northward to retrace their way to their homes on foot." Only Michel Cerre (Cera) and Antoine (Lone Chief), both elderly, almost blind, and physically incapable of walking home, remained. Kemble labeled the eight Poncas as "insubordinate" men who should be arrested and held as prisoners "until such time as they shall consent to yield obedience to the orders of their agent." He also complained to Commissioner Smith that the Indians broke their promises, violated their agreement, and refused to listen to advice. Kemble claimed that the tribe members had "unanimously given their consent" to give up their present lands; this consent, "though not expressed in writing, was fairly and deliberately given in the presence of twenty white witnesses."[45]

In his Senate testimony of February 17, 1880, Kemble insisted that although treated with the "utmost consideration" and in the "most friendly spirit," the chiefs had refused to "listen to reason, [and] to be governed by advice," and thus had endured "the unnecessary hardship" of returning home on foot.[46] Agent Lawrence described the complaints of the eight chiefs as merely an "excuse [to] justify their own unwise and unnecessary action, and [it] had no foundation whatever." Kemble, he said, had treated the Ponca delegation with "kindness, patience, and forbearance."[47] Standing Bear's testimony was quite different. "We talked . . . we begged . . . [and] we pleaded with them [Kemble, Lawrence, and Hinman] to let us alone, to leave us on the land that was our home," he said, "but they showed no pity on us."[48]

Thoroughly dissatisfied with the land and disgusted with Kemble for failing to keep any promises, Standing Bear and the others set out on foot after the angry inspector had tried to force them to take one of the three tracts of land. "If you do not accept these, I will leave you here alone . . . one thousand miles from home . . . [with] no money . . . [and] no interpreter," he had threatened. Then after slamming the door of their room, he sought to force their compliance via messages carried by Le Claire, "from long before sundown till it was nine o'clock at night."[49]

Standing Bear later informed Senator Henry Laurens Dawes of Massachusetts that they finally asked to be taken to the depot so they could return home on the railroad. However, Le Claire told them that Kemble offered only two choices: "either to take the land, or show . . . [themselves] brave, and walk home." And so walk home they did, slowly at first because White Eagle and another chief had not fully recovered from their recent illness. They had no supplies, no interpreter, and only eight dollars among them.[50] Although Kemble denied that they had requested money or passes,[51] both White Eagle and Standing Bear testified that they indeed had asked for money. White Eagle later explained that Kemble left the men "without money, pass, or interpreter, in a strange country, among a strange people, because . . . [we] would not select a piece of land."[52]

Following the chiefs' departure, Kemble and his group traveled east to Independence, Kansas. Sending Agent Lawrence and the others ahead, the inspector and Hinman traveled south to the Quapaw Agency in the northeastern corner of the Indian Territory. They were impressed with the plentiful timber, ample flowing water, and several buildings recently constructed in anticipation of an earlier move there by the Northern Cheyennes, and they declared this land preferable to that of the Kaws. Writing on March 2, 1877, Kemble, Hinman, and Lawrence "respectfully suggested" to Commissioner Smith that he select this tract of land for the Poncas. Five days later Smith authorized the Poncas' removal to the Quapaw Reserve, although the approximately one hundred Quapaws in residence had not been consulted nor had they given their consent for Ponca settlement on their land.[53] Meanwhile Agent Lawrence, Le Claire, Michel Cerre, and Antoine had traveled to the Otoe Agency in southeastern Nebraska in the hopes of intercepting Standing Bear, White Eagle, and the others.[54]

Lawrence, however, had departed by the time the Ponca chiefs arrived at the Otoe Agency on March 7, following a grueling journey. "It was winter," Standing Bear later related. "We started for home on foot. At night we slept in hay-stacks. We barely lived till morning, it was so cold."[55] The Indians followed railroad tracks whenever possible, endured bitter cold weather with only thin blankets for protection, and ate raw corn. "The last few days we were very weak . . . and could walk only a few miles," Standing Bear noted. "When the [Otoe] agent saw how nearly starved we were, and looked at our bleeding feet, for our moccasins wore out [during] the first ten days, he took pity on us, and first gave us something to eat."[56]

In one town they had been befriended by a young man who, in the Kaw language, explained that if they followed the nearby railroad tracks, they would end up near the Otoe Reservation. He drew a map and wrote something on a piece of paper that would elicit food and additional directions from local residents. When the Indians finally arrived among the Otoes, they had only a few tomahawks and some beaded work that they could exchange for horses.[57]

A week later they reached the Omaha Agency in northeastern Nebraska and on March 27, 1877, crossed the Missouri River into Iowa, whereupon they sent President Rutherford B. Hayes a telegram describing their lengthy trip. They informed the president that they were "hungry, tired, shoeless, footsore, sad at heart," and "in trouble," and implored him to answer immediately.[58] This telegram, sent from Sloan, Iowa, at a cost of $6.25, was drafted by Susette La Flesche and edited by William Hamilton, resident missionary among the Omaha. There was no answer. Three days later Standing Bear again crossed the Missouri River and headed north to Sioux City where he delivered a letter to the *Sioux City Daily Journal*. The newspaper called it a "plain unimpassioned statement from the sufferers of a great wrong," who, although threatened with violence and victims of "deceit and subterfuge," had "conducted themselves peaceably and honestly."[59] Finally a delegation of Poncas visited the editorial offices of the *Niobrara Pioneer* in Niobrara, Nebraska. Big Elk, who had accompanied Standing Bear and the others, informed the editor that he had never signed any papers relative to removal and that both Hinman and Le Claire had lied to them. Only a few "half-breeds" wanted to remove; "the full-bred [*sic*] Indians never wanted to go to the Indian Territory."[60] Conferring with editors in both Iowa and Nebraska, the Ponca chiefs made sure that their unfortunate journey would become public knowledge.

Notes

1. For Ponca ethnology see Howard, *The Ponca Tribe*, 1–12; Jablow, *Ponca Indians*, 8–49; Cash and Wolff, *The Ponca People*, 1–3; Wishart, *An Unspeakable Sadness*, 1–37; and Jacobs, "A History of the Ponca Indians," 1–10.

2. Jacobs, "A History of the Ponca Indians," 79–80, 83–85, 97–101; Lake, "Standing Bear! Who?" 454–56; Barrett, "The Poncas," 12–17; and Jackson, *A Century of Dishonor*, 189–94. For Omaha sale of Ponca land see Wishart, *An Unspeakable Sadness*, 132–33; see also 144–49.

3. Jacobs, "A History of the Ponca Indians," 110–11; Lake, "Standing Bear! Who?" 456–57; Wishart, *An Unspeakable Sadness*, 147–48; and Jackson, *A Century of Dishonor*, 194–98.

4. For "Dorsey's Testimony" see U.S. Senate, *Report of Special Commission to the Poncas*, S. Ex. Doc. 30 (hereafter cited as *Report of Special Commission*), 29 (first quote), 28 (second quote). See also Bourke diary, 38:973. (A microfilm copy of the diary was made available to us courtesy of Dr. Charles Robinson III.) Because Bourke, aide to General George Crook, was one of the recorders of the proceedings of this presidential commission, the *Report of Special Commission* is almost a verbatim copy of his diaries.

In his testimony before the Senate committee (U.S. Senate, *Testimony Relating to Removal*, 17), Standing Bear noted there were nine Ponca bands, while Kemble in his testimony (ibid., 57) stated there were ten bands. According to Wishart (*An Unspeakable Sadness*, 202–3), there were three villages with eight bands. With a population of 377, the agency village, adjacent to the Missouri River, was the largest. To the south was the Hubdon village, with a population of about 144, while Point Village, on the north bank of the Niobrara River close to the town of Niobrara, held about 250. Dorsey (U.S. Senate, *Report of Special Commission*, 27) testified that there were two villages eight miles apart, one on the Niobrara River and the other at the agency where his mission was located.

5. Barrett, "The Poncas," 18.

6. "Standing Bear's Testimony," Bourke diary, 38:1017; U.S. Senate, *Report of Special Commission*, 38; "Standing Bear's Testimony," in U.S. Senate, *Testimony Relating to Removal*, 11–12; "T. H. Tibbles's Testimony," in ibid., 41. See also Tibbles, *The Ponca Chiefs*, 13.

7. "E. C. Kemble's Testimony," in U.S. Senate, *Testimony Relating to Removal*, 49–51. For a brief discussion of Kemble's role in removal, see Lake, "Standing Bear! Who?" 467–68; for a general discussion of the impoverished condition of the Poncas, see Wishart, *The Unspeakable Sadness*, 204–7. For a biography of White Eagle, see Zimmerman, *White Eagle*. Kemble had served as editor of the *California Star* (San Francisco) during 1847–48, before establishing the *Placer Times* and the *Alta California*. In the 1870s he became one of the first Indian inspectors hired to make routine investigations of Indian agencies.

8. Cox, "Soldiering in Dakota Territory in the Seventies," 65. For Dorsey's comments on the grasshopper infestations before President Hayes's commission, see U.S. Senate, *Report of Special Commission*, 28. This particular grasshopper plague not only ate through the Great Plains but extended into the northern prairies as well.

9. "Extract from the Annual Report of Bishop Hare," in U.S. Senate, *Testimony Relating to Removal*, 383; see also "Bishop Hare's Testimony," in ibid., 116–33. Hare

resided at the Yankton Indian Agency in Dakota. For additional information on Ponca problems with the Lakotas, see Jacobs, "A History of the Ponca Indians," 102–16.

10. For Birkett's reports see U.S. Senate, *Testimony Relating to Removal*, 385–92. For more on the Lakota raids, see Mulhair, *Ponca Agency*, 43–62, and Wishart, *An Unspeakable Sadness*, 135–39. For Ponca conditions during the 1860s see Wishart, *An Unspeakable Sadness*, 144–53, and Hayter, "The Ponca Removal," 266–67.

11. "A. J. Carrier to the Indian Commissioner, August 11, 1875," in U.S. Senate, *Testimony Relating to Removal*, 395–96 (all quotes); see also Mulhair, *Ponca Agency*, 65–70.

12. "James Lawrence to Major Fergus Walker, June 20, 1876," in U.S. Senate, *Testimony Relating to Removal*, 398.

13. "Philip H. Sheridan to the Adjutant-General of the Army, August 1, 1876," in U.S. Senate, *Testimony Relating to Removal*, 399.

14. "Barclay White's Testimony," in U.S. Senate, *Testimony Relating to Removal*, 135 (quote), 136; see also Minutes of a Council of Poncas and Omahas, in ibid., 399–400. White was a Hicksite Quaker. Lake ("Standing Bear! Who?" 459) notes there was some evidence that the Omaha/Ponca agreement failed because some important Omaha chiefs were absent.

15. "A. J. Carrier's Testimony," in U.S. Senate, *Testimony Relating to Removal*, 152.

16. "A. J. Carrier to E. P. Smith, September 30, 1875," in U.S. Senate, *Testimony Relating to Removal*, 397.

17. "A. J. Carrier to E. P. Smith, February 5, 1875," in U.S. Senate, *Testimony Relating to Removal*, 402–3.

18. "A. J. Carrier's Testimony," in U.S. Senate, *Testimony Relating to Removal*, 145–46. For a longer study of the Indian Territory see Burton, *Indian Territory and the United States*.

19. See "Morgan's Testimony," in U.S. Senate, *Testimony Relating to Removal*, 301–4. Bourke, in Bourke diary, 25:77, described Morgan as a "full-blooded Omaha Indian."

20. "Ponca Agency, Dakota, September 23, 1875," in U.S. Senate, *Testimony Relating to Removal*, 405 (quote); see also "A. J. Carrier's Testimony," in ibid., 37, 143–50, and Lake, "Standing Bear! Who?" 460–61.

21. "A. J. Carrier's Testimony," in U.S. Senate, *Testimony Relating to Removal*, 145.

22. "Standing Bear's Testimony," in U.S. Senate, *Testimony Relating to Removal*, 157.

23. Ibid., 39, 157–58.

24. "A. J. Carrier's Testimony," in U.S. Senate, *Testimony Relating to Removal*, 148.

25. "White Eagle's Testimony," in U.S. Senate, *Testimony Relating to Removal*, 214; see also "Standing Buffalo's Testimony," in ibid., 222.

26. "Hinman's Testimony," in U.S. Senate, *Testimony Relating to Removal*, 336.

27. "Standing Bear's Testimony," in U.S. Senate, *Testimony Relating to Removal*, 157.

28. Ibid., 160–61; "Susette La Flesche's Testimony," in U.S. Senate, *Testimony Relating to Removal*, 37. For more on the language barrier, see Lake, "Standing Bear! Who?" 497–99.

29. U.S. Senate, *Testimony Relating to Removal*, vi (first quote), 466 (second quote), 151 (third and fourth quotes). See also "A. J. Carrier's Testimony," in ibid., 143–56; "Standing Bear's Testimony," ibid., 157–61, and the text of the October letter, ibid., 464–69.

30. "Removal of the Ponca," in U.S. Department of the Interior, Office of Indian Affairs, *Annual Report of the Commissioner of Indian Affairs* (1876), xvii. For the congressional appropriation see U.S. Senate, *Testimony Relating to Removal*, vii (quote). See also "James Lawrence to the Indian Commissioner, August 16, 1876," in U.S. Senate, *Testimony Relating to Removal*, 406; Jacobs, "A History of the Ponca Indians," 101–16; and Lake, "Standing Bear! Who?" 461, who listed four possible reasons why the government chose to relocate the Poncas. A former congressman from Ohio, John Quincy Smith had succeeded Edward Parmelee Smith in December 1875. For more on Edward Parmelee Smith and John Quincy Smith see Kvasnicka and Viola, eds., *The Commissioners of Indian Affairs*, 141–47 and 149–53, respectively.

31. "A. J. Carrier's Testimony," in U.S. Senate, *Testimony Relating to Removal*, 153–54.

32. "Extract of March 24, 1880, letter from John Quincy Smith to Kemble," in U.S. Senate, *Report of Special Commission*, 47.

33. "Commissioner Smith's Instructions to Kemble," in U.S. Senate, *Report of Special Commission*, 49. In his defense, Kemble quoted these instructions in a letter to Massachusetts Governor John D. Long, December 8, 1880, reprinted in U.S. Senate, *Report of Special Commission*, 46–50.

34. "John Q. Smith to Edward C. Kemble, January 15, 1877," in U.S. Senate, *Testimony Relating to Removal*, 407–9; see also "Kemble's Final Report of July 28, 1877," in ibid., 450–56.

35. "E. C. Kemble's Testimony," in U.S. Senate, *Testimony Relating to Removal*, 52 (first quote), 53 (second quote). For additional testimony on the three Ponca councils see U.S. Senate, *Testimony Relating to Removal*, 83–96.

36. "Standing Bear's Testimony," in U.S. Senate, *Testimony Relating to Removal*, 4 (quote); see also 14.

37. "E. C. Kemble's Testimony," in U.S. Senate, *Testimony Relating to Removal*, 99; for letter see Kemble to Smith, April 10, 1877, in ibid., 409–14. Extracts from the minutes of the January 27, 1877, council are included in Col. E. C. Kemble, "The Story of the Poncas," *New York Independent* (hereafter cited as *Independent*), December 18, 1879, 4–5.

38. "Kemble to Smith, February 10, 1877," in U.S. Senate, *Testimony Relating*

to Removal, 415–16, and "E. C. Kemble's Testimony," in ibid., 58. For a general discussion of this tour see Jacobs, "A History of the Ponca Indians," 119–24; see also Lake, "Standing Bear! Who?" 463.

39. "Smith to Kemble, February 7, 1877," in U.S. Senate, *Testimony Relating to Removal*, 416–17.

40. "Weary and Footsore: The Poncas Tell the Story of Their Grievous Wrongs," *Sioux City Daily Journal*, March 31, 1877, 1. Osage men traditionally shaved their heads, leaving a roach of hair about two inches high and three inches wide from forehead to neck.

41. Kemble, "The Story of the Poncas," 5.

42. "Standing Buffalo's Testimony," in U.S. Senate, *Testimony Relating to Removal*, 225.

43. "White Eagle's Testimony," in U.S. Senate, *Report of Special Commission*, 14.

44. "Kemble, Hinman, Lawrence to Smith, February 20, 1877," in U.S. Senate, *Testimony Relating to Removal*, 418–19. For Hinman's testimony on the trip to the Indian Territory, ibid., 327–29, and for Kemble's testimony, ibid., 58–63.

45. "Kemble, Hinman, Lawrence to Smith, February 20, 1877," in U.S. Senate, *Testimony Relating to Removal*, 419 (all quotes). See also page 15, and letter dated February 23, 1877, 419–20, as well as Hinman's version of the Indian Territory tour, 327–29, all in U.S. Senate, *Testimony Relating to Removal*. Standing Buffalo in his testimony (ibid., 226) noted that they had encountered some Pawnees before he and the seven other chiefs walked home. These Pawnees informed them that they and their horses were "dying off very fast" in the Indian Territory. The Pawnee removal treaty had been negotiated in October 1874. See also Kemble's comment on the Pawnees, ibid., 61.

46. "E. C. Kemble's Testimony," in U.S. Senate, *Testimony Relating to Removal*, 111.

47. "Sworn Statement of Lawrence, November 29, 1880," in U.S. Senate, *Report of Special Commission*, 51–52.

48. "Standing Bear's Testimony," in U.S. Senate, *Testimony Relating to Removal*, 20; see also page 14.

49. Standing Bear quoted in H.H. [Helen Hunt Jackson], "Standing Bear and Bright Eyes," *Independent*, November 20, 1879, 2; see also "Standing Bear's Testimony," in U.S. Senate, *Testimony Relating to Removal*, 16, 18.

50. "Standing Bear's Testimony," in U.S. Senate, *Testimony Relating to Removal*, 4–6 (quote), 15, 105. See also "The Poncas Desert," *Niobrara Pioneer*, March 8, 1877, 1.

51. Kemble, "The Story of the Poncas," 5; see also "E. C. Kemble's Testimony," in U.S. Senate, *Testimony Relating to Removal*, 62–63.

52. "White Eagle's Statement," in U.S. Senate, *Testimony Relating to Removal*, 460. This statement was made to Susette La Flesche on May 20, 1879, while she and her father were visiting the Poncas in the Indian Territory at the request of Tibbles. For additional testimony from White Eagle and a reiteration of Kemble's

refusal to give them money, see U.S. Senate, *Report of Special Commission,* 15, and Bourke diary, 37:887–88.

53. According to Baird (*The Quapaw Indians,* 114–21), in 1874 Enoch Hoag, superintendent of the central superintendency, headquartered at Lawrence, Kansas, believing that the Quapaw had "too much land," recommended part of it be purchased and used as a home for displaced tribes. The following year C. F. Larrabee, an employee of the Indian Office, pressured "a poorly attended council" to cede forty thousand acres to the government, land that would be compensated for in the future. However the same band of resident Quapaws refused to sell their remaining land and also refused to move with the rest of their tribe to live with the Osages.

54. "Kemble, Hinman, Lawrence to Smith, March 2, 1877," in U.S. Senate, *Testimony Relating to Removal,* 422–24; "Smith to Kemble, March 7, 1877," in ibid., 424–25; and "E. C. Kemble's Testimony," in ibid., 64, 66, 106–7.

55. Standing Bear, quoted in Jackson, *A Century of Dishonor,* 201; for Standing Bear's entire account see 199–204. See also H.H., "Standing Bear and Bright Eyes," 1–2, and Tibbles, *The Ponca Chiefs,* 6–16, for Standing Bear's account. For confirmation of the date of arrival see "Kemble to Smith, March 16, 1877," in U.S. Senate, *Testimony Relating to Removal,* 426.

56. Standing Bear quoted in Tibbles, *The Ponca Chiefs,* 8. See also Standing Bear's interview in "Seeking Redress in the East," *New York Daily Tribune* [hereinafter cited as *Tribune*], December 8, 1879, 3; "Standing Bear's Testimony," in U.S. Senate, *Testimony Relating to Removal,* 5–8; and Lake, "Standing Bear! Who?" 464.

57. "White Eagle's Testimony," in U.S. Senate, *Testimony Relating to Removal,* 196.

58. "Susette La Flesche's Testimony," in U.S. Senate, *Testimony Relating to Removal,* 22, 23 (quote), 107–8, 432; see also Tibbles, *The Ponca Chiefs,* 9. The text of the telegram is reproduced in *The Ponca Chiefs,* 60–61, as is a letter written at the request of Reverend Dorsey by Susette La Flesche, dated April 29, 1879, 58–59.

59. "Weary and Footsore," 1; the *Niobrara Pioneer* reprinted the entire letter as "Swindled Poncas," April 5, 1877, 1. Signed by all eight of the chiefs, the letter included the text of the telegram to Hayes.

60. "A Ponca Pow-Wow," *Niobrara Pioneer,* March 29, 1877, 8. The Ponca visit was on March 26.

CHAPTER TWO

FORCED REMOVAL

Returning to the Ponca Agency on April 2, 1877, Standing Bear and his seven companions learned that Chiefs Michel Cerre and Antoine, the elderly men who had accompanied Kemble home, had "acquiesced in the decision of the interior department, and agreed to . . . advise the [tribe] to prepare for removal."[1] Kemble had deliberately chosen to ignore the eight defiant Ponca chiefs and considered their leaving him as "an act of insubordination."[2] The inspector later informed the Senate Select Committee that he was not obligated "to consider the will of the chiefs in the matter at all" and then asserted that when the Poncas agreed to send the ten chiefs to the Indian Territory, they in effect had agreed "to give up their lands." He reported that Antoine and Michel Cerre thought that "more than half the tribe would consent to go to the Indian Territory without trouble."[3]

The two elderly chiefs and Kemble, however, failed to consider the impact of Standing Bear's account of the hardships endured on the return trip. Tribal members became excited, confused, and even divided over the prospect of leaving their homeland. Standing Bear's brother, Big Snake, head of the Ponca military society, adamantly opposed removal and threatened to drive Kemble off the reservation. Denouncing both brothers as troublemakers, the Indian inspector portrayed them as defiant and disobedient, inciting disturbances, standing in the way of those willing to remove, and imperiling reservation peace.[4] Fearful for his safety and interested in preserving order, Kemble requested that troops be dispatched from Fort Randall, north of the reservation. When Captain Fergus Walker and a mounted company of thirty men arrived, Kemble ordered the arrest of both Standing Bear and Big Snake. An additional army detachment of thirty men followed, and all remained on the reservation until removal was completed.

The brothers, confined at Fort Randall for ten days, appeared before a military tribunal and were released by the fort commander, who telegraphed President Hayes requesting that Ponca removal be abandoned.[5] Other supporters, including preachers in Yankton, Niobrara, Sioux City, and Omaha, as well as missionaries assigned to various Indian agencies, publicly denounced the government's treatment of the Poncas. One of the more active objectors was the Reverend Alfred L. Riggs, a Congregational missionary serving the Santee Sioux. In a letter to the newly appointed secretary of the interior, Carl Schurz, Riggs noted that the Poncas were "wholly opposed to moving to the Indian Territory" and had not given "their consent" or "relinquished" any rights. Title to their land was still clearly based on two federal treaties. Furthermore, white settlers preferred the Poncas as neighbors instead of the Brulé, and the haste of the process lent credence to the impression that something was "crooked." Riggs therefore requested that "a stay" be put on removal. Repeating his arguments, the determined clergyman then wrote Kemble. The Poncas, he informed the inspector, were "more hostile to the removal than you think." Accusing the missionary of misrepresenting the facts, Kemble forwarded this letter to Commissioner Smith.[6]

Riggs had a second opportunity to express his strong opposition to removal when he spoke before the Senate committee. For nine years he had lived at the Santee Indian Agency in Nebraska, less than twenty miles from the Ponca Agency, and frequently had heard from Ponca chiefs and headmen about their difficulties with Indian officials. He was well aware of the pressure Kemble had exerted. Riggs informed Senator Dawes that the Poncas, who knew of the hardships suffered by the Pawnee following their removal to Indian Territory, were "determined never to be taken there." The Poncas had "never [given] their consent" to remove; they had agreed only to send a delegation south to look at the land. Upon their return from their tour, "a forced consent" had been given by a few; it was a consent reached only after Kemble had threatened to use military force. This latter fact, Riggs acknowledged, had been revealed to him by Charles Le Claire, the interpreter.[7]

Others who opposed removal included Solomon Draper, an attorney who also was an editor of the *Niobrara Pioneer*. Draper had resided in Niobrara since 1875 and knew the Poncas, for one of their villages was only three miles away across the Niobrara River. He became professionally interested in their plight after the eight chiefs, "excited and worked up by the treatment they had experienced" on their Indian Territory tour, came to town seeking advice. He testified before the Senate committee that the Indians "were fearful that they were going to be taken away from their lands."[8]

Acting out of friendship, Draper visited the Ponca Agency to confer with Kemble. He asked that removal be suspended for ten days until he could telegraph government officials. Kemble responded that removal had been decided and "the dignity of the government demanded that it should go ahead, and not back down from its position in that manner." Furthermore, Draper had no authority to act as counsel for the Indians.[9] When the inspector was later summoned to Washington, White Eagle personally drove thirty-two of his own horses to Niobrara to pay Draper for representing the tribe.[10]

Accompanied by Algernon S. Paddock, a senator from Nebraska, Draper reached Washington in late April and met first with Indian Commissioner Smith. The attorney informed Smith that agents and other officials were not reporting the facts accurately: the Poncas "never had agreed to leave their lands." Draper also noted that following their return from the Indian Territory, the chiefs had hired him. At that point "they did not want to go [there] on any consideration." Draper later testified that for whatever reason, "Commissioner Smith was very desirous of their removal."[11]

The two men then called on Interior Secretary Carl Schurz, who "promised that he would look into the matter." Draper, who had requested a delay until a proper investigation could be made, suggested Henry B. Whipple, the first Episcopal bishop of Minnesota, for the task.[12] His recommendation fell on deaf ears. At first, Schurz appeared inclined to grant the delay "but finally made up his mind that his official information was of such a nature that he ought to act." The secretary's change of heart might have been because part of the tribe had already begun to move, but also because Smith had remarked in front of Draper and Paddock that "agents were the sworn officials of the government, and . . . their reports must be the basis of all official action." Thus Schurz, still learning about Indian affairs, had deferred to the professionals in his department.[13]

Draper and Paddock then conferred with Generals William Tecumseh Sherman and Philip H. Sheridan. Although Sheridan thought that the Indians should be allowed to remain, members of the military had been given no orders, and removal was deemed "not properly a question for them to determine." Draper explained to the generals that local residents were anxious to keep the Poncas as neighbors for they served as a buffer against the more aggressive Lakotas.[14]

After leaving Washington, Draper visited Michigan, where he was detained by an unexpected illness. When he returned home, he found that the removal process was underway. Thus despite the groundswell of local support, the many letters written to government officials, and Draper's extensive conferences with government officials, both Smith and Schurz remained committed to removal. Draper believed that Smith favored it because the "half-breed" members of the tribe had already started on their journey, encouraged to do so after receiving numerous gifts and trinkets, "which put them in good humor." It was the contention of the government that if officials sent those Poncas back to their reservation, it would "interfere with the dignity of the government." Nevertheless, the full-bloods had remained on the reservation until Draper had written from Washington that he could not help.[15]

Later Draper explained to the Senate committee that ministers in neighboring communities such as Sioux City and Yankton supported the Poncas, both for humanitarian reasons and because they were preaching among them. However, merchants from these same towns, who made money from government contracts, were anxious to have the larger Lakota tribe replace the smaller Ponca tribe. In this way they could increase their profits. On the other hand, businessmen in Omaha and along the Union Pacific Railroad were opposed to the Lakotas moving to the Missouri River reservation, preferring that they remain more centrally located to ensure the businessmen's profit margins.[16] Furthermore, Draper accused Kemble of siding with Agent Lawrence and the contractors hired to implement removal for there was a "constant communication and manifest sympathy" between them.[17]

A *Niobrara Pioneer* editorial presented the situation in more conspiratorial terms, providing some evidence that local officials had benefited. It described the 1868 Sioux treaty as "the origin of the removal of the Poncas" and informed readers that Governor Newton Edmunds of Dakota Territory, a resident of Yankton, had served as one of the commissioners negotiating the treaty. In addition, Agent Lawrence, who assisted "in managing the dastardly deception" upon the Poncas, was rewarded with an appointment as agent to the Spotted Tail Brulé "with the intention of bringing them where the Poncas now are." The paper described the Poncas as friendly, while it depicted the Spotted Tail band as "red devils" and "outlaws" whom the gentlemen of Yankton wanted settled near Niobrara so they could engage in a profitable trade "without regard to safety of the property or the lives of our citizens."[18]

Safety was of utmost importance to the residents of Niobrara, Nebraska. The commissioners of Knox County openly expressed their concern on April 3, 1877, by unanimously approving a resolution addressed to President Hayes, the full text of which was published by the *Pioneer*. While the commission's president, A. W. Hubbard, and his fellow members portrayed the Poncas as peaceful neighbors, they described the Brulés' summer forays against local settlers. These Indians had driven off livestock, frightened residents, and once "massacr[ed] children." The presence of the Poncas as a buffer had "made the settlement of the Niobrara Valley possible." Their removal and replacement by the Lakotas would not only be grossly unjust but "an experiment, fraught with so much danger to us, that we tremble at the thought of its accomplishment," concluded the commissioners.[19]

While Draper, Riggs, and others actively opposed removal, some worked to implement the process, notably the Reverend Samuel Dutton Hinman, the first Episcopal missionary to the Lakotas. Conversant in Siouan, Hinman was assigned to the Santee Sioux Agency in 1866 and was frequently in contact with the Poncas, who lived only twenty miles away. Standing Bear's son lived with the Hinman family for a time. During the Senate hearings, the missionary defended Kemble, describing him as a "straight man, ... so straight that he leans over backward[s]" and always acts toward the Poncas to the "best of his knowledge and ability, honestly and fairly."[20]

Not as supportive of removal as Hinman, Bishop William H. Hare, the Protestant Episcopal missionary to the Poncas, assumed their consent had been obtained and therefore made no objection. He later informed the senators that by the time he had learned otherwise, all negotiations and arrangements had been completed. Hare deemed it essential that the process proceed. He feared "anarchy . . . would result if the government receded from its position." Thus he and Kemble agreed to telegraph the Interior Department to stand firm.[21]

The *New York Tribune,* which consistently supported the Ponca position, responded sharply to Bishop Hare's testimony. The paper held that blame did not lie with Kemble or Hare, but in a law that gave two men, even if the "most honest and godly on earth," the power "to eject, at their will, seven hundred men, women and children from the farms they owned and the houses they had built, and banish them for life." As long as the Indians remained without legal protection, the editorial concluded, "our Government is as autocratic to-day as that of Russia or Persia."[22]

Thus the government's decision to remove the Ponca caused serious divisions not only within the tribe itself, but between neighboring communities and among government officials and religious leaders. Sympathy for the Poncas in the towns around their reservation forced Kemble to justify his actions to his superiors. In his final report to Commissioner Smith, on July 28, 1877, the inspector claimed that the Indians "invented a story of injustice and oppression with which they extorted sympathy and assistance along the road."[23] When the New England–born author Helen Hunt Jackson eloquently presented Standing Bear's version to a much wider audience in a *New York Independent* article, Kemble immediately declared Standing Bear's tale as fictitious, "invented to cover [the Poncas] bad faith and shortcomings." In rebuttal, Standing Bear accused Kemble not only of attempting to force them to sign a treaty giving up their Dakota lands but of treating them badly."[24]

While the missionary community and local residents were split over the issue of removal, the tribe of seven hundred forty Indians, divided into numerous bands, was further splintered between full-bloods and mixed-bloods at a ratio of approximately 80 to 20. Full-bloods often viewed those of mixed ancestry as "tools" of the local settlers. According to Kemble, the full-bloods, numbering some four hundred, lived beside the Niobrara River about eight miles from the agency. And the "'half-breed band' embracing many full-bloods" lived near the agency on the Missouri River. The elderly Michel Cerre and Antoine, who had returned from the Indian Territory with Kemble, represented this latter band, "which was altogether favorable to removal from the start."[25]

Although some mixed-bloods were willing to remove, most full-bloods were not, including Standing Bear and his brother Big Snake, who endured temporary imprisonment because of their opposition. However, Kemble convinced the mixed-bloods and others in the upper camps near the agency to prepare for removal. A lengthy train of forty-six wagons carrying various portable goods, agricultural machinery, and other supplies crossed the Niobrara River on April 4, 1877, one month after the inauguration of Rutherford B. Hayes. Full-bloods opposed to removal attempted to prevent the wagons from departing.[26]

A week later Kemble received a telegram from Indian Commissioner John Quincy Smith advising, "Strong opposition to removal of the Poncas. Give facts and your views by telegraph." After conferring with Hinman and Bishop Hare, Kemble responded that the three men were united "in asking [the] department to stand firm." They mistakenly assumed that "the Niobrara opposition alone [was] obstructing removal."[27] Obviously local residents did not want the more peaceful tribe removed, but officials in Washington failed to take into consideration that the majority of the Poncas did not want to move either. Ties to the land were extremely strong among all native peoples who consistently resisted removal.

On April 7, Kemble ordered the various camps to prepare for immediate departure. He informed the remaining Poncas that he had one week's rations on hand and that wagon teams would be arriving in several days. After ordering Captain Fergus Walker to read his instructions to the Indians, Kemble met with Draper and those Poncas reluctant to leave. He denied Draper's request of a temporary suspension. Then on April 11, the teams arrived. Four days later, Kemble, accompanied by what he described as nearly half of the tribe, moved down to the Niobrara, escorted by soldiers dispatched by Col. Pinkney Lugenbeel, commander of Fort Randall. Many of these Indians, mostly from the upper camps, drove their own wagons.[28]

A late departure forced them to camp for the night among the full-bloods who opposed removal. The following day, instead of half of the tribe, only 170 to 180 Poncas finally waded across the river. The full-bloods had convinced many to remain behind.[29]

Chief White Eagle later testified that Kemble had promised money to those who would move, and Standing Buffalo complained that for over two months the agent "tried to starve us into it." However, Kemble insisted that he "withheld no rations so long as rations remained at the agency, and committed no act of cruelty or unjust oppression."[30]

Turning over to Agent James Lawrence the group that had just crossed the Niobrara River, Kemble returned to Washington on April 19 to explain the opposition he had encountered. Schurz reiterated that removal would occur, with force if necessary. Meanwhile Lawrence and the party of Poncas headed for the Indian Territory. After traveling for thirteen days in rainy, snowy weather on muddy roads, they arrived on April 28 at Columbus, Nebraska. They had covered only 130 miles.[31]

On April 30, Kemble arrived at Columbus and directed Lawrence and his replacement, E. A. Howard, to return to the agency to await the arrival of troops from Fort Sully, South Dakota, on the Missouri River to the north of Fort Randall, before moving the remaining Indians. Kemble now assumed control of the mixed-bloods and continued the journey.[32] On May 10, delayed by heavy rains, swollen streams, and nearly impassable roads, they reached Beatrice, Nebraska. They had averaged only eleven miles a day. Forced to remain almost a week at the Otoe Reservation along the Big Blue River, waiting for the water to recede, the removal party finally passed through Manhattan, Kansas, on May 24.[33] Reaching the Osage Mission on June 8, the wagon train was caught by rising waters, which required a rapid forced march and a detour around the streams. Two days later the party reached the road leading to Baxter Springs, Kansas, and continued its southward journey. The group finally arrived at the Quapaw Reservation in northeastern Indian Territory on the twelfth of June. The inspector described the Indians as "exceedingly well pleased" with their new home. They immediately set out to select farm and home sites. Although government officials had planted a 300-acre field in corn, little had been done about housing, thereby forcing the weary Poncas to live in army tents. While awaiting the arrival of the rest of the tribe, Kemble kept his son with him as proof of the healthful climate of this new tract.[34]

Under Kemble's direction the Poncas had endured a six-hundred-mile journey that lasted fifty-nine days. The total cost amounted to approximately $8,200, including $6,759 to cover the hauling of agency equipment, sup-

plies, and the Indians' private property. This was double the time and expense anticipated. The inspector admitted in his final report that it would
have been far cheaper to have moved the Indians by river and rail.[35]

In the meantime, Lawrence and Howard returned to the Ponca Agency
on May 6, met with the chiefs and headmen, and informed them that four
companies of soldiers were on their way to "compel" their removal if they
failed to go peacefully. In council the Poncas agreed to comply.[36] The process, however, was not quite that simple. Chief White Eagle later recounted
that although they were impressed with Howard's kindness and finally consented, they returned home after a council meeting one day to find soldiers
"standing guard" over their women and children. After witnessing these
soldiers kicking in locked doors and loading household goods onto wagons, White Eagle and an interpreter traveled to Niobrara and hired Draper
to telegraph the president. Again Hayes failed to reply.[37]

Although Kemble emphatically denied that force was ever used, Standing Bear's testimony substantiated everything White Eagle claimed. When
soldiers with poised bayonets approached the Poncas' homes, Standing Bear
told the senators, "we locked our doors, and the women and children hid
in the woods." After loading the household goods, the soldiers gathered
agricultural equipment, including plows, mowers, hay forks, reapers, and
other items too heavy to take along, and locked them in an agency building. A flour mill and a saw mill as well as 236 Indian-built log houses soon
stood empty. "Many of these things of which we were robbed," White Eagle
noted, "we had bought with money earned by the work of our hands."[38]

Final departure was delayed by inclement weather. Not until May 16 were
the Poncas safely across the turbulent Niobrara, with its dangerous bottom
of quicksand. Wagons were emptied and pulled across, their contents carried on the shoulders of young Ponca men. Severe thunderstorms continually prevented travel. On Saturday, May 19, the clouds began to lift and at
ten in the morning, escorted by twenty-five mounted soldiers commanded
by Captain Walker, an estimated 523 Poncas started out for Columbus. At
this point Lawrence turned control over to Howard and departed. The group
traveled a dozen miles the first day.[39]

The tremendous hardship endured by this party of Poncas on their fifty-
two-day march was graphically presented by Agent Howard in his first
annual report. While researching the ordeal of the Poncas, Helen Hunt Jackson was so moved by Howard's almost daily journal that she included much
of it in her chapter on Ponca removal in *A Century of Dishonor*.[40] The first
death occurred on Sunday, May 20, the second day of the journey. The child
was buried the following day, after the group had marched thirteen miles.

The next day in cool weather the party covered twenty-five miles on mostly dry roads. However, on May 23 they were drenched in a two-hour thunderstorm, followed by continual rain. They remained in camp and another child died. Rain, cold weather, swollen streams and rivers, muddy roads, and a lack of wood for campfires became commonplace.[41]

On May 27, several Indians became seriously ill. Prairie Flower, Standing Bear's daughter, was dying of consumption and it was almost impossible to move her "with any degree of comfort."[42] Roads mired in mud had to be covered with willow brush and wheat straw, and two teams were often hitched together to pull one wagon. The party struggled for seven hours to cover the last five miles to Columbus.[43] The Poncas were greeted by a dozen Omaha Indians gathered to bid good-bye to relatives and friends. Susette La Flesche was there because her uncle, Frank La Flesche (White Swan), a Ponca chief, had sent word to meet them. Susette, her father, Joseph, and eight or ten other Omahas witnessed the approach of the long train, with its wagons and livestock. "We met them on the road," she later remarked, "the men as well as the women—all were crying." White Swan and others informed their Omaha friends "that the soldiers counted them at every bridge they crossed, and called their names over, to see that all were there." Despite these precautions, some families slipped away. Susette reiterated that not one of those gathered wanted to go south.[44]

After the military escort left Columbus, the removal party struggled on, usually starting their day between six and seven in the morning, traveling as much as seventeen or as few as eight miles daily. At two o'clock on June 5, near Milford, Nebraska, Prairie Flower died. Travel in an open wagon in inclement weather and living in tents had been too much for the young woman. On the following day, her body, carefully prepared for burial by local white residents, was given a Christian burial in the Milford cemetery.[45]

That afternoon a heavy rain, accompanied by tornado-like winds, destroyed all the tents, overturned wagons, and hurled equipment "through the air in every direction like straws." Some Poncas were flung as far as three hundred yards, resulting in numerous injuries and the death of a child. The body was sent back to Milford for burial beside Prairie Flower. On June 13, the group camped near the Otoe Agency for two days while waiting for the creek to subside. On June 16, a wagon tipped over, severely injuring a woman; two days later a child died, and that same evening a severe rainstorm flooded the camp. Roads became impassable. On June 25, two elderly women died, and five days later another child died. Then on July 2, an attempt was made on Chief White Eagle's life. Howard successfully forced the assailant to leave the camp. When the rains finally ceased, the weather turned exceptionally hot; flies tormented the oxen. And on July 9, 1877, the last day of their journey, a severe thunderstorm struck with gale-force winds.[46] Nine Poncas died during the lengthy journey.

Almost from the very beginning, the Poncas disliked their new location, a rocky and swampy site some three miles from Baxter Springs, Kansas. They called it "the stony place." The only existing structure was a commissary building. Howard settled his new arrivals in tents north of this structure, while Kemble's group camped to the south. The Indians, accustomed to living in secure log cabins, found these flimsy tents inadequate. But housing was the least of their worries. Malaria became the real scourge; many took sick and died, despite all efforts of the resident physician. White Eagle recalled how difficult it was to adjust to the new climate; although none of his immediate family died during their first two summers, his wife and four children died of fever and ague in the summer of 1879.[47]

Although Kemble had brought his own son along to prove to the Indians that their new home was healthy, he nevertheless was troubled about future hazards to their health. He had indicated to Commissioner Smith as early as March 2, 1877, that a "thoroughly good and attentive physician" should be appointed, and the tribal "diet and mode of life during the first year or two" should be carefully supervised. Otherwise he feared a large number would be doomed "to inevitable death from the sudden change" in climate.[48] Agent Howard, in agreement, predicted "a great mortality [would] surely follow" once the Poncas had settled in.[49] Within two years, one-third of the tribe had died.

Malaria, fever, and ague were not the only dangers that doomed the Poncas. Their removal had threatened their ability to farm. They raised livestock, using their horses for travel and their oxen for plowing. By cutting rations, Kemble had forced the Indians to sell most of their horses to buy food. Other animals died or were run off by thieves. The Poncas had sold some of their oxen during their journey and the remainder soon died of disease. Since most farming implements had been left behind, the Indians' situation was now desperate. Not only were many Poncas too sick to work, those willing to farm did not have the tools to do so.[50]

Moreover, title to this new reservation was unclear. No arrangement had been made for purchase of any portion of the Quapaw land. In fact the government had not even secured the Quapaws' consent. The first time Kemble met in council with them was in June after he arrived with the first group of Ponca immigrants. He did not even try to "win their consent. Instead he informed them somewhat peremptorily that the great father had given their lands to the Poncas and that they must go and live with the

Osages."[51] The Quapaws did not leave; the issue became moot when the Poncas were relocated. In addition to this problem about the current Ponca home, there was no arrangement to compensate the Poncas for their former reservation along the Niobrara River. The Indians, therefore, requested that Agent Howard arrange for a delegation to visit President Hayes to settle these issues.[52] In early November 1877, Howard, accompanied by his clerk, two interpreters, and ten chiefs, including White Eagle and Standing Bear, traveled to Washington, where, on Friday, November 9, 1877, they were received at the executive mansion. During ceremonies in the mansion's cabinet council chamber, the chiefs detailed their removal and subsequent hardships and asked to be returned to their former Missouri River home.[53]

The following day the delegation returned to the executive mansion to hear the president's response. In the presence of Secretary Schurz and Ezra A. Hayt, recently appointed to replace John Quincy Smith as Indian commissioner, the Poncas listened as President Hayes described them as "good friends to the white people" with no blood on their hands. Their removal had been necessary "to guard [them] from collision with other Indians who [were] unfriendly." Now with more friendly tribes as their new neighbors, Hayes recommended against returning them to their old reservation. But when the Poncas informed the president that their livestock was being stolen by "bad men," who demoralized them with whisky, he agreed that they could send a delegation to select a new tract from government land in the Indian Territory. In addition, he guaranteed that they would be supplied with tools, cattle, and houses, which they would be paid for building.[54]

The Poncas listened as Hayes, sympathetic to their predicament, assured them that if they "go to work with a good heart, making good use of [their] time in planting fields and raising crops, [their] condition will soon be better, and [they would] be as prosperous and contented as the many thousand Indians who settled there before." They were admonished to follow the example of white farmers, who "suffered much hardship," but who with "courage and industry" had become "as rich and happy as you now see them." If they took his advice, he would always remember them as "good Indians" and "lend . . . a helping hand."[55]

The delegation emphatically rejected the Indian Office's proposal of a tract between the forks of the Arkansas and Cimarron rivers. Instead the chiefs selected land between the Chikaskia and the Salt Fork of the Arkansas.[56] However, small family groups, demoralized by the death and illness surrounding them in the Indian Territory, slowly began returning north to Nebraska and Dakota Territory where they settled among various local tribes. Others, including some twenty families from Standing Bear's band, headed west for the new location. By the end of April almost three hundred Poncas resided near the Salt Fork. Not until May 1878 were funds available to move the remaining Indians.[57] On the fifteenth of the following month, William H. Whiteman, a lawyer from Baxter Springs, Kansas, a small town due north of the Poncas' former home on Quapaw lands, was appointed as the new agent. He took charge of the agency during the first week of July and immediately prepared to relocate the remaining Indians. The approximately 185-mile journey to the west was begun during the week of July 21. Temperatures soared daily to almost 100 degrees. "Jaded and exhausted," the Indians arrived on July 28, with the loss of only one horse. They did not receive title to this new tract of land until March 3, 1881.[58]

In his annual report, Whiteman noted that there was "a restless, discontented feeling pervading the whole tribe." Nevertheless, he was impressed with his charges, deeming them "good Indians . . . superior to any tribe [he had] ever met." He only wished for them "the prompt and generous consideration of the government, whose fast and warm friends they have ever been."[59] His pleading fell on deaf ears.

Notes

1. "Kemble's Final Report," in U.S. Senate, *Testimony Relating to Removal*, 451.

2. "E. C. Kemble's Testimony," in U.S. Senate, *Testimony Relating to Removal*, 106 (quote); see also pages 81, 109, 111.

3. Ibid., 110 (all quotes).

4. U.S. Senate, *Testimony Relating to Removal*, xii; "E. C. Kemble's Testimony," in ibid., 66, 113–14, and "Standing Bear's Testimony," in ibid., 8–9. For more on Standing Bear, see H.H. [Helen Hunt Jackson], "Standing Bear and Bright Eyes," *Independent*, November 20, 1879, 2.

5. Tibbles, *The Ponca Chiefs*, 10–11.

6. "Alfred L. Riggs to the Secretary of the Interior, March 19, 1877," in U.S. Senate, *Testimony Relating to Removal*, 177, 428 (quotes); "Riggs to Kemble, March 20, 1877," in ibid., 429–30; and "Kemble to Smith, March 22, 1877," in ibid., 430–31. Riggs worked for the American Board of Commissioners for Foreign Missions. For a short list of other critics of removal see U.S. Senate, *Testimony Relating to Removal*, 177–78, 433–34.

7. "Alfred S. Riggs's Testimony," in U.S. Senate, *Testimony Relating to Removal*, 172; also see 173.

8. "Solomon Draper's Testimony," in U.S. Senate, *Testimony Relating to Removal*, 306. For more on Draper see *Niobrara Centennial: 1856–1956*, 13–14.

9. "Solomon Draper's Testimony," in U.S. Senate, *Testimony Relating to Removal*, 307 (quote); see also "E. C. Kemble's Testimony," ibid., 68–69, and "Kemble to J. Q.

Smith, April 12, 1877," ibid, 437. Also consult "Colonel Kemble and the Poncas," *Niobrara Pioneer*, April 26, 1877, 4, and Lake, "Standing Bear! Who?" 465.

10. Draper's report from Washington, dated April 27, 1877, appeared in "The Poncas Must Go," *Niobrara Pioneer*, May 3, 1877, 1. For Draper's complete testimony see U.S. Senate, *Testimony Relating to Removal*, 305–21; see also "Alfred S. Riggs's Testimony," ibid., 178–79. For Draper's payment in horses see "White Eagle's Testimony," in U.S. Senate, *Report of Special Commission*, 15.

11. Quotes from "Solomon Draper's Testimony," in U.S. Senate, *Testimony Relating to Removal*, 309.

12. Whipple established a mission among the Santee Sioux. During the 1862 Minnesota Sioux uprising, he attended to the wounded and comforted the bereaved. Convinced that cheating agents and traders and the ineffectiveness of the government's Indian policy had exacerbated the Indians' condition, he appealed to President Abraham Lincoln on their behalf. Instead of executing over three hundred Sioux prisoners, the government hanged thirty-eight. For more see Nichols, *Lincoln and the Indians*, 104–7, 123–24, 133–50, 157–59.

13. "Solomon Draper's Testimony," in U.S. Senate, *Testimony Relating to Removal*, 309–10.

14. Ibid., 310.

15. Ibid., 310, 312.

16. Ibid., 312–13. The Ponca removal resulted in cries of fraud and investigations; see Phillips, "The Indian Ring in Dakota Territory," 360–63.

17. "Solomon Draper's Testimony," in U.S. Senate, *Testimony Relating to Removal*, 317–18.

18. "Removal of the Poncas," *Niobrara Pioneer*, April 5, 1877, 4. The name Edmunds does not appear anywhere in the 1868 Sioux treaty, either among the commissioners or among those in attendance; however, the name of the Reverend Samuel Dutton Hinman does. Hill, *The Office of Indian Affairs*, 176, does not list James Lawrence as agent at the Spotted Tail Agency.

19. "Our County Fathers," *Niobrara Pioneer*, April 12, 1877, 8.

20. "Hinman's Testimony," in U.S. Senate, *Testimony Relating to Removal*, 339. In a February 15, 1877, editorial on page 4, the *Niobrara Pioneer* said of Hinman: "This exemplary Christian missionary humbug is at the head of the whole business, and with the aid of whisky in high places and Hiawathas in low places, has a wonderful influence with the heads of the Indian Department at Washington. . . . We look for better work in this respect under [the] Hayes . . . administration."

21. U.S. Senate, *Testimony Relating to Removal*, 116–33 (quote, 133); "The Removal of the Poncas," *Tribune*, February 17, 1880, 1.

22. "Bottom Facts in the Indian Matter," *Tribune*, February 29, 1880, 6.

23. "Kemble's Final Report," in U.S. Senate, *Testimony Relating to Removal*, 451.

24. For Kemble's comment, see Col. E. C. Kemble, "The Story of the Poncas," *Independent*, December 18, 1879, 5, and for Standing Bear's rebuttal see Machunahzhe (Standing Bear), "The Man from Washington," ibid., January 1, 1880, 3.

25. "Kemble's Final Report," in U.S. Senate, *Testimony Relating to Removal*, 451–52. Wishart (*An Unspeakable Sadness*, 206) notes that the Ponca had a higher number of mixed-bloods than other Nebraska tribes—some 150 individuals, or 20 percent.

26. "Kemble to J. Q. Smith, April 5, 1877," in U.S. Senate, *Testimony Relating to Removal*, 434–35. For a general discussion of the removal see Jacobs, "A History of the Ponca Indians," 125–33.

27. "Smith to Kemble, April 10, 1877," in U.S. Senate, *Testimony Relating to Removal*, 436 (first quote); Kemble to Smith, April 12, 1877, ibid., 436–37 (second quote); and "E. C. Kemble's Testimony," ibid., 69 (third quote).

28. Thomas Henry Tibbles, an Omaha newspaperman, regarded the removal as a scheme by designing contractors to make money from the government appropriations of $25,000 and $15,000 and the additional $30,000 to be paid after the Poncas were settled. He informed the Senate investigating committee that the Indians used their own wagons, teams, and food during the journey, not commodities belonging to the contractors. "T. H. Tibbles's Testimony," in U.S. Senate, *Testimony Relating to Removal*, 43.

29. "Kemble to J. Q. Smith, April 12, 1877," in U.S. Senate, *Testimony Relating to Removal*, 437–38; "April 16, 1877," ibid., 439; and "E. C. Kemble's Testimony," ibid., 70–71.

30. For White Eagle's statement see "John Springer's Testimony," in U.S. Senate, *Testimony Relating to Removal*, 163, and "White Eagle's Testimony," ibid., 197. For the quote from Standing Buffalo see "Standing Buffalo's Testimony," ibid., 228. For Kemble's statement see Kemble to Governor John D. Long, December 8, 1880, in U.S. Senate, *Report of Special Commission*, 50.

31. "E. C. Kemble's Testimony," in U.S. Senate, *Testimony Relating to Removal*, 70–71. For telegrams see "Smith to Kemble, April 12, 1877," "Kemble to Smith, April 16, 1877," "Smith to Kemble, April 17, 1877," and "Kemble to Smith, April 19, 1877," ibid., 439; see also "Kemble to Smith, May 1, 1877," ibid., 443, and "Kemble's Final Report," ibid., 453.

32. "Kemble to J. Q. Smith, May 1, 1877," in U.S. Senate, *Testimony Relating to Removal*, 442–43; "E. C. Kemble's Testimony," ibid., 72.

33. "Kemble to J. Q. Smith, May 12 and May, 24, 1877," in U.S. Senate, *Testimony Relating to Removal*, 445–46 and 446, respectively; and "Kemble's Final Report," ibid., 454.

34. "Kemble's Final Report," in U.S. Senate, *Testimony Relating to Removal*, 455 (quote), and "E. C. Kemble's Testimony," in ibid., 75, 77–78. See also "Removal of the Ponca," in U.S. Department of the Interior, Office of Indian Affairs, *Annual Report of the Commissioner of Indian Affairs* (1877), 21–23, and Lake, "Standing Bear! Who?" 466–67.

35. "Kemble's Final Report," in U.S. Senate, *Testimony Relating to Removal*, 455.

36. Ibid., 453–54.

37. "White Eagle's Statement," in U.S. Senate, *Testimony Relating to Removal*, 462.

38. For Standing Bear's testimony see H.H. [Helen Hunt Jackson], "Standing Bear and Bright Eyes," 2; for White Eagle's remark see "White Eagle's Statement," in U.S. Senate, *Testimony Relating to Removal,* 463. See also Tibbles, *The Ponca Chiefs,* 119–20.

39. "Kemble's Final Report," in U.S. Senate, *Testimony Relating to Removal,* 454. For Howard's first annual report and "Journal of the March," see "Howard to the Indian Commissioner, August 25, 1877," in U.S. Department of the Interior, *Annual Report of the Secretary of the Interior* (1877), 492–98. See also Hayter, "The Ponca Removal," 269–70, and Sheldon, *History of Nebraska,* 1:115.

40. H.H.J. [Helen Hunt Jackson], "The Poncas," in Jackson, *A Century of Dishonor,* 186–217. Jackson's "How the Indians Were Moved," *Independent,* February 5, 1880, 9–10, is essentially pages 207–17 of the longer chapter in *A Century of Dishonor.* The *Boston Daily Advertiser* (hereafter cited as *Advertiser*) also reprinted part of Howard's journal; see "As You Were," March 8, 1880, 2. See also Schmitz, *White Robe's Dilemma,* 86–99.

41. Howard, "Journal of the March," 493–94. In "Howard to Kemble, May 30, 1877," Howard described almost two weeks of the journey, in U.S. Senate, *Testimony Relating to Removal,* 446–48.

42. Howard, "Journal of the March," 494.

43. Jackson, "The Poncas," *A Century of Dishonor,* 209.

44. "Susette Le Flesche's Testimony," in U.S. Senate, *Testimony Relating to Removal,* 24 (first quote), 25 (second quote); see also "The Visiting Poncas," *Advertiser,* October 30, 1879, 1; and "Bright Eyes" [Susette La Flesche] to the Omaha Agent, April 29, 1879," in Tibbles, *The Ponca Chiefs,* 58–59. See also Green, *Iron Eye's Family,* 56–57.

45. Howard, "Journal of the March," 494. See also "Standing Bear," *Advertiser,* November 15, 1879, 2; Jackson, "How the Indians Were Moved," 10; and "Standing Bear's Testimony," in U.S. Senate, *Testimony Relating to Removal,* 19.

46. Howard, "Journal of the March," 494–95; and "Howard to Smith, June 22, 1877," in U.S. Senate, *Testimony Relating to Removal,* 448–50. See also Lake, "Standing Bear! Who?" 468–69.

47. "White Eagle's Testimony," in U.S. Senate, *Testimony Relating to Removal,* 199, 209–10; Howard, "Journal of the March," 495–96. For conditions after their arrival see Wishart, *An Unspeakable Sadness,* 210–11.

48. "Kemble to Smith, March 2, 1877," in U.S. Senate, *Testimony Relating to Removal,* 424.

49. "Howard to the Indian Commissioner, August 25, 1877," in U.S. Department of the Interior, *Annual Report of the Secretary of the Interior* (1877), 496. In his February 1, 1881, letter to Congress, President Hayes quoted Howard's report; see "Message from the President of the United States," in U.S. Senate, *Report of Special Commission,* 2. See also Sheldon, *History of Nebraska,* vol. 1, 115.

50. "White Eagle's Testimony," in U.S. Senate, *Testimony Relating to Removal,* 211. See also Lake, "Standing Bear! Who?" 470.

51. Baird, *The Quapaw Indians,* 117.

52. "Howard to Smith, May 31, 1877," in U.S. Senate, *Testimony Relating to Removal,* 470; "Howard to Nicholson, July 17, 1877," ibid., 472; and "Howard to Smith, August 7, 1877," ibid., 473–74. For the *New York Times* coverage of this delegation see Coward, *The Newspaper Indian,* 203.

53. Jacobs, "A History of the Ponca Indians," 135–36. The other members of the delegation were Standing Buffalo, Smoke Maker, Big Elk, Black Crow, Hairy Bear, Michel Cerre, Big Snake, and Frank La Flesche.

54. "Remarks of the President at Council held with the Ponca Delegation, November 10, 1877," Ponca Biographical File, Rutherford B. Hayes Presidential Center. The center holds both a handwritten copy and a typescript of this speech. See also "Indian Pow-Wow," *Cincinnati Commercial,* November 10, 1877.

55. "Remarks of the President," Hayes Presidential Center.

56. On February 23, 1878, Albert G. Boone, Ponca Agent, informed the Indian commissioner that the "Poncas positively refused to accept any selection but that between the Arkansas and Chikaskie [*sic*] rivers. Claim this from promises made by Department." Ricker Manuscript, box 28, folder 76, Nebraska State Historical Society.

57. Jacobs, "A History of the Ponca Indians," 135–39 [his pages 135–49; while paging this dissertation, Jacobs transposed some page numbers]. For more details see also Brown, "In Pursuit of Justice," 54–59, and Wishart, *An Unspeakable Sadness,* 211.

58. "Whiteman's Report," in U.S. Department of the Interior, Office of Indian Affairs, *Annual Report of the Commissioner of Indian Affairs* (1878), 64. For the congressional act see U.S. Department of the Interior, Office of Indian Affairs, *Annual Report of the Commissioner of Indian Affairs* (1881), xlvii–xlviii.

59. "Whiteman's Report," in U.S. Department of the Interior, Office of Indian Affairs, *Annual Report of the Commissioner of Indian Affairs* (1878), 65; see also Hayter, "The Ponca Removal," 271.

CHAPTER THREE

STANDING BEAR FLEES

By denying the Poncas' request to return to their homeland and ordering them instead to move to yet another tract in the Indian Territory, the Hayes administration set in motion events that would result in a complex public drama. The president was concerned with achieving justice for the Indians, promoting their education, and helping them achieve a better livelihood. But more immediately, he was interested in improving the Indian Office, known for its fraud, corruption, and inefficiency. To clean up the mess, he chose as interior secretary Carl Schurz, a liberal Republican who shared his interest in civil service reform. Yet on that November day in 1877, as the Ponca delegation stood before both men in the executive mansion, both officials ignored a unique opportunity to right a wrong. Only Hayes was up to the task, although it would take him another three years to recognize the "great and grievous wrong . . . done to the Poncas."[1]

Over the next several years, the Ponca controversy became not only complicated but emotionally charged as each observer, government official, minister, and humanitarian reformer viewed the situation from his or her own perspective. For example, while Agent William H. Whiteman described the Poncas as "restless and discontented" in their new home, Indian Commissioner Ezra Hayt portrayed an idyllic scene: their new land was "admirable in quality" and "surrounded on three sides by water, and fringed by fine forest trees," land that anyone would be pleased to call home.[2]

Standing on this "admirable" new home between the Chikaskia and the Salt Fork of the Arkansas was a commissary building with two small offices, built earlier by the government. Once again the Indians were forced to live in tents, initially in one large village. Whiteman encouraged them to scatter and select lands for future homes. The lateness of the season made it impossible to plant crops, which meant the Poncas would have to depend upon the government for subsistence. In addition, their 1877 annuities had not been paid. And the chills and fevers experienced on the Quapaw reserve continued to plague them. The tribe, which numbered 639, had lost forty-five members during 1878. "Their sufferings," Whiteman noted, had "greatly discouraged [them]," making them "dissatisfied with this location." They had expressed "a strong desire" to return home to their Dakota Reservation.[3]

Although Agent Whiteman appeared sympathetic to their plight, there was little he could do but write to his superiors. Like all "reservation Indians," whose lands had been set aside by a treaty, a statute, or an executive order, the Poncas were at the mercy of government officials, especially the interior secretary and his handpicked Indian commissioner, Ezra Hayt, a former wholesale dry-goods merchant from New York and a member of the Board of Indian Commissioners. Hayt had not been Schurz's first choice. The secretary appointed him after learning that two bank presidents endorsed him while certain corrupt government contractors opposed him. Hayt was independently wealthy and thus presumably had "no pecuniary interest in the job."[4]

Hayt visited the Poncas in the Indian Territory in October 1878 and described their new lands "as far superior to their old location in Dakota." The tribe had been provided with cattle, agricultural implements, a sawmill, timber, and all necessary tools to construct their own homes. Although numerous deaths occurred during the first four months of their residency there, Hayt informed Secretary Schurz that this was "inevitable in all cases of removal of Northern Indians to a Southern latitude." He assured the secretary that they would soon become acclimated to this new location.[5]

In his 1878 annual report, the commissioner described the Poncas as "becoming more reconciled to their new home." However, recognizing the "blunder" by which their lands were ceded to the Lakotas, the chagrined Hayt agreed that "the Poncas were wronged, and restitution should be made as far as it is in the power of the government to do so." True to his word, on February 3, 1879, he forwarded a draft of "A Bill for the Relief of the Ponca Tribe of Indians in the Indian Territory" to Secretary Schurz. Hayt recommended that they be paid $140,000. Of this, approximately $82,000 was earmarked for the purchase of their new Indian Territory lands, which belonged to the Cherokee Nation. The remainder was to be invested and the interest annually dispersed to the tribe. However, the bill was not passed.[6]

The Poncas' situation improved slightly with the arrival of farm implements. While the government paid to break ground for White Eagle and Standing Buffalo, the remaining tribesmen plowed their own land and were paid for their work. The chiefs' fields averaged between four and five acres each. By the summer of 1879 there were about eighty plots planted in corn, potatoes, and melons. Because the fields were not fenced, livestock foraged through the new growth. In addition the lack of rain caused the remaining plants to wither. For the third year in a row, the Poncas had an unsuccessful harvest. On the positive side, house construction got underway with the government furnishing doors and windows. Unfortunately, unseasoned green lumber was used. When the wood dried, there appeared cracks large enough for a man to put his hand through.[7]

In his second annual report, Whiteman recorded that the Poncas constructed over seventy houses of hewed logs and were issued one hundred fifty cows with calves, forty wagons, twenty-five yoke of oxen, and various agricultural implements. The Indians planted over 350 acres in corn and various vegetables, and their children attended the new day school. Whiteman's report reflected satisfaction with the Poncas' progress. The Indians, he noted, were "making rapid improvement both mentally and morally."[8]

Whiteman probably also took pleasure in relating the births of sixteen Ponca children. But he no doubt was saddened by the deaths of twenty-six members of the tribe and by the fact that sixty-six Poncas fled the reservation. Late in 1878 Chief Smoke Maker and nine followers walked away, seeking refuge at the Yankton Agency in Dakota Territory. No retaliatory action occurred although he had been one of the ten chiefs to tour the Indian Territory and had accompanied Agent Howard to Washington in 1877.[9] However, when Chief Standing Bear, his wife, and thirty followers fled the reservation in January 1879, an order for their arrest was issued. Government officials probably followed a hard line toward Standing Bear because some three hundred fifty Northern Cheyennes had left the Indian Territory the previous September. These Cheyenne, after participating in the Battle of the Little Big Horn, had surrendered and had been sent south to live at the Darlington Agency on the Southern Cheyenne and Arapaho Reservation, where, like Standing Bear's people, they suffered from starvation, homesickness, and especially malaria. Accustomed to the high plains of Montana, the Northern Cheyennes were unused to the humid climate of the south, and one-tenth of their numbers died during the first winter. After leaving the Indian Territory, the Northern Cheyennes split into two groups. Those under Dull Knife headed for Fort Robinson, Nebraska, where they were imprisoned. Threatened with a return to the Indian Territory, they tried desperately to escape in early January, and almost one-half of the group were killed. Fortunately, the other group, comprised of Little Wolf and his followers, was able to avoid capture and eventually signed on as army scouts at Fort Keogh, Montana. Ultimately the Cheyennes were allowed to remain in the north, some among the Lakotas at Pine Ridge and others on the Tongue River reserve (renamed the Northern Cheyenne Reservation) near Fort Keogh.[10]

Standing Bear was probably unaware that the Northern Cheyennes had been forced to the Indian Territory scarcely two months after the arrival of his tribe at the Quapaw Reserve. Their final destinations were miles apart. Despite improvements in housing and the arrival of farm implements and food supplies, the Poncas continued to fall ill and die. Standing Bear, much like Dull Knife and Little Wolf, stood by helplessly as his people, including his sister, perished. "I was in an awful place," the Ponca chief later remarked. "I had been taken by force from my own country to a strange land, and was a captive. . . . I could see nothing ahead but death for the whole tribe."[11]

When his sixteen-year-old son died of malaria in late December 1878, Standing Bear vowed to bury him in the old Niobrara homeland as promised. Determined also to save at least a few of his followers, on January 2, 1879, the chief, his wife, nine men, and twenty-one women and children slipped away during a heavy snowstorm and headed north in three covered wagons and one light spring wagon. "If I failed it could be no worse than to stay there" he later remarked. They had meager rations and only twenty dollars, which quickly ran out during the ten-week journey.[12]

The Poncas found white farmers along their route most generous. In only two places were they refused help; Standing Bear simply assumed these settlers had scarcely enough for their own families. One individual, seeing the sorry condition of the horses, offered hay and a large bag of corn. When the Indians shelled and parched some of the corn for the children, who ate "ravenously," the farmer then provided them with meat, flour, and coffee. Thus unlike the Northern Cheyennes, who in their odyssey through Kansas and Nebraska fled government troops, fought several battles, killed a number of settlers and cattlemen, and stole livestock, Standing Bear and his party bothered no one. Writing about the Ponca journey twelve years later, Lieutenant John Gregory Bourke, aide-de-camp to Brigadier General George Crook, described them as "walking every foot of the way, molesting nobody, and subsisting upon charity. Not a shot was fired at any one; not so much as a dog was stolen."[13]

On March 4 the Poncas arrived at the Omaha Reservation. They were warmly welcomed by Chief Joseph La Flesche, who provided food, land, and seeds for planting. Omaha Agent Jacob Vore's welcome was not as friendly. He had them arrested.[14]

Because the Poncas departed during inclement weather, Agent Whiteman remained unaware of their escape for six days. Upon discovering them missing, he notified the Indian Office, which had already been alerted by Vore's March 4 telegram to the Indian commissioner. Three days later Interior Secretary Schurz informed Secretary of War George McCrary of their presence at the Omaha Agency and requested that the nearest military commander detail a guard to return them to their own agency. An order, following the chain of command, was forwarded to General William Tecumseh Sherman; to Lieutenant General Philip Sheridan, commander of the Military District of Missouri; and finally to General George Crook, commander of the Department of the Platte. From his headquarters at Fort Omaha, on March 19 Crook ordered Lieutenant William L. Carpenter of the Ninth Infantry to arrest the runaways.[15]

On March 23, accompanied by a corporal and an interpreter, the lieutenant and four others marched to the Ponca camp. Although ordered to escort them to the Indian Territory, Carpenter, in the presence of principal members of the Omaha tribe and their agent, listened to Standing Bear's recitation of their sufferings. Impressed by the chief's "able speech" and concerned about the Poncas' "pitiable condition from the effects of chills and fever," the lieutenant took them to Fort Omaha to confer with General Crook.[16]

The following day, J. Owen Dorsey, an Episcopal priest living among the Omaha, wrote a desperate appeal to A. B. Meacham, who had a long history of reform work among the Indians.[17] Appointed as superintendent of Indian affairs for Oregon in 1869, Meacham worked hard to implement Grant's "peace policy." Seeking to resolve the conflict between the Klamath and Modoc, who occupied the same reservation, he headed a peace commission in 1873 to mediate with Captain Jack and other Modoc leaders who had fled the reservation. Captain Jack and the other delegates murdered several members of the commission, including General Edward R. S. Canby, and shot and partially scalped Meacham.[18]

Following his recovery, Meacham lectured on the causes of the Modoc War and in 1878 founded the *Council Fire*, a monthly journal, which he hoped would be to Indian reform what the *Liberator* had been to the abolition movement. "Its chief and determined purpose," wrote Meacham, "is to ascertain and define the right, and expose and condemn the wrong."[19] In 1879 Meacham moved the journal to Washington, where he could more closely follow congressional Indian policy.

Dorsey happened to be at the Omaha Agency when Standing Bear and his followers were arrested. The chief informed the priest, "We could not live down there where the Great Father put us, so we came here to live and work the land." Moved by Standing Bear's words and witnessing the Poncas walking about a mile in advance of the military escort, Dorsey told Meacham that this was not a war party but a group of families, with their wagons, pigs, and chickens. Fearful that military force would be needed to keep the remaining Poncas in the Indian Territory, or that this situation might escalate into another massacre, like that of the Northern Cheyennes, Dorsey appealed to Meacham to find out who "caused the arrest of the thirty Poncas." He had been told that because the Omahas were willing to allow them to live on their reservation "they would not be disturbed."[20]

Meeting with Hayt and Schurz, Meacham read Dorsey's letter to them, and he reported in the April issue of the *Council Fire* that both men insisted they were powerless "without the authority of Congress, to move any tribes of Indians." More to the point, they claimed if Standing Bear and his followers were allowed to remain in the North, other tribes, including the Pawnees, Northern Arapahoes, Northern Cheyennes, and Nez Perces, would all be "clamoring to return" to their northern homes. Meacham ended his column with a question: "will not the time come when the Indian will be treated as a man?"[21]

Dorsey's letter prompted a sharp rebuke from the Ponca agent, William H. Whiteman. He reported that Standing Bear and some two-thirds of the tribe had run away from the Ponca Agency at Quapaw and moved to their new home without government permission. As a consequence, they lived without rations and medical attention for several months until he arrived with the remaining Poncas. By this time Standing Bear's group was sick with ague and malaria "brought upon them by their own misconduct, in running away from the Agency." Whiteman believed it was the duty of missionaries to "allay discontent," to encourage a "spirit of content, hope, and faith in the Government and obedience to its wishes." Instead, Dorsey and residents of Niobrara and neighboring towns had engaged in "propagating and intensifying a spirit of discontent among the Poncas."[22]

Unaware of Dorsey and Meacham's efforts on his behalf, Standing Bear and his followers arrived at Fort Omaha on March 27, 1879, under guard. A short distance south of the main entrance, the Poncas built three lodges, two with wagons as the foundation. Because over half of the adults were sick and their horses were in a weakened state, the post commander, Colonel John H. King, determined that they were incapable of enduring the long trek to the Indian Territory and would be temporarily detained at the fort.[23] James Lawrence, the former Ponca agent, who was now in business with his brother in Nebraska, learned of the arrest and visited Standing Bear, "advis[ing] him to be patient and not to make any resistance."[24]

King's commanding officer, General George Crook, displeased with having been ordered to arrest the Poncas, visited the editorial office of the *Omaha Daily Herald* at nearly one in the morning on March 30, 1879, to confer with the assistant editor, Thomas Henry Tibbles. Years later in his memoirs, Tibbles claimed that the general had asked for his support, remarking that "if we can do something for which good men will remember us when we're gone, that's the best legacy we can leave." Crook promised that he would stand by Tibbles if he took up this work.[25]

By this time Crook had had a distinguished military career. After graduation from West Point in 1852, he served with the Fourth Infantry stationed on the Pacific Coast, where, until the opening salvos of the Civil War, he built military posts and fought in several Indian wars. During the Civil War, among other assignments, he commanded the Thirty-sixth Ohio Volunteer Infantry and later the Second Cavalry Division. At war's end he was appointed lieutenant colonel of the Twenty-third Infantry stationed in the Pacific northwest. After successfully subduing the Paiutes, he moved to Arizona where, as commander of the Department of Arizona, he placed many Apache bands on reservations. Four years later he commanded the Department of the Platte. His defeat at the Rosebud by Lakota warriors prevented his command from joining in the pincer movement against Sitting Bull and Crazy Horse at the Little Bighorn.[26]

For almost a decade, Crook opposed the government's Indian policy but considered it improper to take a public stand. Well aware that various tribes could be warlike, Crook understood that if they deemed it to be in their best interest, they would accept peace. "I will say, without hesitation," he wrote Tibbles, "that our Indians have adhered more closely to the spirit of treaty stipulations than the white men or the white man's Government has ever done." A quick glance at treaty provisions, he noted, revealed how many had been broken, giving the Indians strong grounds for "their distrust and contempt." Crook claimed tribes that remained at peace were starved, while those that went to war were made "every promise, [and] yield[ed] concession[s]." Indians learn that by being "bad," they were "all the more certain to be the recipient of kind treatment."[27]

Particularly critical of the Indian's lack of legal protection, Crook commented that it was "an odd feature of our judicial system that the only people in this country who have no rights under the law are the original owners of the soil." If, instead, the Indian possessed the same rights as white men, he concluded that "self-interest [would] impel him to imitate us, to send his children to school, to adopt clothing, perhaps our language, and to devote his attention to raising cattle and horses and eventually to qualify himself for citizenship."[28] Because Crook's command was located near the Omaha

Reservation, this latest example of government treatment of the Indian had been thrust upon him. The Poncas would gain a sympathetic friend.

"Beyond question, the most important . . . [case] occurring within General Crook's jurisdiction after the pacification of the Sioux" was that of the Poncas, noted Lieutenant John Gregory Bourke of the Third Cavalry.[29] Bourke, the general's aide-de-camp since September 1871, was involved with the Ponca controversy from the initial meeting of Crook and Standing Bear through the tenure of President Hayes's Ponca Commission, for which he served as one of the recorders. His diary entries reflect at times daily contacts with Standing Bear, White Eagle, and other Poncas.

Although Crook had disagreed with federal Indian policies for some time, the fact that a fellow Ohioan and former comrade in arms, Rutherford B. Hayes, was now president gave him a sense of security in acting as he did. Not only did Hayes serve under Crook as a colonel of the Twenty-third Regiment, the Ohio Volunteers, but when Lucy Hayes and her three children visited the camp, Crook was included in family activities. Crook, who had no children, often acted as a surrogate father to the Hayes children, becoming particularly close to Webb Hayes. A child born to the family during the war was named George Crook Hayes.[30]

Crook may have sought out Tibbles because he considered him a kindred spirit. The journalist had known John Brown and had been an abolitionist in Kansas Territory, where he participated in the bitter guerrilla warfare. After numerous adventures, Tibbles moved farther west, spending two years among the Potawatomi and Iowa Indians. By the time he arrived in Omaha, he was regarded as a warm friend of the Indians.[31]

After a lengthy conversation with Crook on that early morning of March 30, Tibbles left his office, headed home for a few hours of sleep, and then set out to interview the Indian prisoners at Fort Omaha. He later recalled that Standing Bear was reluctant to tell his side of the removal and journey until the Indians had met formally with Crook. "But as soon as I tried on him some of the Soldier Lodge signs," wrote Tibbles, Standing Bear "called a council to smoke the pipe of peace with me."[32] For the next three hours, Tibbles listened and asked questions as the Poncas related their recent experiences, while Charles P. Morgan, who lived among the Omahas, interpreted.

The first to speak was Buffalo Chips, who, gesturing gracefully, remarked: "I sometimes think that the white people forget that we are human . . . that we require food and clothing." He queried: "Am I not a man?" After a long silence he continued. "Eight days ago I was at work on my farm which the Omahas gave me. . . . I was arrested and brought back as a prisoner. . . . I have been told since the great war that all men were free men, and that no man can be made a prisoner unless he does wrong."[33] He inquired of Tibbles if there were different laws for those who were not white. He simply wanted to work his land and provide for his family. Instead he was arrested and forced to depend upon the government for rations. "We want land which shall be our own," he told Tibbles, and then added, "we want a court."[34]

Standing Bear spoke next, briefly summarizing the move to the Indian Territory. He informed Tibbles that during their first four months there Agent Howard "never issued a pound of rations," thus forcing them to beg from neighboring Modocs, Quapaws, and Cherokees. Then the sickness came, one hundred fifty died and the others suffered severe head and back pains. Their new home, he said, was "the worst country in the world." All he desired was to send his remaining children to school, raise his livestock, and plant his fields. "I can raise this year enough wheat, potatoes and other things to have plenty to eat next winter," he told Tibbles, "but the government won't let me." What most concerned him, however, was keeping the promise made to his son to bury his bones where he was born.[35]

With the interview concluded, Tibbles set out to enlist support. As a former Methodist circuit rider, he turned to Omaha ministers in the hope they might appeal to government officials to allow the Indians to remain on the Omaha reservation. At the First Presbyterian Church, the Reverend William Justin Harsha permitted Tibbles to appeal to his parishioners while the Reverend Alvin F. Sherrill, pastor of the First Congregational Church, let him speak between the opening hymns. E. H. E. Jameson, pastor of the Baptist Church and a friend of Schurz, sent the secretary a telegram signed by local ministers, requesting that the order to return the Poncas to the Indian Territory be rescinded.[36] To coordinate their collective efforts, leading laymen and clergy established the Omaha Ponca Relief Committee, chaired by the Right Reverend Robert H. Clarkson, Episcopal bishop of Nebraska.[37]

Methodist, Congregational, and Episcopal ministers in Yankton, joined by prominent citizens, also organized on behalf of the Poncas. They sent to Senator Alvin Saunders of Nebraska a communiqué the *Yankton Daily Press and Dakotaian* described as an "uncommonly interesting memorial," and Saunders in turn presented it to Congress in late April 1879. The ministers and their supporters described the Ponca move from the Dakotas to the Indian Territory as "fatal." Because Spotted Tail and his people had recently abandoned the lands, the group called for the return of the Poncas to their old home or permission to join whichever tribe they preferred, such as the Omahas, the Santee, or Yankton Siouan people. If neither solution was possible, they recommended the appointment of a commission to investigate the case.[38]

The Poncas also received sympathetic treatment at the hands of the local military. Summoned to Crook's Fort Omaha office on March 31, 1879, Standing Bear—described by Bourke as a "noble looking Indian, tall and commanding in presence, [and] dignified in manner"—was resplendent in blue flannel leggings, beaded belt, a grizzly bear claw necklace, and a red blanket trimmed with blue stripes. The seven other Ponca men and Charles Morgan wore green Mexican blankets over their clothing. According to Bourke, Morgan's excellent command of English had been gained as a scout in the 1st Nebraska Volunteer Infantry during the Civil War. After being formally presented to General Crook by Lieutenant Carpenter, the Poncas shook hands with all the officers, "squatted in a semi-circle on the floor," and then, through the interpreter, related the story of their removal. In his diary Bourke included a verbatim transcript of the conference "merely to show the cruel and senseless way in which [the] government of the United States deals with the Indian tribes who confide in its justice or trust themselves to its mercy."[39]

Standing Bear, speaking first, lamented his inability to read. He detailed his visit with the president and mourned the deaths of hundreds of his fellow Poncas. "It just seems . . . to me as if a big prairie-fire was coming toward me," he informed the assembled group, "I would take hold of my wife and baby boy and run with them to a safe place." He informed the officers and Tibbles that he felt as if "somebody [was] clamping [him] down to the ground. I need help to get that man off me, so I can stand up."[40]

At the conclusion of the conference, General Crook agreed that it was "a very hard case," but he was in no position to help them. He must obey his orders "from Washington, where they know all these facts and still order . . . [you] down [to the Indian Territory.]" He said that it would do no good to telegraph, but he could allow them to stay for a few days at Fort Omaha, where they and their livestock would be rested and fed before undertaking the return journey. The conference ended with handshakes all around.[41]

Although General Crook proved unable to help the Poncas, Thomas Henry Tibbles did. The only civilian present at the conference, he would be responsible for turning the ordeal of the Poncas into a national controversy, one that accelerated the cause of Indian reform. He tirelessly transcribed the conversation during the early morning hours at Fort Omaha on March 30 and the speeches delivered in Crook's offices. He telegraphed them to newspapers in New York, Chicago, and other cities. On April 1, his article based on these speeches appeared in both the daily and weekly *Omaha Herald*. Tibbles also published an interview with the interpreter Charles P. Morgan, who had firsthand knowledge of the conditions at the Quapaw Agency, the

Poncas' first home in the Indian Territory. Not only had Morgan visited the agency but his brother, a resident at the Otoe Agency, wrote monthly letters about the sick and dying Poncas. Once, Morgan informed Tibbles, the Indians had gone about a month without receiving any governmental provisions. Tibbles skillfully used these details to elicit sympathy.[42]

"Clearly I was in for another fight on the very same principle which had carried me to Bleeding Kansas in 1856," Tibbles wrote in his memoir, "namely: that before the law all men are equal." Research in a law office led him to believe that the key was the Fourteenth Amendment, which "defined the right of any *person* in the United States to his life, liberty, and property unless these were removed by due processes of law." According to his reasoning, the amendment gave "these Indians as *persons* a right to call upon the courts to defend them."[43] With no funds to pursue a legal defense, Tibbles asked John Lee Webster, an Omaha lawyer, if he would take the case with no fee and file an application for a writ of habeas corpus on behalf of the Poncas. Calling the matter "a question of vast importance," and interested in the constitutional issue it posed, Webster agreed. He stressed clearly that the application "must be based upon broad constitutional grounds" and should focus on the issue of "personal liberty." He was concerned, however, that the writ might not hold because of the wardship relation of Indians to the federal government, but he concluded it would "do no harm to try." He believed that "this inhuman cruelty" must stop and hoped the power to change it rested in the courts.[44]

Aware of the magnitude of the case, Webster suggested that Tibbles enlist the support of the older, more experienced legal counsel for the Union Pacific Railroad, Andrew Jackson Poppleton. Years later in a pamphlet entitled *Reminiscences*, Poppleton wrote that to the best of his "personal knowledge" it was General Crook who "suggest[ed] the remedy of habeas corpus."[45] Regardless of who made the suggestion, Poppleton agreed to assist. He remarked to Tibbles that even though Indians were viewed by the government as "wards of the nation," it did not mean that guardians "can imprison, starve or practise [*sic*] inhuman cruelty upon the ward." He concluded that "the courts always have, and always will interfere in such cases," and told Tibbles to inform Webster that he would "give to it close attention and [his] best efforts."[46] The judge that Tibbles wanted was Elmer Scipio Dundy, who was then on a hunting trip. Several days passed before the judge could be located; Tibbles described Crook during that time as "the most anxious person I ever saw to have a writ served on him."[47]

Webster, Poppleton, and Dundy were well-respected members of their community at the time of the Ponca removal. Webster, a native of Ohio, had settled in Omaha in 1869 and for the next four decades had practiced law. Prior to his selection by Tibbles, he served in the Nebraska state legislature, was president of the Nebraska Constitutional Convention that drafted a new state constitution in 1875, and earned a reputation as an excellent debater.[48]

A native of Michigan, Andrew Jackson Poppleton arrived in Omaha in 1854. He had served as attorney for the plaintiff in the first lawsuit tried in the territory and won the case. From then on he never lacked clients. He served in Nebraska's first legislature in 1857 and the following year became Omaha's second mayor. Between 1863 and 1888 he served as chief counsel for the Union Pacific Railroad Company.[49]

Born in Ohio, Elmer Scipio Dundy moved with his family to Pennsylvania in 1850, where three years later he was admitted to the bar. He arrived in Nebraska in 1857 and the following year was elected to the upper house of the territorial legislature, where he served two terms and continued his law practice until Abraham Lincoln appointed him an associate justice of the Supreme Court of Nebraska Territory. Andrew Johnson appointed him to the United States District Court, a position he held at the time of his death in 1896. By the time of Standing Bear's arrest, Dundy had already presided over several cases involving Indians. In the most recent, he ruled "that federal courts had no jurisdiction over crimes committed on Indian reservations."[50]

Tibbles enjoyed a significant connection with Webster. They both had attended Mount Union College in Ohio where the journalist had been much in demand as a campus speaker at a time when the student body was thoroughly abolitionist in its sympathies. Although Webster attended later, those sympathies undoubtedly affected him, and help explain his favorable response to Tibbles's request.[51]

Thomas Henry Tibbles emerged as a major instigator of the reform movement that sprang from the Ponca court case. Relying on his skills as a journalist to promote the Ponca cause, Tibbles chose the legal counsel and the court. It was he, in conjunction with prominent citizens, who organized the Omaha Ponca Relief Committee. His endeavors along with those of the committee suggest a strong western impulse in the burgeoning Indian reform movement. A biographical sketch of John Lee Webster published in the 1894 edition of *History of the City of Omaha, Nebraska* confirms this western origin. Its authors concluded that Standing Bear's case "first awakened the people of New England to a sense of the wrongs done the Indians by our federal government, and . . . led to the formation of a strong philanthropic society for their protection."[52]

Although New Englanders participated in efforts to right the wrongs that the Poncas suffered, it was initially western voices that were raised on their behalf. A petition sent to President Hayes from Yankton, Dakota Territory, by prominent members of that community described the removal of the Poncas from their Dakota homeland as fatal. It informed the president that one-fourth of the tribe had died. Like Reverend Dorsey of the Omaha Agency, the petitioners feared there was "imminent danger of another Cheyenne horror," a reference to the massacre of Northern Cheyennes attempting to return to their Northern Plains homeland only three months earlier. Because Spotted Tail and his band were no longer living on the former Ponca Reservation, the petitioners suggested that the Poncas be allowed to return home.[53]

On April 4, 1879, the same date as the Yankton petition, Webster and Poppleton filed an application for a writ of habeas corpus in the Federal Circuit Court for the District of Nebraska. The petition, witnessed by Tibbles and Lieutenant William L. Carpenter, appeared as *Ma-chu-nah-zha (Standing Bear) v. George Crook* and listed twenty-six Poncas who were described as "unlawfully imprisoned, detained, confined and in custody, and . . . restrained of their liberty" under "the alleged authority of the United States." The complainants were represented as "separated from the Ponca tribe," self-supporting, and at the time of their arrest residing peacefully on the Omaha Reservation.[54]

The writ, signed four days later, was issued from Lincoln and served on General Crook, the respondent. In a sworn statement on April 11, Crook informed Dundy that he had detained the Indians under orders from the secretary of the interior and his key associates.[55] On the second day of the ensuing trial Crook learned that an amendment, which noted that the complainants still retained "their tribal relations" and were "not pursuing the habits and vocations of civilized life," had been appended to his response by Genio Madison Lambertson, the federal district attorney for Nebraska. Because this amendment appeared over his signature, and because it was not accurate, Crook protested first to Major Horace B. Burnham, departmental judge advocate, and later to Judge Dundy. The judge explained to Crook that he was signing only as a brigadier general in the United States Army and not as an interested individual. Although Crook continued to protest, the offending amendment was never removed.[56]

Two days later, Commissioner Hayt informed Secretary Schurz that there was no law in place that would allow the Poncas to return to their old reservation. If the system was to work, "discontented and restless or mischievous Indians cannot be permitted to leave their reservation at will and go where they please." Discipline would break down, and the West would soon be swarming with "roving and lawless bands of Indians, spreading a spirit of uneasiness and restlessness even among those Indians who are now at work and doing well." The civilization process, Hayt observed, required rules that "sometimes produc[e] individual hardships, and which cannot be abandoned without detriment to the best interests of the large majority of our Indian wards." He singled out Standing Bear as the only chief who "showed a bad spirit, constantly grumbl[ed], and held [himself] aloof from the other chiefs." He "seemed full of discontent, which he took no pains to conceal, while the other Poncas were at work." Hayt added that Agent Whiteman had expected Standing Bear to flee the agency at the "first favorable opportunity."[57]

Shown Hayt's letter, Standing Bear went to a trunk and produced numerous letters dating back to 1865, written by agents and military men testifying to his good character. Agent Arthur J. Carrier described him as "reliable and trustworthy," "industrious," and possessing a "real zeal in setting a good example." First Lieutenant William H. Hugo called him "civil, quiet and well-behaved, a warm friend of the whites, and loyal to the government." And even Commissioner Hayt on December 18, 1877, described Standing Bear as desirous of preserving "peace and harmony between the Ponca Indians and the United States, and as such entitled to the confidence of all persons whom he may meet."[58]

Standing Bear agreed that he was not liked and respected by all Ponca chiefs. He explained that like many tribes, his people divided into two groups, the traditionalists, who wanted to retain their old customs and religion, and those willing to send their children to school, build homes, and become self-sufficient. He identified with the latter group.[59] A week or so after Standing Bear's response, a petition dated April 21, 1879, arrived from the Omaha Agency addressed to "the friends of the Poncas." Drafted by Charles P. Morgan and signed by twenty Omahas, it expressed the tribe's willingness to share their lands with the Poncas.[60]

Two powerful forces in Nebraska had combined to defend Standing Bear and his band of followers—General George Crook, commander of the Department of the Platte, and Thomas Henry Tibbles, assistant editor of the *Omaha Daily Herald*. Together they had prevented the Poncas' return to the Indian Territory, thus enabling Tibbles time to get the story of their plight before the public, both locally and nationally. They had carried the issue as far as they could. The next step was to determine what rights if any these Indians had before the federal courts. Their destiny would be decided by Federal District Court Judge Elmer Scipio Dundy in his Omaha courtroom.

Notes

1. Hayes, *Diary and Letters,* 3:629. For Hayes's Indian policy, see Weeks, "Humanity and Reform," 174–88.

2. "The Poncas," in U.S. Department of the Interior, Office of Indian Affairs, *Annual Report of the Commissioner of Indian Affairs* (1878), xxxvi.

3. "Whiteman's Report," in U.S. Department of the Interior, Office of Indian Affairs, *Annual Report of the Commissioner of Indian Affairs* (1878), 64–65 (quote, 65); see also Brown, "In Pursuit of Justice," 58.

4. Kvasnicka and Viola, eds., *The Commissioners of Indian Affairs,* 156; see pages 155–66 for discussion of Hayt's tenure as commissioner. Hayt was dismissed from service in 1880 due to alleged improprieties relative to the San Carlos Agency in Arizona.

5. "Mr. Hayt's Assault on Standing Bear, and the Reply the Old Chief Made," in Tibbles, *The Ponca Chiefs,* 47. This letter also appeared in the *Council Fire,* May 1879, 76.

6. "The Poncas," in U.S. Department of the Interior, Office of Indian Affairs, *Annual Report of the Commissioner of Indian Affairs* (1878), xxxvi (quotes). For the draft of the relief bill, see "The Poncas," in U.S. Department of the Interior, Office of Indian Affairs, *Annual Report of the Commissioner of Indian Affairs* (1879), xiv–xv; see also "Hayt to Schurz, February 3, 1879," in U.S. Senate, *Testimony Relating to Removal,* 478–79.

7. "Standing Buffalo's Testimony," in U.S. Senate, *Testimony Relating to Removal,* 231–32, and "Joseph Esaw's Testimony," in ibid., 240–41. See also Brown, "In Pursuit of Justice," 59.

8. "Whiteman's Report," August 31, 1879, in U.S. Department of the Interior, Office of Indian Affairs, *Annual Report of the Commissioner of Indian Affairs* (1879), 72–75 (quote, 75).

9. Jacobs, "A History of the Ponca Indians," 157.

10. The most comprehensive history of the flight of the Northern Cheyennes is Monnett, *Tell Them We Are Going Home;* see also Andrist, *The Long Death,* 320–30.

11. "The Trials of a Tribe: The Two Sides of the Ponca Indian Story. The Other Side. Statements of White Eagle and Standing Bear," *Advertiser,* August 23, 1879, 2. This statement by Standing Bear is an extract from an interview at Fort Omaha on April 13, 1879, translated by William W. Hamilton, resident missionary among the Omaha for twelve years. For the entire text see Tibbles, *The Ponca Chiefs,* 7–17.

12. "The Trials of a Tribe," 2; see also Tibbles, *The Ponca Chiefs,* 15.

13. Bourke, *On the Border with Crook,* 427.

14. "The Trials of a Tribe," 2.

15. Tibbles, *The Ponca Chiefs,* 40–44.

16. "Indian Victims," *Omaha Herald,* March 30, 1879, 5, and "An Army Officer's Statement," 42, 64 (first quote), 65 (second quote), both in Tibbles, *The Ponca Chiefs.*

17. "Dorsey to Meacham, March 24, 1879," *Council Fire*, April 1879, 61. For more on Meacham, see Prucha, *American Indian Policy in Crisis*, 78, 86–90.

18. For more on the Modoc War see Mardock, *The Reformers and the American Indian*, 134–37, and Jones, "Toby Riddle, Catalyst," 37–38.

19. *Council Fire*, August 1879, 120. Meacham noted that because the journal represented the "highest civilized moral sentiment of the age," it was not often a popular publication, yet it had its "warm, ardent and substantial" supporters (ibid.).

20. "Dorsey to Meacham, March 24, 1879," 61 (all quotes). Part of this letter can be found in Tibbles, *The Ponca Chiefs*, 55.

21. *Council Fire*, April 1879, 61; see also Tibbles, *The Ponca Chiefs*, 56–57.

22. "From Wm. H. Whiteman, April 28, 1879," *Council Fire*, August 1879, 117 (all quotes).

23. Tibbles, *The Ponca Chiefs*, 41. For newspaper coverage see Coward, *The Newspaper Indian*, 204–6.

24. Seymour, *Indian Agents of the Old Frontier*, 292.

25. Tibbles, *Buckskin and Blanket Days*, 195–96; see also 193–94, 197–99. In *The Ponca Chiefs*, 18, Tibbles states that the city editor and not Crook had initially informed him of the arrest. For a comprehensive study of Crooks's involvement with the Ponca see Robinson, *General Crook and the Western Frontier*, 232–46; see especially 235–36, for Crook's initial contact with Tibbles.

26. King, "'A Better Way,'" 241–47.

27. Crook to Tibbles, June 19, 1879, reprinted as "General Crook's Letter," *Tribune*, October 10, 1879, 1–2. See also Robinson, *General Crook and the Western Frontier*, 232, and King, "'A Better Way,'" 250–52, for a discussion of the importance of this letter, which had been reproduced in the *Council Fire*, December 1879, 178. For Bourke's view of the Ponca matter see Bourke, *On the Border with Crook*, 427–29, and Porter, *Paper Medicine Man*, 69–70.

28. "General Crook's Letter," 1–2.

29. Bourke, *On the Border with Crook*, 427.

30. See Hoogenboom, *Rutherford B. Hayes*, 175, for a comment about Crook's confidence in Hayes. See also Robinson, *George Crook and the Western Frontier*, 67, 82. Crook's namesake died before his second birthday.

31. For biographical background on Tibbles see his memoir, *Buckskin and Blanket Days*, written in 1905. However this volume must be used with great caution as Tibbles, writing from memory, presents the gist of conversations occurring during previous decades. As a good storyteller, at times he embellished a tale to make it even better. An indication of his warm friendship with Indians can be found in letters sent to him in 1879 by members of the Omaha Tribe. See Dorsey, *Omaha and Ponka Letters*, 29–33. See also Prucha, "Historical Introduction," and DeFrance, "Some Recollections of Thomas H. Tibbles."

32. Tibbles, *Buckskin and Blanket Days*, 196 (quote), and idem, *The Ponca Chiefs*, 19. In the mid-1850s Tibbles lived with a band of Indians he described as "a mixed

lot belonging to the tribes along the Missouri River." He was invited to become a member of the "Soldier Lodge, the secret society to which only their bravest men were admitted." Tibbles, *Buckskin and Blanket Days*, 74 (first quote in note), 112 (second quote in note).

33. "Criminal Cruelty. The History of the Ponca Prisoners Now at the Barracks," *Omaha Herald*, April 1, 1879, 4 (the same article was reprinted in the *Omaha Weekly Herald*, April 4, 1879, 1, 4). Tibbles, in *The Ponca Chiefs*, 20–27, reproduced parts of the Indian speeches and Bourke pasted the April 1 *Omaha Herald* article into his diary, 25:89–105).

34. Tibbles, *The Ponca Chiefs*, 23.

35. "Criminal Cruelty," *Omaha Weekly Herald*, 1; see also Tibbles, *The Ponca Chiefs*, 25. Although there is no historical evidence, it is likely that the young man was buried with honors.

36. "Criminal Cruelty," *Omaha Weekly Herald*, 4, and Tibbles, *The Ponca Chiefs*, 27–28; see also Lake, "Standing Bear! Who?" 473.

37. "Condition of the Poncas in the Summer of 1880," Jackson, *A Century of Dishonor*, 370. Committee members included Rev. Alvin F. Sherrill, Rev. William Justin Harsha, Leavitt Burnham, W. M. Yates, and P. L. Perine.

38. "The Sad-Hearted Poncas," *Yankton Daily Press and Dakotaian*, April 29, 1879, 4, and see the editorial on p. 2; see also the editorial in the *Niobrara Pioneer*, May 2, 1879, 2. See also J. Clark, "Ponca Publicity," 497–98.

39. Bourke diary, 25:71 (third quote), 76 (first and second quotes); see 89–104 for discussion of the entire conference. For more on Crook's conference see "Criminal Cruelty," *Omaha Weekly Herald*, 1, 4, and Tibbles, *Buckskin and Blanket Days*, 196–98.

40. Bourke diary, 25:82 (first quote), 83–84 (second quote). Parts of this and other speeches were printed in "Criminal Cruelty," *Omaha Weekly Herald*, 1 and 4.

41. Bourke diary, 25:86; see also U.S. Senate, *Report of Special Commission*, 32.

42. "Criminal Cruelty," *Omaha Herald*, April 1, 1879, 4–5.

43. Tibbles, *Buckskin and Blanket Days*, 199. Congress had debated this very issue, not only in the passage of the Fourteenth Amendment, but in the earlier Civil Rights Act of 1866. Furthermore, Chief Justice Roger B. Taney, in his Dred Scott decision, argued that Indians who separated from their tribes were entitled to the rights of a foreign immigrant. "Presumably this would include the right to vote once naturalized," argues Bodayla, in "'Can an Indian Vote?'" 372–73. For a contemporary article by the federal district attorney who prosecuted Standing Bear see Lambertson, "Indian Citizenship," 183–93; see also M. Smith, "The History of Indian Citizenship," 25–35.

Deloria and Wilkins (*Tribes, Treaties and Constitutional Tribulations*, 142) note that in 1870 the Senate Judiciary Committee, as directed by Congress, investigated the issue of whether or not the Fourteenth Amendment made Indians citizens. The authors concluded that the committee "suggested that it would be abhorrent for the

United States to make any changes in its fundamental organic laws that would affect Indians without seeking their consent or ratification" (144). Thus citizenship had not been granted to Indians via this amendment.

44. Tibbles, *The Ponca Chiefs,* 34–35.

45. Poppleton, *Reminiscences,* June 11, 1915.

46. Tibbles, *The Ponca Chiefs,* 35.

47. Tibbles, *Buckskin and Blanket Days,* 199. According to Milner (*With Good Intentions,* 176), Dundy had earlier ruled in the murder trial of the Pawnees, in *Yellow Sun et al.*

48. In a 1917 tribute in an Omaha newspaper, Webster was described as "the central figure of a group of Omaha people devoted to the cultivation of artistic ideals." He was "a remarkable figure, mentally keen as a lance, towering as a giant in his profession . . . a poetic soul; [and] a forceful personality that never lacks confidence in his ability to overcome all obstacles." See Sheldon, *Nebraska: The Land and the People,* 1:12–13. For additional material on Webster see Morton, *Illustrated History of Nebraska,* 2:798–800; Savage and Bell, *History of the City of Omaha,* 584–85; Sorenson, *The Story of Omaha,* 371–74; and Wakeley, *Omaha,* 986–89.

49. Sorenson, *The Story of Omaha,* 338–42; Wakeley, *Omaha,* 5–7

50. Milner, *With Good Intentions,* 72. A brief sketch of the judge's life can be found in the Elmer Dundy Papers, Nebraska State Historical Society. For his legal career see Price, "The Public Life of Elmer S. Dundy," 72–107.

51. Osborne, *A Select School,* 59–60.

52. Savage and Bell, *History of the City of Omaha,* 584a. Nichols (*Lincoln and the Indians,* 160) also attributes the roots of reform, which led to severalty and ultimately to the passage of the Dawes Act, to western supporters. The reason, Nichols noted, that the severalty movement is perceived as an eastern movement in part comes "from the scholar's neglect of Indian policy during the Civil War years."

53. "The Poncas and Their Friends," *Council Fire,* June 1879, 84.

54. The application is quoted in Tibbles, *The Ponca Chiefs,* 36–39; see also Lake, "Standing Bear! Who?" 474–75.

55. Tibbles, *The Ponca Chiefs,* 39–41. The May 1879 issue of the *Council Fire,* 74, quoted a *Chicago Tribune* byline relative to the writ.

56. For a text of the amendment see Tibbles, *The Ponca Chiefs,* 44; see also 45. See also Lake, "Standing Bear! Who?" 475, and "A Plea for the Poncas," *Omaha Herald,* May 4, 1879, 2.

57. "Mr. Hayt's Assault on Standing Bear," in Tibbles, *The Ponca Chiefs,* 48.

58. Ibid., 49–50.

59. Tibbles, *The Ponca Chiefs,* 51–52.

60. Ibid., 53–54.

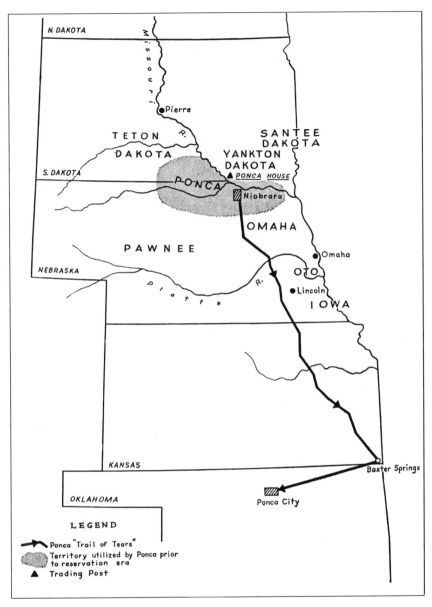

The Poncas' "Trail of Tears." From James H. Howard, *The Ponca Tribe*, Bureau of American Ethnology, Bulletin no. 195 (Washington, D.C.: Government Printing Office, 1965).

Standing Bear, second chief of the Poncas, fled the Indian Territory in 1879 with the body of his son and a few followers. His arrest, trial, and eastern lecture tour brought the plight of Indians in general to the attention of the American public. (South Dakota State Historical Society–State Archives)

White Eagle, principal chief of the Poncas, was removed with his followers by government orders from their Dakota home to the Indian Territory. He died there in 1914 at age seventy-four. Photo taken in 1877. (Western History Collections, University of Oklahoma Library, Norman, Oklahoma)

Standing Bear and his remaining family were allowed to return to their former Dakota lands following the successful conclusion of *Standing Bear v. Crook*. Until Standing Bear and the Northern Poncas were self-sustaining, however, they were assisted by members of the Omaha Ponca Relief Committee. (Special Collections, Tutt Library, Colorado College Library, Colorado Springs, Colorado)

The Right Reverend Robert H. Clarkson, Episcopal
bishop of Nebraska and chairman of the Omaha Ponca
Relief Committee (neg. MS 4751 [042], 01220900,
National Anthropological Archives, Smithsonian
Institution)

Thomas Henry Tibbles, an
Omaha, Nebraska, journalist,
hired lawyers to defend Standing
Bear and then organized and escorted the Ponca chief, his interpreter, and her brother on the
successful eastern speaking tour.
(Nebraska State Historical Society Photograph Collections)

General George Crook, commander of the Department of the Platte, was ordered to send troops to arrest Standing Bear. Disapproving of the Poncas' treatment, he allowed himself to become part of the important case of *Standing Bear v. Crook*. (Rutherford B. Hayes Presidential Center)

John Lee Webster, an Omaha lawyer, was hired by his friend Thomas Henry Tibbles to defend Standing Bear in Judge Elmer Scipio Dundy's district court room. Several years later Webster also defended John Elk in the unsuccessful case of *Elk v. Wilkins*. (Nebraska State Historical Society Photograph Collections)

Andrew Jackson Poppleton, legal counsel for the Union Pacific Railroad, along with John Lee Webster successfully defended Standing Bear. He also worked with Webster on *Elk v. Wilkins*. (Nebraska State Historical Society Photograph Collections)

Judge Elmer Scipio Dundy, federal district court judge, presided over the trial of *Standing Bear v. Crook*. (Nebraska State Historical Society Photograph Collections)

Francis and Susette La Flesche on tour. When Susette, a member of the Omaha tribe, was chosen as Standing Bear's interpreter, her father requested that her brother Francis accompany her. (Nebraska State Historical Society Photograph Collections)

Henry Laurens Dawes, senator from Massachusetts, took up the Ponca cause, serving on the Senate Select Committee ordered to investigate the Ponca removal. (Library of Congress)

Carl Schurz, secretary of the interior, ordered the removal of the Ponca to proceed despite opposition from both the Indians and local residents. When Standing Bear fled the Indian Territory, Schurz ordered the chief's arrest, thus putting into motion a highly publicized trial and eastern lecture tour. (Library of Congress)

President Rutherford
B. Hayes created a
presidential com-
mission headed by
General George Crook
to investigate the
circumstances of the
Ponca removal.
(Rutherford B. Hayes
Presidential Center)

Big Snake, Standing Bear's brother, was killed at Fort Reno, Indian Territory, in a scuffle with soldiers in 1879. (neg. 04178, 0662000, National Anthropological Archives, Smithsonian Institution)

Standing Bear, 1881 (neg. 9N 04176–A, 06619801, National
Anthropological Archives, Smithsonian Institution)

White Eagle and Standing Bear, leading Ponca chiefs (neg. Bell 9N, 06637000, National Anthropological Archives, Smithsonian Institution)

Standing Bear's home in Nebraska near the end of the nineteenth century (neg. 54,538, National Anthropological Archives, Smithsonian Institution)

CHAPTER FOUR

STANDING BEAR V. CROOK

The case of *United States ex rel. Standing Bear v. Crook* began in Omaha on May 1, 1879, in the Federal Circuit Court for the District of Nebraska. United States District Attorney Genio Madison Lambertson, representing the defendant, General George Crook, hoped to "establish the jurisdiction of the military to hold the Indians."[1] Slightly over a month had passed since Standing Bear's arrest, and Tibbles's publicity campaign on behalf of the Poncas had reached a national audience. The front page of the *New York Times* informed readers of the importance of the "first case of the kind ever brought before a United States court." The *Chicago Tribune* alerted readers to Standing Bear's promise to bury his son's body with the bones of his ancestors.[2]

Those present in the courtroom on the first day included Standing Bear, his wife, their two orphaned grandchildren, Yellow Horse (identified as Standing Bear's brother), Buffalo Chips, and Episcopal Bishop Robert H. Clarkson. Willie W. Hamilton, the twenty-two-year-old son of the missionary on the Omaha Reservation, was the first witness for the plaintiff. Employed at the agency store and a twelve-year resident of the area, Hamilton was fluent in the Omaha language. He testified that he became acquainted with Standing Bear and the other Poncas when they arrived at the agency on March 4, 1879.[3] All the Indians, except for those too sick to help, he asserted, were busy planting crops on lands provided by the Omahas when they were arrested on that Sunday morning. When asked by John Lee Webster if the Poncas were in the habit of resting on the Sabbath, the young man responded, "some do, and some do not," much like white men. When queried by the court if this question was necessary, Webster quipped that "the theory of this government is to Christianize these Indians, I believe."[4]

Webster intended to prove that Standing Bear and his followers had made great strides toward assimilation. They separated from their tribe, actively farmed, and neither received nor requested government support. He noted that Standing Bear also accepted Christianity.[5] This approach suggests that Webster and Poppleton were interested in "liberal law and personal liberty, not tribal sovereignty" and that they framed their appeal on individual rights "owed to Standing Bear as a person."[6] To reinforce this contention, Webster asked Lieutenant William L. Carpenter how the Poncas were dressed on the day of their arrest. In "citizens' clothes," the lieutenant responded; only two wore traditional blankets and leggings.[7]

During cross examination, Lambertson, determined to prove that the Ponca petitioners still depended upon the government, sought to show that some of their possessions were government issued. Hamilton agreed that some were, but he also testified that the Poncas made the tents they were living in at the time of their arrest. Although Omaha tribal police planted three or four acres for Standing Bear, the missionary's son remarked that the chief had helped them. When Webster asked if the Indians were receiving annuities while at the agency, the witness answered no, although a day or two before their arrest they had received some agency rations. Standing Bear acknowledged that two of the wagons he used in the flight from Indian Territory were government property. The third wagon, a light spring wagon, he had purchased himself.[8]

Following a recess for lunch, the court reconvened at two in the afternoon with Standing Bear as the final witness. Lambertson, challenging his right to testify, queried, "Does this court think an Indian is a competent witness?" Judge Dundy responded that Indians were competent in civil and criminal courts and that the "law makes no distinction on account of race, color, or previous condition."[9]

The chief, through an interpreter, informed Webster that he lived well on his Niobrara reservation. He had land, and his children attended school. He "want[ed] to work, and become like a white man, and . . . he [had] tried his best." But in the Indian Territory, he could not sow wheat because the land was rocky, his children could not go to school because there was no school, and everyone got sick. One hundred fifty-eight Poncas died. "It seemed," he lamented, "as though I had no strength in my body at all." But after fleeing to Nebraska, he told Webster, he grew stronger daily. If only he could return to his old reservation, go back to working the land, and feed his family, he concluded, God "will let me live."[10] In desperation, Standing Bear, whose band in the Indian Territory numbered some fifty members, explained that he had set out for Nebraska with his family and only a few followers. The rest of his band had remained behind.[11]

Since Lambertson called no witnesses, both sides presented their summary arguments at the end of Standing Bear's testimony. Webster argued that the Omahas' title to their land was as good as a fee simple title and therefore they had the right to invite friends to share it. Furthermore Indians could not be moved "at the whim and pleasure of the commissioner at Washington." He quoted Thomas Jefferson, who "held . . . that they were entirely independent and the government could in no way interfere with their internal relations." Webster insisted that Indians were not "wild animals, deer to be chased by every hound." The Omahas and Poncas particularly were not "savages" or wanderers but cultivators of the soil.[12]

He then spoke to the core of Tibbles's argument—the application of the Fourteenth Amendment. Quoting from a report made by Senator Matthew H. Carpenter of Wisconsin, holding that when tribal relations were dissolved, the Fourteenth Amendment applied, Webster cogently claimed that the amendment made Indians born in this country "who did not owe allegiance to any other form of government, a citizen beyond all dispute." His next point focused on the use of the army by the commissioner. Situations in which military force could be used were clearly defined by statute. They included open hostilities, the removal of unauthorized persons, who by law had to be remanded to civil authorities, and the necessity of arresting someone who committed a crime.[13]

Lambertson, whose summation lasted three hours, praised Poppleton and Webster "for their generosity in coming to the assistance of these poor people, prisoners and friendless in a strange land." He followed with a discussion of the origin of the writ, questioning the jurisdiction of the court to issue such a document. He based his remaining "arguments principally upon Chief Justice Roger B. Taney's decision" in *Dred Scott v. Sandford*.[14] Taney determined that Scott, a Missouri-born slave who resided in a free state and free territory with his owner, was "not a citizen of Missouri within the meaning of the constitution of the United States, and not entitled as such to sue in its courts."[15] Therefore, Lambertson concluded that the "Indian could not appear in court, was not entitled to the writ of habeas corpus, . . . [and] was not a citizen."[16] When Lambertson finished, the court adjourned until after supper.

In his two-hour summation, reported in three issues of the *Omaha Herald,* Poppleton informed the court that he never had "been able to deal with questions affecting liberty without a feeling of apprehension which, at times, [was] almost appalling." The feeling, he confessed, had intensified in this case.[17] He could not believe that a beneficent country would claim the right "to place [the Poncas] in a condition which is to them worse than slaves, without a syllable of law." If the court agreed with Lambertson's proposition that Indians enjoyed no status in the courts, then, Poppleton said, churches should not attempt to "induce them to lead a civilized life if they have no rights, not even a right to that salvation which has been proclaimed as free to all." Poppleton insisted the only crime the Poncas committed was desiring to earn their own living. "What shall be done with that kind of an Indian?" he asked. The government says send him to the Indian Territory where he will die; "we say he shall be allowed to prosecute his own fortune, to become rich or poor."[18]

Poppleton inquired why immigrants could become American citizens, "while the primitive possessors of this soil—who are not their inferiors in many respects either of body or mind—are alone barred from the right to become citizens and participate in that government." He could find no authority limiting any human from testing "the question as to his right to the possession of liberty." Therefore he concluded that liberty was a right under the law.[19] Following a lengthy discussion of the writ of habeas corpus, Poppleton queried how anyone could "assault these people as savages." We are an impatient people, he said; "because we cannot civilize these Indians in a single generation we conclude that we cannot civilize them at all."[20]

After these lengthy summations, Standing Bear addressed the court, which by this time was filled with military officers and prominent citizens. Turning toward the audience, he extended his hand and looked up at Dundy. "That hand is not the color of yours," he said, "but if I pierce it, I shall feel pain. . . . The blood that will flow from mine will be of the same color as yours." Reminding the judge that he was a man and that the "same God made [us] both," he gazed out the window and described a scene he imagined. He and his wife and daughter were standing on a river bank. The river was wide, and steep cliffs rose up behind them. The water began to rise, but a steep path opened before them; as they started up the cliff to safety, their way was barred by a powerful man, behind whom stood many soldiers. "We are weak and faint and sick. I cannot fight," he told Dundy. "You are that man." Standing Bear then informed the judge that only he had the power to allow his Ponca family to return to "the Swift Running Water that pours down between the green islands," to the land of his fathers' graves, where again they can set up their lodge and light their fires. At the conclusion of Standing Bear's speech, there were no dry eyes in the courtroom. The judge had tears running down his face, and Crook, leaning forward, had covered his eyes. The sobs of women in the audience were easily heard. At once the audience arose and General Crook was the first to shake Standing Bear's hand. The court then adjourned, and Dundy took the evidence under advisement. He rendered his decision on May 12, 1879.[21]

"I have never been called upon to hear or decide a case that appealed so strongly to my sympathy as the one now under consideration," explained the judge. One side was "a weak, insignificant, unlettered, and generally despised race," while the other was the "representative of one of the most powerful, most enlightened, and most Christianized nations of modern times." The representatives of this "wasted race" asked only "for justice and liberty to enable them to adopt our boasted civilization"; the government was determined to send them back to a distant territory, which to them was "less desirable than perpetual imprisonment in their own native land."[22] Standing Bear wanted to return to his old home, where "he might live and die in peace, and be buried with his fathers." The love of their native land was so intense, noted Dundy, that the Poncas were willing to "brave every peril to return home."[23]

The judge acknowledged that federal courts had the power to issue writs of habeas corpus to "persons" or "parties." Nowhere did they stipulate citizenship as a qualification for suing out such a writ. Just because an Indian never "invoked the aid of this writ in a federal court" did not mean that "the rightful authority to issue it does not exist." Dundy observed that since every "person" in the United States was required to obey the laws of the land, this included Indians, "especially off [their] reservation. It would . . . be a sad commentary on the justice and impartiality of our laws to hold that Indians, though natives of our own country, cannot test the validity of an alleged illegal imprisonment in this manner." Pursuing his argument to its logical conclusion, Dundy held "that Indians . . . are 'persons,' such as are described by and included within the laws before quoted." Thus the writ in question was properly issued and the relators (Standing Bear et al.) were "within the jurisdiction conferred by the *habeas corpus* act."[24]

Once Dundy determined that jurisdiction was established, he addressed the issue of "whether or not an Indian can withdraw from his tribe, sever his tribal relation . . . , and terminate his allegiance . . . for the purpose of making an independent living and adopting our own civilization." He remarked that from the very beginning of the country, many heated debates over the issue of expatriation had occurred until finally in 1868 Congress passed an act declaring that "the right of expatriation is a natural and inherent right of all people." Thus he concluded that "the individual Indian possesses the clear and God-given right to withdraw from his tribe and live away from it, as though it had no further existence."[25]

Dundy then considered the presence of the Poncas on the Omaha Reservation. He stressed that federal law granted some officials authority to decide who could enter a reservation. One such official was the Indian commissioner, while the most logical arm of government to implement the removal of intruders was the military. Dundy observed that the Poncas were on the Omaha Reservation "without lawful authority." Therefore, if the commissioner "deemed [their] presence [as] detrimental to the peace and welfare of the Omaha Indians," he could employ the military, and General Crook was "justified in removing them therefrom." However, the law further provided that arrested parties must be conveyed to the nearest civil authority. Instead government officials had ordered Crook to remove the Poncas "by force to the Indian Territory."[26] While absolving Crook because he was "simply obeying the orders of his superior officers," Dundy concluded this unprecedented decision by stating that he could find no authority that justified the commissioner's forcing the Poncas "back to the Indian Territory, to remain and die in that country, against their will." The Poncas therefore must be set free.[27]

Two years after Dundy's decision, George F. Canfield, writing in the *American Law Review,* carefully distinguished between the rights of Indians living on a reservation with their tribe and the rights of those living in white society. Describing Standing Bear's Poncas as "visitors among us," who "claimed that they had severed their tribal relations," he concluded that "they were entitled to all the rights of a white man." He believed that it "was a strange misconception of the powers of government to suppose that they could be taken back by force and held down in the Indian Territory."[28] More than half a century later, Felix S. Cohen, special assistant to the attorney general, in *A Handbook of Federal Indian Law,* published in 1942 by the Department of the Interior, described the "right of expatriation," established in *Standing Bear v. Crook,* as a "significant human right," the "answer not only to federal oppression but to tribal oppression as well." He observed that history had shown "that nations lose in strength when they seek to prevent such unwilling subjects from renouncing allegiance."[29]

Dundy's decision, rendered only ten years after the ratification of the Fourteenth Amendment, reflected the humanitarianism of former abolitionists and reformers in the process of expanding their concern from freedmen to Indians. That concern was evident in the congressional debate framing first the Civil Rights Act of 1866 and then the Fourteenth Amendment, which for the first time defined citizenship. Since freedmen were to become citizens just like persons born or naturalized in the United States, some senators raised the question whether Indians should fall within the scope of this definition. While most agreed that tribal Indians would not be considered, discussion centered on Indians who had dissolved their tribal membership and were taxed. Such Indians were "domesticated" and qualified as citizens.

An amendment providing citizenship for Indians along these lines was defeated by a vote of ten to thirty, but the Senate's discussion brought the ideal of Indian citizenship to public attention. Some judicial officials, like Elmer Dundy, whose appointments had been approved by Radical Republicans during Reconstruction, undoubtedly were aware of the congressional debate and incorporated both moral idealism and equal justice in their rulings.[30] Dundy's decision, however, extracted a heavy price because it divided Indians into two classes, those who chose to maintain their tribal status and those who chose to separate. Although his opinion rendered them "persons" in a legal sense and "free from the 'whims' of Washington bureaucrats," they achieved this new position "*only* if they abandoned their tribe as an instrument for social, economic, and political advancements."[31]

Prior to the Dundy decision, congressional members were not the only individuals interested in granting citizenship to American Indians. As early as 1869, only a year after the ratification of the Fourteenth Amendment, the Board of Indian Commissioners, which was composed of Christian philanthropists and established during the administration of U. S. Grant, proposed the elevation of Indians "to the rights of citizenship" in its first annual report. A decade later, at roughly the same time as Standing Bear's trial, the first national Indian reform organization, the Women's National Indian Association, was established. This group too urged citizenship granted "at once to all Indians who so desire."[32] But citizenship rights would have to wait.

Reactions to Dundy's decision varied. General William Tecumseh Sherman, for example, strongly disapproved. He wrote to Secretary of War Mc-Crary on May 20, 1879, that the Poncas, formerly "fed and maintained by the Indian Bureau," were now "paupers turned loose on the community" by Dundy, who should assume the expense of their care.[33] While Sherman merely voiced his opinion, United States District Attorney Lambertson took action and filed an appeal. Samuel F. Miller, associate justice of the Supreme Court, however, ordered a continuation because the Poncas were not in court, having been freed under Dundy's orders. On January 5, 1880, the appeal was dismissed on Lambertson's motion.[34] After reading a copy of the brief, Interior Secretary Carl Schurz would not "approve the principles upon which the argument was based" and instructed the attorney general to drop the suit.[35]

While some officials voiced their disapproval, Helen Hunt Jackson and Lieutenant John G. Bourke predictably penned strong, favorable statements. "There are times when one *habeas corpus* is better than a thousand howitzers or bloodhounds," wrote Jackson, in "Standing Bear and Bright Eyes," which appeared in the *New York Independent*. She believed that when Judge Dundy "made free men" of the Poncas, he initiated a reform movement "in the only direction where lies any hope for the rest of the Indian race in this country." While Jackson expressed her satisfaction with the decision in a very public manner, Bourke simply wrote in his diary that the decision was "a complete victory for the Poncas."[36]

Newspaper reactions to the decision varied. The Ponca issue enabled the press to serve as "a platform for the humanitarians and their opponents to debate the 'Indian problem,'"[37] which was further complicated by American society's failure to evaluate the Indian. Was he good—that is, noble, innocent, the "child of nature"—or bad, that is, degraded or a "barbaric savage"? The Poncas represented the good Indian: peaceful, hardworking, self-sufficient agriculturalists, dispossessed of their land by their more warlike neighbors, the Lakotas. That the Poncas were dependent upon the government for subsistence and were not literate was often overlooked. While newspaper accounts during the late 1860s and 1870s had been full of the activities of Red Cloud, Sitting Bull, Crazy Horse, Captain Jack, and Chief Joseph—names that elicited fear and represented violence—Standing Bear and his tribe were different. They had not engaged in hostilities; instead they were innocent victims of a government blunder. Readers were suddenly presented with a different image: an Indian desirous and capable of adapting to the dominant culture.[38]

Eastern journals tended to be more sympathetic than those in the West because Indians had essentially been removed from the East decades earlier, while western settlements were still enduring resistance by various tribes. The *Rocky Mountain News,* a Denver paper, for example, described the court decision "as a heavy blow to the present Indian system," dangerous to both whites and Indians; the latter would soon become a "body of tramps moving without restraint wherever they pleased," subject to attacks by frontiersmen and unable "to secure any redress from government."[39] On the other hand the *Chicago Tribune* editorialized that if the principle behind Dundy's decision was sustained, far more would be accomplished than by "a continuance of the present system."[40] An editorial entitled "Indian Civil Rights" in the *New York Times* informed readers that the Ponca court proceedings were a "novelty" in that Indians were defendants in criminal cases, not petitioners in civil proceedings. Finally the Poncas understood that "the Indian is just as good as a white man, as long as he behaves himself."[41] The *New York Tribune,* which had described the treatment of the Poncas as "probably the most cruel among the many outrages committed" against Indians, called Tibbles "fifty years in advance of his generation" and praised the city of Omaha for seeing the Indian as "a man with human rights," not as livestock to be shipped from place to place, starved to death, and imprisoned.[42]

The *Council Fire* also alerted its readers to the continuing Ponca saga. Although supposedly "a friend of the Indian," A. B. Meacham was almost as negative as the *Rocky Mountain News* editorialist. The Dundy decision would not have a "beneficial influence upon the Indians generally," wrote Meacham, because they "cannot maintain . . . [themselves] against the encroachment of civilization," and therefore their best hope was government paternalism. Because the Indian would be fed and clothed and his children educated, in return the government "should have something to say about where [the Indian] goes and what he does." Although Meacham admitted that corruption existed in the Indian service, he nevertheless believed that the government "means well, and really desires the welfare of its wards." He could "see no other way for [the Indian] but obedience to the law and dependence upon the government until he shall have advanced sufficiently to take [his] place as a citizen of the United States."[43]

Several days after Dundy's decision, Secretary of War McCrary ordered Crook to free the Ponca defendants. Before leaving Fort Omaha, Standing Bear asked to speak with Tibbles. The old chief, the newspaperman, and an interpreter went out to a small hill where Standing Bear often had stood during his long days as a prisoner at the fort. Thanking Tibbles for his help, he remarked, "While there is one Ponca alive you will never be without a friend. You are my brother." Standing Bear then returned to his lodge on the fort grounds and from a trunk took out a war bonnet, a tomahawk, and a pair of beaded buckskin leggings. He offered the leggings to Tibbles and asked that he give the tomahawk to Webster and the war bonnet to Poppleton. Tibbles suggested that the Ponca chief present the items personally.[44]

So Standing Bear journeyed into town on Sunday and met first with Webster. The chief related how in the past the Poncas had taken up the tomahawk and gone to war to avenge wrongs and assert rights. "But you have found a better way," he told Webster, as he placed the weapon on the floor near his feet. "You have gone into the court for us." As he bent to pick up the weapon, he informed Webster, "now I have no more use" for it, and he handed it over. Accepting the gift, Webster portrayed his work on behalf of the Poncas as "a labor of pleasure" and promised to preserve the tomahawk "through the years to come, in memory of the effort made to prevent the extermination of [the Poncas]."[45] Standing Bear then visited Poppleton, who graciously accepted the war bonnet, which allegedly had been worn at the first Ponca treaty, negotiated in 1817.[46]

Now that the trial was over, Tibbles, with approval and financial support from the Omaha Ponca Relief Committee, arranged for Susette La Flesche and her father to travel to Indian Territory and visit her uncle, White Swan (Frank La Flesche), and his ailing wife. During her weeklong visit, Susette saw many recent graves, few roads, six little shanties interspersed between white tents, and a "handsomely built" home for the agent, a structure that looked "strangely out of place among the tents and graves."[47] Her report furnished the Omaha clergy with details of Ponca hardships, which they wove into Sunday sermons.[48]

Discovering her aunt's condition to be more serious than previously thought, La Flesche and her father requested permission from Agent White-man to allow the elderly couple to move to the Omaha Reservation. White-man refused. La Flesche again witnessed the agent's inflexibility when, several days before she and her father returned home, a party of some fifty Poncas had been escorted back to their reservation by troops from Fort Reno, Indian Territory. Because most of the Poncas' horses had either died of disease or been stolen by local whites, members of the neighboring Cheyenne tribe offered them replacements. When Whiteman refused to allow the transfer of the horses, several Poncas, without official permission, went to retrieve them. The agent contacted the commander at Fort Reno, and the Indians were returned under escort; soldiers remained to prevent other transgressions.[49]

Despite concern over the poor health of her aunt, La Flesche found the countryside to be quite beautiful. That beauty, however, was offset by the fact that the water was unfit to drink; huge horseflies were infecting and killing many horses; and housing was inadequate. She later informed Senator Henry Laurens Dawes that "the Omaha would not have those houses for chicken houses." She prepared for Chief White Eagle a lengthy description of the tribe's experience during the removal process.[50] This document was later described by the Reverend Joseph (Flavius Josephus) Cook, a prominent Boston minister, as "eloquent" and "in many passages . . . as touching as the historic speech of Logan."[51]

La Flesche reported to the *Omaha Herald* upon her return that none of the Poncas liked their new home or their agent. Twenty-four families had "become entirely extinct" because of family deaths, one hundred ten new graves had been dug in sight of the agency, and half of the tribe members were barely able to walk. She predicted that sixteen more would be dead by the end of the month.[52]

Shortly thereafter, A. B. Meacham arrived in the Indian Territory eager to present his readers with an eyewitness account. His assessment, much like William H. Whiteman's second annual report, told of new houses and planted fields. Meacham praised the agent as "active, earnest, [and] competent" and the land as "excellent." He wrote Carl Schurz that he saw "no sickly, discontented Indians" and "heard no serious complaint about the country or the Government." He concluded that he found the Indians "more comfortably and happily situated than [he] had expected."[53]

Contradictory assessments only confused government officials and the public. La Flesche's observations suggested that Standing Bear and his followers had made the correct decision to flee. Other disillusioned tribal members would soon follow. In June 1879 twenty-five Poncas led by Walks Over the Other, Whistler, and Woodpecker arrived at the Santee Agency, intending to settle on their old reservation. Carefully following the route taken two years previously, they sold their horses along the way to pay for food. Several paid a call at the offices of the *Niobrara Pioneer,* informing the editor that Reverend Riggs had advised them to begin farming on their former lands. The newspaper's staff was pleased with their return, remarking that old settlers "now look back with great pleasure to the days when the [Indians] used to come down from the agency." It was a reminder of a familiar time when "Niobrara had name and fame but little money." The *Pioneer* predicted that, with the aid of citizens and missionaries, this small band of Poncas would not be bothered by the government.[54]

While Walks Over the Other and his followers were probably secure at the Santee Agency, Standing Bear's group faced a dilemma. They were no longer wards of the government and could not live on any government reservation. Ironically, they had gained their freedom but possessed no land. Temporarily they camped near Decatur, Nebraska, struggling to survive. Finding employment with local whites was difficult because the Indians spoke no English. Standing Bear and his family regularly attended church on Sunday, and once at a district Sunday school convention he gave a speech, translated by several English-speaking Omahas.[55] Eventually the small group found refuge in a willow thicket on a private island in the Niobrara River, two miles from the town of Niobrara.[56] Unable to plant crops because of the lateness of the season, the Poncas became dependent upon the charity of the Omaha Ponca Relief Committee. The committee was determined to return them to their former lands now that Spotted Tail and other Lakota tribal leaders "were willing to bury the feuds of former days" and permit the homeless Poncas to "occupy their old reservation without further interference."[57]

The committee's goal was shared by Thomas Henry Tibbles, who along with General Crook and John Lee Webster, spent hours in discussion. Their planning went beyond the immediate circumstances of Standing Bear and his party and the Poncas in the Indian Territory. They intended to include freeing all Indians from "the whims of anyone in Washington" who could control them or their belongings or hinder their "liberty to live [their] own life reasonably."[58] By "fighting to extend liberal law to Standing Bear," the Ponca Relief Committee, Tibbles, and other reformers "aided the move away from original principles guaranteeing tribal sovereignty and land rights" and toward government "exercise [of] extensive power over tribes and acculturation."[59]

Since funding was essential, Tibbles resigned his position at the *Omaha Daily Herald* and began soliciting letters of support from Albinus Nance, governor of Nebraska, and General Crook, as well as endorsements from Bishop Clarkson and leading clergymen. Sponsored by the Ponca Relief Committee, in late June 1879 he embarked on a short speaking tour to Chicago, Boston, and New York. It had been five years since he made a similar journey to raise money for the victims of the grasshopper plague.[60]

Not only was Tibbles welcomed by a large audience at Farwell Hall in Chicago, but the proceedings were summarized sympathetically on the front page of the *Chicago Tribune*. After relating details of Ponca removal and of Standing Bear's flight, Tibbles informed the audience that while Webster and Poppleton were willing to carry the Ponca case without a fee to the Supreme Court, the effort to regain the Poncas' former Dakota lands would be costly. He appealed for contributions and later noted that six hundred dolars was turned over to the Reverend A. F. Sherrill, committee treasurer.[61]

Tibbles traveled on to Boston where Delano Alexander Goddard, editor of the *Boston Daily Advertiser,* promised his support, and Edward Everett Hale, the noted author, longtime minister of the South Congregational Church, and later chaplain of the United States Senate, wrote a sympathetic editorial describing Tibbles's efforts as a "laudable undertaking, which should be encouraged."[62] The editorial, titled "Indians and the Law," appeared on the same page as a lengthy article with the same headline, in which White Eagle's account "of the woes of his tribe" was printed. Included were extracts from letters written by General George Crook; a former New York governor and presidential candidate, Horatio Seymour; and Julius H. Seelye, former pastor and congressman and the current president of Amherst College. Seelye, elected to the House of Representatives in 1874, served on the Indian Affairs Committee and had recommended that Ponca removal not proceed without the Indians' consent. Despite this precaution, removal went forward, and now Seelye felt motivated to work on the Poncas' behalf.[63]

On July 30, 1879, after an editorial and article had alerted Bostonians to the Ponca tragedy, the Society for Propagating the Gospel Among the Indians and Others of North America held a meeting at the Hospital Life Insurance Company. A committee of five, including B. W. Williams, of the Boston lecture bureau, and the Reverend Edward Everett Hale, was elected to organize a mass meeting to discuss the Ponca matter further.[64] This new group, called the Ponca Indian Committee, was to solicit and receive monies to bring suit "to settle the status of the Indians." The committee soon included Frederick Octavius Prince, mayor of Boston; Hon. Levi C. Wade, speaker of the Massachusetts House of Representatives; Reverend S. K. Lothrop; the publisher Henry Oscar Houghton, of Houghton and Osgood; and Henry Mason, partner in the organ manufacturing firm of Mason and Hamlin.[65]

Interested individuals not in attendance at the July 30 meeting could read Tibbles's comments the following day on the front page of the *Advertiser*. Sympathetic to the Poncas and to Tibbles's version of the removal, the article's author mentioned that an "Indian ring" was determined "in cold blood to rob [the Poncas] and get possession of their lands and houses." As in Chicago, Tibbles appealed for funds. Although those attending the meeting clearly favored the Ponca cause, not until months later did the society vote to donate $425 to the fund.[66]

The Ponca Indian Committee called a noon meeting on August 5 at Tremont Temple in Boston. Upon arrival, Tibbles sat in a corner of the platform next to B. W. Williams and watched the hall fill with "poets, historians, scientists, [and] lecturers." On the far side of the platform, Tibbles could see the former abolitionist Wendell Phillips.[67] Following introductory remarks by Williams, Mayor Prince opened the meeting by expressing surprise that in a country boasting "so much philanthropy and refinement," some men could "dare so to outrage public sentiment and defy public opinion." He described the treatment of the Poncas as "transcend[ing] in cruelty and atrocity all the wrongs perpetrated by the strong against the weak yet disclosed in that part of the country."[68]

By the time Tibbles got to his feet, he was "trembling so badly [that he] could hardly walk." His manuscript fell from his shaking hands. The thud brought him back to his senses. Putting his notes aside, he began speaking. "I make no assault upon any individual," he told the audience; instead he was attacking a system with its inherent evils. His remedy was to allot lands in severalty to the Indians and bring them "*as persons* under the protection of the courts." Tibbles was greeted with lengthy applause when he repeated Judge Dundy's statement, "Any human being that God ever made can come into my court."[69]

Phillips spoke last, and Tibbles described his address as "a masterpiece." The eloquent speaker compared the federal government's Indian policy with that of Canada, where Indian outbreaks did not occur. He placed blame for the American "outbreaks" upon the "desire of money." Contractors and merchants "scheme[d] to have troops ordered to the remote frontier," where they could sell their wares. Under such conditions, flour peaked at eighty dollars a barrel. Because Indians were on the road to becoming "civilized," Phillips said they needed access to courts to protect their property. "The audience gave liberal applause through the long speech and every praise of the Indian or censure of the [Indian] ring was evidently relished," wrote the *Advertiser* reporter. At the end of the address, resolutions drafted by Hale were unanimously adopted. These resolutions declared that Indians had certain rights that the Supreme Court should determine and that whites would be "bound to respect." To "press the appeal of the Ponca Indians," and to raise money to pursue the case, Hale recommended that a committee of ten prominent Bostonians be appointed.[70] Following the meeting Tibbles and Phillips met over dinner, and Phillips encouraged the former Omaha newsman to continue his work on behalf of the Indians.

The escalating criticism of Indian policy by humanitarian reformers caused the Indian Office to question the activities of the Ponca supporters and to discredit Tibbles. In defense, Goddard in an editorial defined "the truth of the matter" based on three critical issues. First, Tibbles was not accepting money under false pretenses. All monies collected went directly to the Reverend Sherrill, treasurer of the fund. Second, the government was incorrect in its contention that the Poncas were "contented in the Indian Territory." Finally, not only could a suit "be brought to cover the case of the whole Ponca tribe," but a second suit "might be brought under a writ of ejectment." This second suit could be used "to settle titles involving the questions of the Indian's right to citizenship, title to land, and the adjudication of all matters affecting the Indian's rights under our laws."[71]

A more forceful editorial appeared in the next issue of the *Advertiser,* wherein Goddard posed the question: "Why should not an Indian have justice as a white man has it, by going to court?"[72] These sympathetic editorials, as well as Tibbles's continued public appearances, made government officials determined to defend their position. In one Washington dispatch, the writer commented that "the persistent attempts to make it appear that the present administration is responsible for the wrongs done the Ponca Indians is exceedingly unjust."[73]

It soon became evident that editors of the *Advertiser* and the *Tribune* were openly sympathetic to the Poncas. An August 11 editorial in the *Tribune* described Tibbles as "the heroic Editor of Omaha, who forced Justice, . . . to take off her bandage and deal fairly with Standing Bear."[74] To shift blame from the Schurz administration, however, other newspapers and periodicals questioned Tibbles's motives and facts. In late August the *New York Times* informed readers that while the cession of the Ponca lands was "a blunder of a former Administration," currently the Poncas are "prospering fairly, and are not only contented, but are on the road to civilization."[75] A strong indictment of Tibbles came from the pen of Dr. Thomas A. Bland, a supporter of Meacham and the *Council Fire*. Bland attacked Tibbles's "well-known reputation as a professional adventurer, of what is termed the philanthropic type, and also upon his wild and untruthful utterances and suspicious actions in connection with this Standing Bear Case."[76]

Whatever motives drove him, Tibbles dedicated the next several years of his life to the Ponca cause. Supported by Standing Bear and Susette La Flesche, he launched an eastern lecture tour that effectively presented the Ponca tragedy to a much wider audience. He encountered loyal supporters and hostile critics, and the tour deepened the differences between government officials and their supporters on one side and Standing Bear and the reformers on the other.

Notes

1. "The Ponca Trial," *Omaha Herald,* May 2, 1879, 8; see also Lake, "Standing Bear! Who?" 475; Cohen, *Felix S. Cohen's Handbook of Federal Indian Law,* 177–78; Shattuck and Norgren, *Partial Justice,* 84–88.

2. "Have Indians Any Rights?" *New York Times,* May 2, 1879, 1; "The Poncas: Probability that Justice May Be Done These Unhappy Savages," *Chicago Tribune,* May 2, 1879, 3. See also "The Legal Status of the Indians," *Chicago Tribune,* May 6, 1879, 4; Coward, *The Newspaper Indian,* 206.

3. For Clarkson's presence see entry dated May 1, 1879, Clarkson diaries, 1846–84, Nebraska State Historical Society. For Hamilton's testimony see "The Ponca Trial," 8; and Tibbles, *The Ponca Chiefs,* 66–67; a verbatim account of the testimony of the entire trial can be found in the latter, 66–90.

4. Tibbles, *The Ponca Chiefs,* 71.

5. Ibid., 5–6, 37; for Standing Bear's religious beliefs see 62–64.

6. Shattuck and Norgren, *Partial Justice,* 87.

7. Tibbles, *The Ponca Chiefs,* 78.

8. Ibid., 72–76, 87–89.

9. Ibid., 79; see also "The Ponca Trial," 8.

10. Tibbles, *The Ponca Chiefs,* 80 (first quote), 81 (second quote). Most of Standing Bear's testimony was reported in the May 2, 1879, issue of the *Omaha Herald.*

11. Tibbles, *The Ponca Chiefs,* 85–86. Standing Bear's followers included Yellow Horse, Long-Runner, and Chicken Hunter, with their families, and another chief—although unnamed, presumably Buffalo Chips—and his six men and their families.

12. "The Writ of Liberty," *Omaha Herald,* May 3, 1879, 8, reprinted on a supple-

ment sheet of the *Omaha Weekly Herald,* May 9, 1879, 1.

13. Ibid. Deloria and Wilkins, in *Tribes, Treaties, and Constitutional Tribulations,* 142–44, discuss this 1870 Senate Judiciary Committee report, which Webster used. No mention is made of the specific quote Webster cited. Instead the authors note that the report concluded "that the amendment was intended to recognize the change in the status of the former slave which had been effected during the war, while it recognizes no change in the status of the Indians" (143). Since Tibbles wrote the *Herald* article, he obviously interpreted Webster's reasoning for the benefit of Standing Bear's cause.

14. "The Writ of Liberty," 8.

15. "*Dred Scott v. Sandford,*" 60 U.S. 393, in *A Documentary History of the United States,* 138. See also "The Truth of Misery—What Justice Taney Did Not Say," *Omaha Herald,* May 8, 1879, 4.

16. "The Writ of Liberty," 8.

17. "A Plea for the Poncas," *Omaha Herald,* May 4, 1879, 2.

18. "Mr. Poppleton's Argument," *Omaha Herald,* May 6, 1879, 2.

19. Ibid.

20. "To Every Human," *Omaha Herald,* May 7, 1879, 2.

21. Tibbles, *Buckskin and Blanket Days,* 200–202 (quotes, 201), and idem, *The Ponca Chiefs,* 91–93. See also "The Writ of Liberty," 8; *The Niobrara Pioneer,* May 9, 1879, 2; King, "'A Better Way,'" 248–49. A transcription of the decision can be found in "Standing Bear's Victory," *Omaha Herald,* May 13, 1879, 2, with a reprint in the *Omaha Weekly Herald,* May 16, 1879, 1, 4; Tibbles, *The Ponca Chiefs,* 94–111; and Armstrong, comp., *I Have Spoken,* 164–78. See also *Niobrara Pioneer,* May 16, 1879, 2.

22. *United States ex rel. Standing Bear v. Crook,* 25 F. Cas. 695 (C.C.D. Neb. 1879) (No. 14,891), p. 695. This opinion was also reported by Circuit Judge John F. Dillon, 5 Dill. 453.

23. Ibid., 698.

24. Ibid., 697 (all quotes).

25. Ibid., 699; see also Lake, "Standing Bear! Who?" 477.

26. Ibid., 700. Standing Bear and his followers were freed only because the judge "found that procedural due process had been violated." Shattuck and Norgren, *Partial Justice,* 87.

27. *U.S. ex rel. Standing Bear v. Crook,* 700–701. Dundy's five major points are spelled out in "Judge Dundy and the Poncas," *Council Fire,* June 1879, 92; see also *Yankton Daily Press and Dakotaian,* May 14, 1879, 1.

28. Canfield, "The Legal Position of the Indian," 32–33.

29. *Felix S. Cohen's Handbook of Federal Indian Law,* 178. Cohen's *Handbook* was a special study that evolved from his forty-six-volume collection of federal treaties and laws.

30. *Congressional Globe,* 39th Cong., 1st sess., January 30, 1866, 498–99, and May 30, 1866, 2892–97. The vote on the amendment to exclude Indians not taxed

from citizenship is noted on p. 2897. For a lengthy study of Indian citizenship see Priest, *Uncle Sam's Stepchildren*, 198–216, and Lee, "Indian Citizenship and the Fourteenth Amendment," 208–11. Lee offers a masterful discussion of this provocative theme. For an example of evenhanded justice toward minorities during Reconstruction, see Zhu, "'A Chinaman's Chance' on the Rocky Mountain Mining Frontier," 45–46. See also James, *The Framing of the Fourteenth Amendment*, 78, 143.

31. Lake, "Standing Bear! Who?" 497n.

32. Prucha, *Documents of United States Indian Policy* 133 (first quote); *Annual Meeting and Report of the Women's National Indian Association* (1883), 18 (second quote).

33. "Sherman to the Secretary of War, May 20, 1879," in U.S. Senate, *Testimony Relating to Removal*, 480.

34. "Report of the Attorneys," in Jackson, *A Century of Dishonor*, 372–73; "The Poncas Case Continued and the Last Jury Trial On," *Omaha Herald*, June 4, 1879, 8; Lake, "Standing Bear! Why?" 479. See also "The Story of Standing Bear," *Advertiser*, August 13, 1879, 2.

35. Carl Schurz to Helen Hunt Jackson, January 17, 1880, in Schurz, *Speeches, Correspondence and Political Papers*, 3:497. This letter is reprinted in Jackson, *A Century of Dishonor*, 361–62.

36. H.H. [Helen Hunt Jackson], "Standing Bear and Bright Eyes," *Independent*, November 20, 1879, 1 (first quote); Bourke diary, 25:106 (second quote).

37. Coward, *The Newspaper Indian*, 197; for press coverage of the Poncas see 201–21, and for imaging Indians see 23–62.

38. Numerous studies on the "noblility" versus the "savagery" of Native Americans include, for example, Billington, *Land of Savagery*, esp. 105–28; Berkhofer, *The White Man's Indian*, esp. 72–85; Coward, *The Newspaper Indian*, 23–42.

39. "The Red Man Judicially Declared a 'Sovereign,'" *Rocky Mountain News*, May 15, 1879, 1.

40. "Our Indian Relations," *Chicago Tribune*, May 19, 1879, 4.

41. "Indian Civil Rights," in Hays, *A Race at Bay*, 35–37 (quote, 37); see also 21. According to Hays, during the latter half of the nineteenth century the paper generally supported the Indian cause, "assuring readers that virtually every instance of open conflict could be found to have originated with injustices by whites" (3). Occasionally, however stereotypical images were evident in its pages, thus presenting the reader with a portrayal "of an inferior race decidedly less advanced than white citizens" (4).

42. "The Poncas Again," *Tribune*, May 16, 1879, 4. Some papers even encouraged monetary contributions. In "Standing Bear's Release," a reporter at the *Omaha Herald* (May 15, 1879, 5) wrote that the chief intended to take up a homestead. Apparently the Omaha leader Joseph La Flesche had located land near the Omaha Reservation for Ponca use and requested donations to "repair in some slight degree the great wrong which has been done to Standing Bear."

43. "Judge Dundy's Decision," *Council Fire*, August 1879, 116–17.

44. Tibbles, *The Ponca Chiefs*, 113.

45. "Standing Bear's Farewell," *Omaha Herald*, May 20, 1879, 2; most of this article has been reproduced in Tibbles, *The Ponca Chiefs*, 114–17. See also Mary Clemmer, "A Woman's Letter from Washington," *Independent*, February 17, 1881, 3.

46. Mrs. Caroline L. Poppleton on January 5, 1915, gave a speech describing Standing Bear's gift to her husband; see "The War Bonnet," folder on Standing Bear, Nebraska State Historical Society.

47. "The Visiting Poncas: Arrival of the Chief of the Tribe in This City," *Advertiser*, October 30, 1879, 1.

48. "Susette La Flesche's Testimony," in U.S. Senate, *Testimony Relating to Removal*, 26–27.

49. Ibid., 26–28. See also Tibbles, *Buckskin and Blanket Days*, 205–6.

50. "Susette La Flesche's Testimony," in U.S. Senate, *Testimony Relating to Removal*, 33–35 (quote, 33). For the complete text of "White Eagle's Testimony," see U.S. Senate, *Testimony Relating to Removal*, 458–64. For the text of this letter, written on May 20 by La Flesche, see Tibbles, *The Ponca Chiefs*, 118–21. White Eagle had requested it be published, and La Flesche commented that she had seen portions of it published but was uncertain if it had been reprinted in its entirety.

51. "The Poor Poncas: Suffering of Friendly Indians under Our Laws," *Advertiser*, July 31, 1879, 1; "The Monday Lectures: by the Rev. Joseph Cook—with Preludes," *Advertiser*, November 4, 1879, 4 (quotes); see also Tibbles, *The Ponca Chiefs*, 118. Logan was a Mingo chief who during Lord Dunmore's War in 1774 had lost all members of his family. His poignant letter originally appeared in Thomas Jefferson's *Notes on the State of Virginia*. Cook had learned of White Eagle's letter from La Flesche, who read it to him on June 27 in Omaha.

52. "The Poncas: Their Present Condition in the Indian Territory," *Omaha Herald*, May 29, 1879, 2; see also J. Clark, "Ponca Publicity," 499.

53. "Meacham to Carl Schurz, August 15, 1879," *Council Fire*, October, 1879, 148. This letter was reprinted in "A Talk with Secretary Schurz about the Ponca Indians," *Chicago Tribune*, August 23, 1879, 7; "Wrongs of the Poncas," *New York Times*, August 23, 1879, 2; and "The Trials of a Tribe," *Advertiser*, August 23, 1879, 1. Meacham had arrived in the Indian Territory on July 10.

54. "Returning Poncas," *Niobrara Pioneer*, June 13, 1879, 4.

55. "Among the Indians," *Omaha Herald*, June 14, 1879, 8.

56. Comment by Solomon Draper in his Senate testimony, in U.S. Senate, *Testimony Relating to Removal*, 313.

57. "Returning Poncas," 4.

58. Tibbles, *Buckskin and Blanket Days*, 204.

59. Shattuck and Norgren, *Partial Justice*, 88.

60. Tibbles, *Buckskin and Blanket Days*, 204–7; see also King, "'A Better Way,'" 259.

61. "The Aborigines: Mass-Meeting in Their Interest at Farwell Hall," *Chicago*

Tribune, July 1, 1879, 1; see also J. Clark, "Ponca Publicity," 500. For the six hundred dollars, see Tibbles, *Buckskin and Blanket Days,* 206.

62. "Indians and the Law" (editorial and article of same title), *Advertiser,* July 29, 1879, both on p. 2. Hale concluded that the "arbitrary, forcible and causeless removal of the Poncas" was one of the "most flagitious of recent outrages." See also Tibbles, *Buckskin and Blanket Days,* 207.

63. "Indians and the Law" (editorial). For the comment about Seelye see "Indian Rights: A Boston Audience Speaks in Faneuil Hall," *Advertiser,* December 3, 1879, 1.

64. "The Poor Poncas," 1. Other members included Rev. William Bradley, Baxter Perry Smith, and the Hon. Charles R. Ladd. Tibbles, in *Buckskin and Blanket Days,* noted, "My plain statement of facts resulted in the birth of a Ponca committee of five leading Bostonians who promptly planned a big public gathering" (207).

65. "The Ponca Indian Committee," *Advertiser,* August 11, 1879, 1; "Local Miscellany," *Advertiser,* August 12, 1879, 4. The other members were Frank Wood, John S. Lockwood, and Edward J. Thomas. For additional material on Wade see Davis, *History of the Bench and Bar,* 1:605.

66. "The Poor Poncas," 1. For reference to the $425, see *Advertiser,* November 7, 1879, 2.

67. Tibbles, *Buckskin and Blanket Days,* 208 (quote). After slavery was abolished, some abolitionists shifted their interest to Indian reform. Mardock (*The Reformers and the American Indian,* 1) claims that most post–Civil War Indian reformers had been involved in the antislavery movement. Prucha disagrees, noting that the evidence in Mardock's "own book tends to disprove this statement" (*American Indian Policy in Crisis,* 26). Prucha further argues that those abolitionists cited by Mardock, primarily Lydia Maria Child, Wendell Phillips, and Henry Ward Beecher, "had no sustained effect on the Indian reform movement after the war" (ibid.). Helen Hunt Jackson, whose role in Indian reform cannot be denied, was not an abolitionist. The Quaker participation in both the abolition and Indian reform movement is well documented; however, no study has been undertaken to see if those in the antislavery movement continued to work on behalf of the Indians. Therefore, although there is assuredly a connection between the two reform movements, it is tenuous at best.

68. For Mayor Prince's statements see "The Ponca Indians: The Public Meeting in This City Yesterday Noon," *Advertiser,* August 6, 1879, 4. See also "Local Miscellany," *Advertiser,* August 4, 1879, 4. Because mechanics were busy in the hall above, the meeting was actually held downstairs in the Melonaon.

69. Tibbles, *Buckskin and Blanket Days,* 208–10; "The Ponca Indians: The Public Meeting in this City Yesterday Noon," *Advertiser,* 4.

70. Tibbles, *Buckskin and Blanket Days,* 209–10; "The Ponca Indians: The Public Meeting in This City Yesterday Noon," *Advertiser,* 4 (quotes). For more on Phillips's work with the Indians see Mardock, *The Reformers and the American Indian,* 16–18, 38–39, 56–57, 71–72, 111–12, 134–37. This new committee included

Williams, Hale, Smith, Bradley, and Ladd, who were authorized to appoint five more men. Rev. Dr. Lothrop served as treasurer.

71. "The Courts and the Indians," *Advertiser,* August 5, 1879, 2. This editorial was in answer to such *Advertiser* articles as "The Ponca Indians," August 2, 1879, 1, and "The Indian Office and the Poncas Again," August 4, 1879, 1.

72. "The Indian Bureau and the Poncas," *Advertiser,* August 6, 1879. 2.

73. "The Ponca Indian Wrongs," *Advertiser,* August 11, 1879, 1. For other editorials sympathetic to the Poncas and critical of the government see "The Poncas Once More," "The Story of Standing Bear," and "The Indian Problem," *Advertiser,* August 12, August 13, and August 23, 1879, 2.

74. "A Shameful Story," *Tribune,* August 11, 1879, 4. Coward noted that although the *Tribune's* positive position clearly aided the cause, "it was not an entirely realistic assessment" of the Ponca situation (*The Newspaper Indian,* 212). By focusing almost exclusively on the plight of the Poncas, it contributed to the confusion of facts that exacerbated the differences between government officials and the reformers.

75. *New York Times,* August 23, 1879, 5. This news item concluded that "this careful presentment of the case may not please the sentimentalists who have been so vociferous over 'the wrongs of the Poncas,'" but nevertheless "it bears the unmistakable impress of an absolute truthfulness." See also Coward, *The Newspaper Indian,* 212. For a slightly more positive view of the *Times* and the Ponca issue see Hays, *A Race at Bay,* 12, 21–22, 35–40, 43–44, 76, 221–23, 236, 248–50.

76. T. A. Bland, "The Last Ponca Sensation," *Council Fire,* August 1880, 122; for a criticism of this point of view see Bland, "The Council Fire Criticized," ibid., October 1880, 153.

CHAPTER FIVE

The Tour

Upon his return home on September 6, 1879, Thomas Henry Tibbles was urged by the Omaha Ponca Relief Committee to organize an eastern lecture tour. Indian delegations had been touring the country and meeting with officials since colonial times. These visits to major cities were a government effort to impress Indian leaders with the economic and military power of the country and sometimes to enhance the power of a particular leader, who then could speak for all of his people. However, tribes had their own reasons for visiting the "great white father." For example, in 1870, Chief Red Cloud of the Oglala (Lakota) traveled to Washington on a well-publicized visit to demand additional rations, ammunition, and the removal of a fort, and to deny strongly any knowledge of the 1868 Sioux treaty. Four years later A. B. Meacham led a small group of Modoc and Klamath delegates on a lyceum circuit tour to present the injustices suffered by Captain Jack's band of Modocs.[1]

The month after Standing Bear and his entourage headed east, in November 1879, Sarah Winnemucca, a Paiute spokeswoman, began a monthlong series of lectures in San Francisco, followed by a journey to Washington with her father, Chief Winnemucca, and brother, Natches, to confer with Secretary Schurz and President Hayes. Then beginning in the spring of 1883, for more than a year she lectured over three hundred times in various eastern cities. According to Winnemucca's biographer, Sally Zanjani, "Boston was primed to take up the Indian cause," because ground had been broken by the Ponca visit.[2] Although Winnemucca's schedule was extensive, the Ponca tour stands out because it was well organized, well supported by pastors in Omaha and Boston as well as by influential political and literary figures, and generated extensive news coverage. Furthermore, it raised money to support legal suits aimed at restoring the Ponca homeland. Petitions were filed in both

Nebraska and Dakota Territory during the spring and summer of 1880 in pursuit of this latter objective. Organizers also intended to prepare a suit aimed toward validation of Dundy's decision by the U.S. Supreme Court.[3]

While Webster and Poppleton began their legal research, Tibbles organized the tour. Standing Bear was the main attraction, but the selection of twenty-five-year-old Susette La Flesche, or "Bright Eyes," as the press preferred to call her, was a shrewd decision. As noted earlier, she was the daughter of an Omaha chief, Joseph La Flesche; she had been educated in New Jersey, spoke fluent English, and was well versed on the Ponca controversy. Her uncle, White Swan, was a Ponca chief.[4]

La Flesche was not chosen to accompany Standing Bear simply because she spoke English. Her people, the Omahas, were closely related to the Poncas. They belonged to the same southern Siouan language group and shared common traditions. Therefore, the arbitrary removal of the Poncas had a profound impact upon the members of her tribe, who were fearful that they too could lose their land. Her father, Joseph, who led the more progressive element of the tribe, lived in the southernmost of three villages, called by the others "the village of the 'make-believe' white men." He had encouraged his followers to build frame houses, send their children to school, and accept land allotments in severalty as provided in both their 1854 and 1865 federal treaties. As more land was allotted, small separate farms became the norm. Following the Ponca removal, some Omahas consulted local lawyers about their land rights, only to learn that in fact they did not own the land.[5]

Because of this growing fear for their farms, in the summer of 1879 Joseph La Flesche and other tribal members wrote letters of support for Tibbles. In actuality, these were petitions to Tibbles and eastern humanitarians, criticizing President Hayes for failing to help them and praising Tibbles for his loyal support. In one letter La Flesche remarked that Tibbles had never "spoken even one false word," and that he was "trying to right our wrongs."[6]

Whether she was chosen simply to interpret Standing Bear's words, or to gain support for her tribe, or for both reasons, Susette and her companions attracted the attention as well as the support of eastern audiences when they appeared on the dais. The young Omaha—a graceful figure—was clothed in a plain dark dress set off by a white lace scarf at the neck. She sat next to Standing Bear, who was dressed as a traditional Ponca chief, his long hair flowing freely. Susette's nineteen-year-old brother, Francis ("Woodworker"), accompanied them. Although he wore his hair long, Francis dressed in "civilized style," as did Standing Bear when he was not speaking before an audience. The chief believed the traditional dress reflecting his tribal position made his speeches more official. Tibbles preferred that Standing Bear "dress in citizens clothes," in order to represent "by his attire the idea that he defended, namely, that the Ponca Indians were making an effort to adopt the ways of the whites." At one point the old chief threatened to cut his hair. Fearful that "there would be no end of criticism in the papers," Tibbles urged him to leave it alone. When the journalist failed to convince the Ponca leader, he turned to Helen Hunt Jackson, whose persuasive powers were more successful. After the Senate hearings were completed several months later, Standing Bear went to the hotel barber shop and had his hair cut.[7]

Bishop Robert H. Clarkson, chairman of the Omaha Ponca Relief Committee, asked Susette La Flesche to speak at one of the local Omaha churches before she headed east. When the young woman appeared, the congregation jumped to its feet, clapping and waving handkerchiefs in welcome. "There stood the little figure, trembling, and gazing at the crowd with eyes which afterwards thrilled many audiences," Tibbles later wrote. He described them as "wonderful" because they were capable of smiling, commanding, flashing, pleading, mourning, and playing "all sorts of tricks with anyone they lingered on."[8]

"I love my people," La Flesche informed the audience, and "I have told them that they must learn the arts of the whites and adopt their customs; but how can they, when the government sends the soldiers to drive them about over the face of the earth?" Lamenting the death of Standing Bear's daughter, she exclaimed, "Oh, the perplexities of this thing they call civilization! Part of the white people murder my girl companion and another part tenderly bury her." At this point in her speech, she stopped and hurried from the platform. "Her breakdown had thrilled the audience like an electric shock"; they cried, and even swore, despite the presence of Bishop Clarkson on stage.[9]

The official tour began in Chicago where on Sunday, October 19, 1879, Standing Bear, wearing his bear claw necklace, a white feather in his hair, spoke at the Second Presbyterian Church. Explaining that he had "great reverence for the Bible," the Ponca chief described Indian people as weak because "God has not given the[m] . . . His Book." "I have been told that Jesus the son of God says for us to help one another when in trouble," he continued, "and I hope all of you Christian people will help me, as I am in trouble." The audience contributed several hundred dollars.[10]

Some Chicago residents, however, were not impressed with Standing Bear's piety. They were shocked and dismayed by the massacre of soldiers and agency personnel by Ute Indians in Colorado three weeks earlier. Nathan Cook Meeker, who along with Horace Greeley helped found the utopian community of Greeley, Colorado, had been appointed agent at the White River Agency in 1878. Unable to convince the Utes to give up their roving lifestyle and settle down to farming, the agent had requested military support, which in turn had infuriated the Indians and had driven them to strike back. Thus some Chicagoans regarded Standing Bear's "intrusion into a Christian church as evidence of 'cheek' rather than piety." The Reverend William Justin Harsha, who addressed the audience following Standing Bear's talk, was criticized for not referring "in a deprecating way to the late Ute massacres." Admitting that many Indians were "degraded," Harsha, pastor of the Omaha First Presbyterian Church and a member of the Omaha Ponca Relief Committee, placed the blame for this condition upon the whites.[11]

On October 23, during this tour, a reporter from the *Chicago Inter-Ocean* interviewed Standing Bear and La Flesche. He asked Susette what specific "wrongs" afflicted her tribe. Closing the small volume of poems she was reading, she informed him that Indians had no rights. Agents decided how their annuity monies were to be spent and even opened their personal letters. In addition, the military was "kept to fight the Indians and quell disturbances that the Interior department ha[d] caused." When the reporter interjected that the army killed Indians only in "open battle," she responded: "they kill men, women and children . . . and you cannot deny it, for it is true." The Indian problem could be resolved only when whites treated the Indians honestly and granted them citizenship, she concluded.[12]

At times Standing Bear must have found white Americans' customs peculiar. During dinner at the Palmer House in Chicago with Bishop Clarkson, the Reverend Harsha, members of the Ponca Relief Committee, and several local citizens, Tibbles tipped the waiter to ensure that Standing Bear had plenty to eat, especially well-done roast beef. Toward the end of the meal, the chief informed Tibbles that he could not eat any more, and he had no way to take it away. Tibbles immediately recognized his dilemma, for "among Indians it is compulsory, either to eat all that is given you or take it away when you retire." To do otherwise was an insult to the host.[13]

Although dining out with various supporters of the tour was an occasional diversion, the main work of the Standing Bear party was to lecture in various Chicago churches until they set out for Boston on the Boston and Albany Railroad. In that hub of the antebellum abolitionist movement they experienced overwhelming success, receiving three thousand dollars in contributions within the first two weeks.[14] They arrived the morning of October 29 and went directly to the Tremont House where they had breakfast before attending a private reception hosted by Mayor Frederick Octavius Prince in the hotel parlors. Following brief remarks by the mayor, more than one hundred guests listened as Standing Bear, with La Flesche interpreting, explained that he no longer felt sad. He assured his audience: "It seems that I have come to a place I can call home."[15]

Shortly before that evening's large public reception at Horticultural Hall, B. W. Williams of the Boston lecture bureau, with whom Tibbles had signed a contract for the tour, delivered telegrams, rerouted from Chicago, to Tibbles and Standing Bear. They bore devastating news. Tibbles's wife had suddenly died of peritonitis, and Standing Bear's brother, Big Snake, had been killed when soldiers attempted to arrest him.[16]

"Prostrated, I went to my room and flung myself on my bed," wrote Tibbles years later. Standing Bear and Francis La Flesche soon came to console him. "We both suffer," soothed Standing Bear, "but remember those others who suffer and die in that strange land." Urging him not to go home, the Ponca chief said, "Don't stop trying to help my poor people. . . . Promise me that you will not forsake them." Tibbles took his hand and agreed to continue. Other telegrams relieved his anxiety about the fate of his daughters. The girls, ages eleven and nine, had been placed in a private school under the supervision of Bishop Clarkson.[17]

Standing Bear and the others urged Tibbles to attend that evening's reception. The grief-stricken Indian claimed that one of the group argued that "a soldier on the fighting line, if his brother falls or his wife dies, still must keep his place in the battle." The Ponca chief reminded Tibbles that following the loss of his own children, he had not given up. "I know how sore your heart is," he said, "but do go to the meeting and say one word for those who suffer and die with no one to pity. If you can do that, it will make your burdens lighter, not heavier." Tibbles complied.[18]

Mayor Prince presided at the meeting. The *Boston Daily Advertiser* described the participants and the evening's events: Standing Bear, who was attired in his "picturesque costume" of red, green, and gold, "spoke with great animation and earnest eloquence, using vigorous gestures," while La Flesche read her address in "a modest, natural manner, and with a sweet, girlish and expressive voice which quietly won the hearts of her listeners." She described the tour of the ten chiefs to the Indian Territory and the concern her mother had that they might be left in "a strange place where they cannot find their way home." Laughing at this possibility, she explained to her mother that the federal government would never "treat the chiefs of a nation with whom it made treaties in that dishonorable way." But her mother's worst fears had become a reality. When her uncle and the other chiefs returned, "ragged, weary and footsore," she saw her mother's tears and realized just how powerless her people were. "All we ask of your government is to be treated as men and women, to be allowed to have a voice in whatever concerns us, and last, but not least, we wish to be *allowed* to become civilized."[19]

The public meetings and lectures generally followed a pattern: introductions and speeches by various officials, clergymen, and prominent citizens, followed by the presentations of Tibbles and La Flesche, the latter of whom translated Standing Bear's remarks. Boston residents could easily follow the group's itinerary, but they could also read lengthy excerpts of the delegates' remarks in the pages of the *Boston Daily Advertiser,* owing to the personal attention of the editor, Delano A. Goddard. In addition to writing frequent pro-Ponca editorials, Goddard invited tour members to tea at his home in early November.[20] The editor made certain that news items about Standing Bear and his companions appeared frequently and were prominently positioned in his paper. Secretary Schurz, who described Standing Bear as "a man of morose disposition, . . . sullen and indolent among his followers after their removal," would not have agreed with the *Advertiser*'s portrayal of the chief as "noble [in] appearance [like] the Indian of [James Fenimore] Cooper's tales."[21] Nor for that matter would Schurz have concurred with Jackson's description of Standing Bear as "dignified and courteous," with a gentle face "stamped with unutterable sadness."[22]

At times the Poncas' schedule was grueling. Between the first and the fifteenth of November they were shown through a Cunard steamer, visited several adjacent docks, spoke at the Harvard Congregational Church in Brookline, and appeared at the Clarendon-Street Baptist Church in Boston. They joined with the Reverend Joseph Cook in the Boston Monday lectureship at the Old South Church, gave talks at Union Hall in Cambridge and at the Odd Fellows' Hall in Lynn, and appeared again at Horticultural Hall. Finally on Saturday, November 15, the Fisk University Jubilee Singers gave a benefit concert on their behalf at the Berkeley Street Church. "The scene of emancipated slaves extending their sympathy and help to the wronged, outraged and long-oppressed Indian race was one to touch the hearts of all men who have aught of sympathy for suffering brother men," wrote an *Advertiser* reporter.[23]

On another day they toured the organ manufacturing plant of Mason and Hamlin at the invitation of Henry Mason, a member of the Ponca Indian Committee. When Mason asked if Standing Bear could say a few words to his several hundred employees, the chief willingly mounted a small box in the large hall. He spoke of the journey from Omaha to Boston and how at one point all they "could see in every direction . . . were houses and houses. . . . [and he] began to understand why the white people were so great . . . they work." He noted that "every brick in all those houses were made by some man's hands. The White people are rich and great, and men like you are the ones who make them great." Reflecting on these words several years later, Tibbles mused, "did any labor leader ever make a more appropriate speech to a band of working men?"[24]

Although notices of all these events appeared in the *Advertiser,* the November 3 noon lecture by the Reverend Joseph Cook in the Old South Church was covered extensively. Sharing the speakers' platform with members of the Ponca tour, Cook praised the "Christian sentiment" in Omaha and moved for the adoption of a number of resolutions, including the issuing of homesteads to Indians, revision of laws relative to Indian affairs, and recognition of the Indian as a person, "amenable to civil laws." His final resolution was a recommendation that the Omaha and Boston Committees, the latter represented by Mayor Prince, "take in hand the collection of funds for the expense of this appeal."[25]

As the plight of the Poncas became better known, new supporters joined the cause. Dr. Oliver Wendell Holmes attended the Horticultural Hall meeting, where the governor of Massachusetts, Thomas Talbot, presided.[26] Henry Wadsworth Longfellow and Helen Hunt Jackson would soon lend their support. According to Tibbles, in early November Longfellow was introduced to La Flesche at a dinner reception at the Cambridge home of the publisher Henry Oscar Houghton. A traffic snarl had caused the Ponca delegation to be late. Eagerly staring out of the window, Longfellow opened the door when he saw them arrive. He took La Flesche's hand and earnestly remarked, "*This* is Minnehaha," a reference to the wife of his famous poetic character Hiawatha.[27]

The dates when Holmes and Longfellow joined the Ponca cause are well known, but the time and place of Helen Hunt Jackson's first introduction to Standing Bear and Susette La Flesche remains elusive. However, it is likely she met them in Boston. In mid-November, Jackson asked Charles Dudley Warner, editor of the *Hartford Courant,* to reprint an article on the Poncas she had written for the *Independent,* a New York weekly. She admonished Warner not to be "funny" about the Indians, explaining that their one chance for freedom, "and our one chance for decency as a nation in our treatment of them," lay "in this movement toward the courts, by the Poncas." Jackson also showed Tibbles this article. Later he expressed doubt as to whether the Indians' cause would have garnered as much success without her influence in dealing with congressmen, senators, and editors. More important, Tibbles said, Susette and Standing Bear "quickly became devoted to her."[28]

"I wish that every man and every woman in the United States could have the opportunity which I have had of seeing and conversing with these Indians," wrote Jackson of Standing Bear and La Flesche. Describing the removal in detail, and recognizing the "enormous significance" of Judge Dundy's decision, she asked her readers to "slip a dollar into an envelope" for their cause.[29] This article marked the beginning of Jackson's five-and-a-half-year career researching and writing in defense of America's Indians. The vigor she brought to her crusade was obsessive. "I shall be found with 'Indians' engraved on my brain when I am dead," she wrote in December 1879. "A fire has been kindled within me which will never go out."[30] Her death in 1885 snuffed out the flame.

In late November nearly five hundred Boston businessmen met at the Merchants' Exchange reading room—one of the largest gatherings ever held there. Following speeches by a shipping merchant, William H. Lincoln, and the newly elected Massachusetts governor, John Davis Long, Tibbles took the platform and called for legal rights for the Poncas. He was followed by La Flesche and Standing Bear, both of whom urged sympathy and generosity toward the Poncas. At the end of the meeting, those in attendance resolved that "immediate measures should be taken to secure for . . . [the Poncas] their legal rights and protection in their persons and property." They called for a committee of five to be appointed by the governor "to investigate and report in print."[31]

Governor Long appointed Thomas Talbot, his predecessor, as committee chair. Other members included Mayor Prince, the Reverend Rufus Ellis, John W. Candler, and William H. Lincoln, who served as secretary and treasurer.[32] This committee became formally known as the Boston Indian Citizenship Committee (also called the Boston Indian Committee). Secretary Schurz approved, describing Long's appointees as a "committee of intelligent and competent citizens in whom the people of Boston will have confidence." He graciously invited them to visit the capital, where he promised to supply them with accurate information.[33]

The committee's final report, published in 1880, concluded that the Ponca removal was not only unlawful but disastrous, and that the government was duty bound to restore the Poncas' lands. It recommended that a congressional committee investigate expenditures for Ponca removal and called for the fulfillment of treaty obligations, Indian citizenship, land allotments, and the granting of reservation lands in fee simple. These measures were also championed by subsequent national Indian reform organizations. Once it had formed, the Boston Indian Committee took over all decision-making for the tour.[34]

Several days after the meeting at the Merchants' Exchange, newspapers published excerpts from Secretary Schurz's annual report. In his discussion of the Poncas, he explained that his department had done "all in its power to indemnify the Poncas for the wrong done them," adding defensively, "no tribe has been more liberally cared for, and they have been provided with everything that can make them comfortable and prosperous."[35] In an editorial response, Goddard criticized Schurz's assessment of the Poncas. Then, addressing his remarks directly to the secretary, the *Advertiser* editor wrote that "the wrong which you speak of was the robbing them of this land. They ask you to return it to them." Goddard concluded, "Unhappily an Indian's word counts for little against the great men of this land."[36]

The tour's farewell meeting was held on December 2, 1879, at noon in Faneuil Hall.[37] A large, enthusiastic audience greeted the speakers. As William H. Lincoln noted, "the people of Boston have a keen sense of justice, and they are unable to reconcile [the treatment of the Poncas] with their ideas of right." Bostonians might not be experts in Indian affairs "but when certain facts are brought before us, we consider ourselves capable of deciding upon the justice of such facts."[38] The party then left for New York, but the triumphal nature of the tour's month in Boston was not duplicated. Helen Hunt Jackson wrote to Charles Dudley Warner from her room in the city's Brevoort House that the Poncas had arrived and "New York does not care for them. I have walked, talked, written & spent myself all in vain."[39]

Although she never suggested an explanation for New York's failure to embrace the Poncas, part of the reason could be that in Massachusetts distinguished local, state, and federal officials and well-known literary figures had joined the crusade. The only truly prominent individual supporting the tour in New York was Whitelaw Reid, longtime managing editor at the *Tribune*. Unlike Delano A. Goddard of the *Daily Advertiser,* who wholeheartedly supported the Poncas, Reid was involved only professionally with their cause. The Goddards—both Delano and his wife, Martha Le Baron—remained committed to Standing Bear long after he left Boston.

Tour members arrived at the Fifth Avenue Hotel in New York City on the morning of December 5, 1879. The reception that evening, attended by businessmen and the clergy, was held at the home of Josiah M. Fisk, a leading merchant, who along with Lincoln was in charge of the tour's itinerary.[40] The first public meeting was not held until December 12 at Steinway Hall, where a Unitarian minister, Dr. Henry W. Bellows, presided. Following the same format that had been successful in Boston, Tibbles, Susette La Flesche, and Standing Bear gave their respective speeches. Here too, audiences and reporters were impressed with La Flesche's fluent English, poise, and feminine voice. New Yorkers unable to attend could follow events simply by picking up their daily paper, which often printed excerpts from each speech.

While the *New York Times* described the audience as numbering about a thousand, the *Tribune* reporter remarked that it seemed small when compared to the tour's last Boston appearance, "when the Music Hall was filled to overflowing and two or three thousand persons were turned away unable to secure entrance." Only a small sum was pledged that evening. In addition to contributions to the collection box, however, a pamphlet detailing the history of the Ponca case, with an introduction by La Flesche, was sold at the door.[41]

On the evening of Sunday, December 14, a meeting was held at the Church of the Incarnation; the following Wednesday a free public meeting was scheduled at Association Hall, where both Standing Bear and La Flesche spoke; and on Sunday another public meeting was scheduled in Brooklyn. Near the end of that week, the Ponca tour planned on visiting the towns of Elizabeth and Montclair in New Jersey.[42] While Standing Bear, Tibbles, and La Flesche were making their presentations before these public meetings, newspapers kept the tour continually before the public. Although the lack of interest by New York citizens was apparent, one sympathetic *New York Times* editorial recommended the return of Ponca lands "at any cost to the Government under whose authority they have been so tyrannically despoiled."[43]

Tour members enjoyed a little free time in the city. In his reminiscences, Tibbles related a humorous tale about Standing Bear. One day the chief saw a Thomas Nast cartoon of Carl Schurz in *Harper's Weekly*. He purchased a copy, returned to the hotel, and borrowing scissors from the barber, cut out the cartoon and asked Tibbles to put it in his scrapbook. Periodically Standing Bear would look at it and laugh.[44]

Despite occasional *New York Times* editorials and the efforts of Whitelaw Reid at the *Tribune,* New Yorkers donated far less money than had Bostonians. Although Reid filled columns with the activities of the tour and also published Jackson's lengthy letters along with editorials calling attention to them, New Yorkers were simply not as responsive as Bostonians. On the other hand, Interior Secretary Carl Schurz reacted strongly.

Well before the lecture tour publicized the Ponca removal, Schurz recognized that the action toward the Indians was a mistake. Since the Indians had been "treated by the government in the most shameful manner," the Interior Department endorsed a reparations bill before Congress on February 3, 1879, authorizing $140,000 for their benefit, including the purchase of Cherokee land for their use. The bill failed to pass.[45] Later that year, in the annual reports of the Interior Department, Indian Commissioner Ezra A. Hayt and the Ponca agent William H. Whiteman suggested the Indians' condition had improved. This led the department to insist that the Poncas should not be returned to their former homeland. The Board of Indian Commissioners concurred, asserting that the Poncas were "safer and [in] better condition" than on their old reservation. The board believed that "they should be aided and encouraged in the arts of husbandry, education, improvement, and self-support [and] taught the blessings of civilization . . . and fitted for the exercise and enjoyment of rights of citizenship."[46] Thus Schurz, believing he had acted in good faith and supported by Hayt and the Board of Indian Commissioners, was determined to defend his policies. In Helen Hunt Jackson he found a worthy opponent.

In a December 6 letter to the *Tribune*, Jackson reviewed *The Ponca Chiefs: An Indian's Attempt to Appeal from the Tomahawk to the Courts*, written by Zylyff, a pseudonym used by Tibbles. After describing the book as "a full history of the robbery of the Ponca tribe of Indians," she related a poignant story of Susette La Flesche seated by a window, musing that the "hurrying city crowds" could go anywhere they wanted. "That is being free," the young woman had remarked. Jackson asked her *Tribune* readers, "What could be more profoundly touching than the thought of this Indian girl herself liable to arrest at any moment, as a 'ward' of the United States Government, absent without cause from the 'reservation' appointed for her tribe," witnessing what most people took for granted, the ability to come and go at will.[47]

Jackson also prepared a lengthy review of Tibbles's book for the *New York Evening Post*, stating that its profits would be used to recover Ponca lands and to bring a case before the Supreme Court to settle "whether or not the life and property of an Indian can be protected by law." Urging readers to attend one of Standing Bear's lectures, she speculated that if the chief could visit "every American home, there would be a swift and mighty revulsion of American sentiment upon the 'Indian Question,' for this Ponca case is but one of hundreds."[48]

Jackson's initial Ponca writings were designed to appeal to the emotions; however, at this stage of her quest, she began quoting from documents that she had located in New York City's Astor Library. Incorporating details from the Commissioner's Annual Reports of 1876 and 1878, and writing as "H.H.," she posed ten questions to the American people in a letter to the *Tribune,* which appeared on December 15. In her eagerness, she had expanded her research on Indian policy to include the White River Utes, Nez Perces, and the Omahas. In her last question, she inquired if the American public knew anything about the Poncas' present condition. The Indians were not, as Secretary Schurz had reported, "content and acclimated in their new home in the Indian Territory." Instead they were "waiting with the straining fear and hope of exiles for the result of the effort now being made by their Chief Standing Bear to secure legal redress for their wrongs."[49]

According to a short, untitled item in the *Tribune* dated December 19, "the string of pungent questions on Indian affairs by 'H.H.' . . . has evidently disturbed the serenity of the Interior Department." In fact, "to show how very much mistaken" Jackson was,[50] Schurz submitted to an interview by a *Tribune* correspondent. He defended the federal government's Indian policy, reiterated that Ponca removal had been ordered before he assumed office, and emphasized that he and Hayt were "doing everything in their power to indemnify [the Poncas] for their losses."[51] Infuriated by his response, Jackson scribbled another letter to the *Tribune,* answering the secretary point by point. A week later Charles Dudley Warner enlightened his Connecticut readers by quoting from it in his editorial in the *Hartford Courant.*[52]

Jackson then wrote directly to Schurz, enclosing excerpts from the letter of a Boston woman willing to contribute funds needed to prosecute a suit to regain Ponca lands. Jackson asked whether he approved of such a suit and, if not, whether he would be willing to explain his reasoning.[53] Accepting her challenge, Schurz explained that Indian tribes could not sue the government or any state in federal courts. He suggested that the monies thus far collected in Boston and New York should go toward improving Indian schools and indicated that the solution to Indian landholding was legislation transferring tribal ownership to individual ownership, "to settle them in severalty, and give them by patent an individual fee—simple in their lands." Such legislation would, Schurz said, entitle Indians to the same legal protection for their land and the same standing in court as white land owners.[54]

Troubled by Schurz's response, Jackson wrote to William Hayes Ward, editor of the *New York Independent,* calling Schurz "that false souled man." She informed Ward that the public was *"waking up* at last to this question— to our infamy—& the Indians' sufferings.—We are on the threshold of a great revolution," she asserted, "& the thieves who have been *fattening* on the seven millions a year spent in our Indian Policy, will do well to make all they can this year, for next year they will have small chance."[55]

Although intensely committed to their individual causes, both Jackson and Schurz remained civil and respectful in their letters to one another.[56] More important, they were eager to have their opinions expressed publicly, and the *Advertiser* and the *Tribune* obliged. The publication of these letters generated so much interest that on February 21, 1880, the *New York Times* reviewed them in a lengthy editorial. The paper criticized Schurz for opposing the Indians' attempt to gain legal redress and for suggesting that the solution was individual land ownership in severalty. It was regrettable that the secretary did not adequately show "how the giving to an Indian of 160 acres of land can clothe him with civil rights which he does not now possess," rights that the secretary "thinks that the courts cannot give him."[57]

Jackson's findings awakened her doubts about the secretary's motives. In almost identical letters to Oliver Wendell Holmes and Henry Wadsworth Longfellow, she remarked that Schurz had developed "such malignity towards innocent people, and such astounding and wholesale lying," that true friends of the Indians should denounce him and his methods.[58] She was not alone in her views. Schurz displeased many individuals with a stake in the operations of the Interior Department. Some westerners were upset with his reluctance to use force against unruly tribes; army officials were displeased with his preference for civilian control of Indian affairs; various churches disliked his decision to open reservations to all religious denominations, thus suspending their control over the appointment of agency officials.[59] Added to these detractors were humanitarians searching for a cause to replace the slavery issue. Boston and New York philanthropists who contributed money for the Ponca legal fund opposed Schurz because he claimed their donations could be better spent elsewhere.

Jackson's personal criticism of Carl Schurz resulted from her growing obsession with the Ponca controversy. As she rummaged through New York's Astor Library, she ferreted out evidence of neglect, fraud, and treaty violations by the federal government. Eager to share her discoveries, she inundated her wide circle of literary acquaintances with letters, articles, and editorials. She confided to her husband, William Sharpless Jackson, that Carl Schurz was a "dishonest *minded* man" and that she strongly believed herself "qualified to protest against *broken* treaties—cruel massacres—& unjust laws." In response to his suggestion that she "keep cool" on the Ponca issue, she retorted that Edward Everett Hale, Delano Alexander Goddard, and others "*all* said [she] had not written a word a 'cool headed man might not have written.'"[60]

While Jackson was composing letters to Secretary Schurz and researching other western tribes,[61] Tibbles and the Ponca tour continued their campaign to raise money in New York. On January 5 they appeared at Chickering Hall,[62] returning again on January 16, at which time Susette La Flesche read a "well written statement" challenging Schurz's claim that "the Indians can get no help from the Supreme Court." She also related a story about her father that highlighted the Indian's lack of rights. Joseph La Flesche had entrusted a thousand dollars to a white man, but found himself without any recourse when the man refused to repay the loan. In another incident one of his horses was stolen. When he asked the agent for advice in retrieving the animal, the suggestion was to "steal it back again." These stories lent credibility to Susette's insistence on the need for Indian legal rights.[63]

After their lukewarm reception in New York, the tour members appeared briefly in Philadelphia and several days later, on February 10, 1880, they traveled to Washington, D.C., to testify before the Senate Select Committee investigating Ponca removal. During the late winter and early spring, tour members traveled back and forth between the nation's capital and Philadelphia, where they had speaking obligations. The day after they first arrived in Washington, Standing Bear testified before the committee. Susette La Flesche interpreted his remarks. Two days later she took the stand. On the following day, accompanied by Senator and Mrs. Dawes, La Flesche visited with President and Mrs. Hayes at the White House. During the course of the evening the president expressed deep sympathy for the Poncas.[64] In the weeks that followed, the need for accurate translation intensified, demanding the skills of both Francis and Susette La Flesche. By early April, after Tibbles and his entourage had lectured in Baltimore, the westerners returned to Omaha. From there Standing Bear went to live with his family and followers on their old lands across from the town of Niobrara. In late September a delegation of ministers visited them. They found the Poncas living peacefully, sharing the area with both white settlers and Lakotas. More important, the Poncas were prospering; they had planted 250 acres in corn and had recently received supplies from the Omaha Ponca Relief Committee. The *Niobrara Pioneer* favored giving the Indians "a home of 160 acres if they are made citizens" and recommended that the remainder of their former reservation be opened to white settlement, with all proceeds going to the Poncas.[65]

At year's end, Tibbles organized yet another eastern lecture tour with the usual round of teas, receptions, lectures, and public meetings. One of the most important gatherings was held at Tremont Temple in Boston on December 3, 1880, one day after the Department of the Interior's annual report was made public. In his commentary, Schurz maintained his previous stance, acknowledging the injustice of the Ponca removal but concluding that since the Indians continued to prosper, they would not be returned to their Missouri River home. An editorial in the *Advertiser* reminded Bostonians that it had been three years since the Poncas had been forced from their homes and that "there has not been a day since that time when the Secretary, by a stroke of his plausible pen, might not have sent them back."[66] This editorial set the tone for the meeting.

At Tremont Temple, Tibbles and Susette La Flesche were joined by Governor Long, Mayor Prince, and members of the Boston Indian Committee. An "attentive and sympathetic audience" sat for two and a half hours and heard Long denounce the treatment of the Poncas. His stand was "all the more severe because it was not spoken in the heat of platform inspiration, but was carefully written before speaking, as a deliberate judgment upon the facts." Long's summary of the "Ponca outrage" was in language "strong enough to stir all the blood that ever boiled over the wrongs of African slaves." Wendell Phillips concluded the program, speaking "with masterly and brilliant eloquence. The Indian question never had more powerful or more impressive presentation."[67]

Governor Long stressed the Western origin of this reform movement and praised Tibbles, noting that "if anybody has been instrumental in bringing this outrage before the minds of the people of the East," it was the former Omaha journalist. Tibbles in his remarks emphasized that the movement for granting Indian titles to land and protection of the law originated "right in the heart of Indian country." Local citizens had prompted it, contributed to it, and brought the matter into court where they won a decision that the government refused to contest, thereby stalling the effort to extend the rule of law to Indians. "I tell you," he informed his audience, "the infamy of this business is in Washington, and not in the West."[68]

Secretary Schurz was to blame. "Western lawyers, Western business men, Western clergy, [and] Western settlers," Tibbles insisted, "protested with all the vigor and force of an honest and indignant people." Following the Poncas' exile in the "malarial bottoms of the Indian Territory," western men had "ever since been engaged in trying to right that wrong." Indians, Tibbles said, were human beings, "activated by the same motives that other people would be activated by under the same circumstances." If the equal protection clause of the Fourteenth Amendment applied to Indians, in accordance with Judge Dundy's ruling, the Ponca question, let alone the Indian question, could be resolved. Tibbles quoted from Section 1977 of the Revised Statutes, which stated that "all persons within the jurisdiction of the United States shall have the same right in every State and Territory to make and enforce contracts, to sue, be parties, give evidence," and enjoy "the full and equal benefit of all laws and proceedings for the security of persons and property." Indians, he claimed, should enjoy the same rights as white citizens and should be "subject to like pains, punishments, penalties, licenses, and exactions of every kind, and no other." Why is it, Tibbles asked, that men were afraid to grant Indians rights now accorded "to the negro [sic] and to the Chinaman?" To secure these rights for the Poncas and for Indians in general was at the core of the western impulse for Indian reform.[69]

By early 1880 much of the reading public was aware of Ponca removal,

Standing Bear's flight, and the condition of those remaining behind in the Indian Territory. The well-orchestrated lecture tour of Tibbles, Standing Bear, and Susette La Flesche had kept the Ponca issue continually before the public throughout the previous fall. Helen Hunt Jackson's letters detailing the Ponca affair along with her criticism of Secretary Schurz, which received additional support from the favorable editorials by Whitelaw Reid of the *Tribune* and Delano A. Goddard of the *Advertiser,* also contributed to the cause.

In short, the time was ripe for congressional attention. The westerners' tour could serve only as a catalyst for change. Congressional action was ultimately necessary to ensure the Indian policy sought by the reformers. With this in mind, the Senate created a Select Committee in February 1880, and the focus of struggle shifted to the nation's capital as committee members began their inquiry into the circumstances of Ponca removal. In addition to the participation of Senate committee members, Secretary of Interior Carl Schurz and Massachusetts Senator Henry Laurens Dawes entered the fray.

Notes

1. For Chief Red Cloud see Larson, *Red Cloud,* 129–36. Red Cloud journeyed on to New York where he spoke at Cooper Institute, founded by Peter Cooper, the New York inventor and philanthropist and a member of the Indian Peace Commission of 1867. For the Modocs see Jones, "Toby Riddle, Catalyst," 37–38, and Mardock, *The Reformers and the American Indian,* 134–37. See also Viola, *Diplomats in Buckskins,* and W. Clark, "An Indian Delegation to Washington," 192–205.

2. Zanjani, *Sarah Winnemucca,* 197–218, 244 (quote, 236).

3. Tibbles, *Buckskin and Blanket Days,* 211; J. Clark, "Ponca Publicity," 499–500.

4. For more on La Flesche see Mathes, "Iron Eye's Daughters," 135–52; Wilson, *Bright Eyes;* Crary, *Susette La Flesche;* Green, *Iron Eye's Family,* 56–81, 97–121; and idem, "Four Sisters," 165–76.

5. Milner, *With Good Intentions,* 156 (quote), 157–76; Mark, *A Stranger in Her Native Land,* 66–70.

6. These letters, dictated to the Episcopal minister Dorsey, who was studying the Omaha language, were translated and published as Dorsey, *Omaha and Ponka Letters.* See 29–33 (quotes, 32).

7. J. Stanley Clark stated that Susette La Flesche dressed in moccasins and a beaded doeskin dress when she spoke ("Ponca Publicity," 505), while Tibbles wrote that she usually "would dress like any American lady of the day" (*Buckskin and Blanket Days,* 213). For Tibbles's remark about Standing Bear, see Tibbles, "Anecdotes of Standing Bear," 274.

8. Tibbles, *Buckskin and Blanket Days,* 211.

9. Ibid., 212.

10. "Standing Bear's Appeal," *Chicago Tribune,* October 21, 1879, 4.

11. Ibid.; for an editorial on the Ute massacre see "The Old Story," *Advertiser,* October 3, 1879, 2. On September 29, Ute Indians from the White River Agency in Colorado attacked troops commanded by Major Thomas T. Thornburgh and agency personnel, killing Thornburgh, ten soldiers, and Agent Nathan C. Meeker and nine of his employees. While researching the condition of the Utes, Helen Hunt Jackson learned they had not received their annual supplies for 1877. The Utes "were starving—not simply suffering hunger—starving, dying for want of food," she wrote ("The Indian Problem: Questions for the American People, Propounded by 'H.H.,'" *Tribune,* December 15, 1879, 5, reprinted in Jackson, *The Indian Reform Letters,* 32–38). Jackson and others viewed the Utes as victims of an uncaring government policy.

12. "The Indian Wrongs," *Advertiser,* October 24, 1879, 2; the byline reads "From the Chicago Inter-Ocean."

13. Tibbles, "Anecdotes of Standing Bear," 271–73.

14. "The Poncas," *Advertiser,* November 11, 1879, 1.

15. "The Visiting Poncas: Arrival of the Chief of the Tribe in this City" (quote), and "Summary of the News," both in *Advertiser,* October 30, 1879, 1. See also "Local Miscellany," *Advertiser,* October 29, 1879, 4.

16. U.S. Senate, *Alleged Killing by Soldiers of Big Snake, a Chief Man of the Poncas,* S. Ex. Doc. 14 (hereafter cited as *Alleged Killing of Big Snake*) 14; J. Clark, "The Killing of Big Snake," 302–14. See also "The Poncas," *Advertiser,* November 3, 1879, 4; "The Murder of a Ponca Chief," *Tribune,* March 12, 1880, 1; U.S. Senate, *Testimony Relating to Removal,* 28, 67, 123–14, 206–7, 245–52, 480–84; Lake, "Standing Bear! Who?" 492; Tibbles, *Buckskin and Blanket Days,* 215–16.

17. Tibbles, *Buckskin and Blanket Days,* 214–15.

18. Ibid., 215.

19. "The Visiting Poncas," 1.

20. "The Poncas," *Advertiser,* November 3, 1879, 4; for one of Goddard's editorials see the *Advertiser* for November 1, 1879, 2.

21. "The Trials of a Tribe," *Advertiser,* August 23, 1879, 1 (first quote); "The Visiting Poncas," 1 (second quote).

22. H.H. [Jackson], "Standing Bear and Bright Eyes," *Independent,* November 20, 1879, 2.

23. "The Oppressed Poncas," *Advertiser,* November 17, 1879, 1 (quote). See also "The Poncas," ibid., November 3, 1879, 4; "About Town," ibid., November 5 and 10, 1879, 4.

24. Tibbles, "Anecdotes of Standing Bear," 275.

25. "The Monday Lectures: By the Rev. Joseph Cook—with Preludes," *Advertiser,* November 4, 1879, 4. In his lecture Cook mentioned his friend, the Reverend Alvin F. Sherrill, treasurer of the Ponca fund. They had been roommates at Andover Theological Seminary.

26. "The Poncas," *Advertiser,* November 11, 1879, 1.

27. Tibbles, *Buckskin and Blanket Days,* 218. See also "The Poncas," *Advertiser,* November 11, 1879, 1; "Seeking Redress in the East," *Tribune,* December 8, 1879, 3.

28. Jackson to Warner, November 18, 1879, Charles Dudley Warner Collection, Watkinson Library, letter reprinted in Jackson, *The Indian Reform Letters,* 22–24; see also p. 19. For the Tibbles quote see *Buckskin and Blanket Days,* 216. Tibbles wrote that Jackson traveled with them "for some weeks" ("Anecdotes of Standing Bear," 274). There is no supporting evidence of this statement from her letters. See also "The True Story of the Poncas," *Hartford Courant,* November 25, 1879, 1, and the *Colorado Springs Weekly Gazette,* December 6, 1879.

29. H.H. [Jackson], "Standing Bear and Bright Eyes," 1–2.

30. Jackson to Warner, December 21, 1879, Warner Collection, Watkinson Library, reprinted in Jackson, *The Indian Reform Letters,* 56.

31. "The Poor Poncas: A Noonday Meeting of Busy Boston Merchants," *Advertiser,* November 26, 1879, 4 (quotes); see also editorial entitled "The Meeting at the Merchants' Exchange," ibid., 2

32. For names of the committee members see *The Indian Question: Report of the Committee Appointed by Hon. John D. Long,* 1. It can be assumed that these five men and the earlier Ponca Indian Committee, appointed on July 30 at the meeting of the Society for Propagating the Gospel, merged their efforts for there were names from both groups listed as members of the Boston Indian Citizenship Committee in a later publication entitled *Secretary Schurz: Reply of the Boston Committee,* 23.

33. "The Ponca Indian Troubles," *Advertiser,* December 6, 1879, 1.

34. *The Indian Question: Report of the Committee Appointed by Hon. John D. Long,* 11–12 for conclusions, and 25–26 for the committee's final recommendations. For mention of this report see "The Secretary of the Interior and the Indian Question," February 3, 1880, 2, and a brief notice on February 8, 1880, 2, both in the *Advertiser.* For more on the committee see Hoxie, *A Final Promise,* 9, 11, 32, 74, 227; Prucha, *American Indian Policy in Crisis,* 115, 132–34, 146, 251, 339; Priest, *Uncle Sam's Stepchildren,* 78, 83, 213; Mardock, *The Reformers and the American Indian,* 184, 198, 222, 224.

35. "The Indians: Secretary Schurz's Annual Report to Congress," *Advertiser,* November 28, 1879, 1. See also "Indian Affairs: The Red Man Improving in Civilization and Generally Living a Peaceful Life," *Tribune,* November 28, 1879, 3.

36. "Our Indian Policy," *Advertiser,* November 29, 1879, 2.

37. "The Ponca Indians," *Advertiser,* December 2, 1879, 1; "Indians' Rights: A Boston Audience Speaks in Faneuil Hall" and an untitled news item, ibid., December 3, 1879, 1.

38. "The Indian Problem—A Reply to Carl Schurz," *Advertiser,* December 6, 1879, 2.

39. Jackson to Warner, December 14, 1879, Warner Collection, Watkinson Library, reprinted in Jackson, *The Indian Reform Letters,* 43–45.

40. "Arrival of the Ponca Indians," *Tribune,* December 6, 1879, 2; "Seeking Redress in the East," 3; and "Indian Wrongs: A Reception to the Poncas," *Tribune,* December 9, 1879, 5. See also "Is the Indian a Citizen?" *New York Times,* December 9, 1879, 2; "An Indian Reception," *Advertiser,* December 10, 1879, 1.

41. "Wrongs of the Indians: Cruel Treatment of the Poncas," *Tribune,* December 13, 1879, 5 (quote); "For the Ponca Indians: The Speeches in Steinway Hall," *New York Times,* December 13, 1879, 2; Coward, *The Newspaper Indian,* 215–16.

42. "Appeals for the Poncas," *Tribune,* December 15, 1879, 5; "New York," *New York Times,* December 15, 1879, 8.

43. "The Wronged Poncas," *New York Times,* December 19, 1879, 4. See also Hays, *A Race at Bay,* 221–23.

44. Tibbles, *Buckskin and Blanket Days,* 219–20.

45. U.S. House, *Report [to Accompany Bill H.R. 6332],* H. Rept. 107 (quote); see also "The Poncas," in U.S. Department of the Interior, Office of Indian Affairs, *Annual Report of the Commissioner of Indian Affairs* (1879), xiv, for the text of the bill.

46. *Eleventh Annual Report of the Board of Indian Commissioners for the Year 1879,* 13.

47. Jackson to the editor, December 6, 1879, printed as "An Appeal for the Indians: Full History of the Wrongs of the Ponca Tribe—Bright Eyes on Law and Liberty," *Tribune,* December 9, 1879, 5; reprinted in Jackson, *The Indian Reform Letters,* 27–29. See also *New York Evening Post,* December 26, 1879, 2, for notice of the book's publication.

48. Jackson to the editor, December 14, 1879, printed as "The Story of the Poncas: A Vigorous Rehearsal of a Shameful Tale," *New York Evening Post,* December 17, 1879, 1; reprinted in Jackson, *The Indian Reform Letters,* 38–43.

49. Jackson to the editor, December 11, 1879, printed as "The Indian Problem," *Tribune,* December 15, 1879, 5 (quotes); in the same issue, in "The News This Morning," 4, Reid, in a brief editorial note, directed readers to "peruse" Jackson's letter on the following page. This letter is reprinted in Jackson, *The Indian Reform Letters,* 32–38. See also "Mr. Schurz on Indian Affairs," *Tribune,* December 19, 1879, 1; "The Indian Problem: Questions for the American People," *Hartford Courant,* December 22, 1879, 1; Coward, *The Newspaper Indian,* 216–18.

50. *Tribune,* December 19, 1879, 4 (both quotes).

51. "Mr. Schurz on Indian Affairs: The Secretary Replies to the Letter of H.H. in the *Tribune,*" *Tribune,* December 19, 1879, 1. See also Schurz to Edward Atkinson, November 28, 1879, in Schurz, *Speeches, Correspondence and Political Papers,* 3:485.

52. Jackson to the editor, December 23, 1879, printed as "The Wrongs of the Indians: 'H.H.' Takes up Mr. Schurz's Reply," *Tribune,* December 28, 1879, 5, reprinted in Jackson, *The Indian Reform Letters,* 57–59. For an interesting sketch of the secretary see "Hon. Carl Schurz, Secretary of the Interior," *Council Fire,* May 1880, 68. For the editorial see "A 'Corner' on the Indian Department," *Hartford Daily Courant,* December 30, 1879, 2.

53. Jackson to Schurz, January 9, 1880, printed in Jackson, *A Century of Dishonor*, 359–61, reprinted in Jackson, *The Indian Reform Letters*, 77–79.

54. Schurz to Jackson, January 17, 1880, in Jackson, *A Century of Dishonor*, 362; Schurz, *Speeches, Correspondence and Political Papers*, 3:498. See also J. Clark, "Ponca Publicity," 509.

55. Jackson to Ward, January 27, 1880, [HM 13980], Jackson Manuscripts, Huntington Library, reprinted in Jackson, *The Indian Reform Letters*, 89.

56. In her January 22 letter, Jackson apologized, explaining that it was her "deep interest in the Indians, and in the Ponca case especially," that had prompted her to write. See Jackson to Schurz, January 22, 1880, in Jackson, *A Century of Dishonor*, 363–64; in Schurz, *Speeches, Correspondence and Political Papers*, 3:499–500; and in Jackson, *The Indian Reform Letters*, 87.

57. "Civil Rights in Acres," *New York Times*, February 21, 1880, 4, reprinted in Jackson, *A Century of Dishonor*, 368, and Hays, *A Race at Bay*, 37–40. See also "The Hayt Inquiry—Interesting Correspondence," 2, and "The Ponca Suits: The Letters Between Mrs. Jackson (H.H.) and Mr. Schurz," 1, both in the *Advertiser*, February 7, 1880; "The Poncas' Case," *Chicago Tribune*, February 11, 1880, 4; "The Indian Problem," *Tribune*, February 12, 1880, 2.

58. Jackson to Longfellow and Holmes, March 2, 1881, Henry Wadsworth Longfellow Papers and Oliver Wendell Holmes Papers, Houghton Library, reprinted in Jackson, *The Indian Reform Letters*, 184–88. See also Mathes, "Helen Hunt Jackson and the Campaign for Ponca Restitution," 36–40, for the Holmes letter.

59. Prucha, *American Indian Policy in Crisis*, 57–61 (regarding the religious issue), 99–102 (regarding the military issue).

60. Jackson to Will Jackson, December 26, 1879, William Sharpless Jackson Family Papers, Tutt Library, reprinted in Jackson, *The Indian Reform Letters*, 61–64.

61. Jackson defended the Utes, condemned the Sand Creek massacre of the Cheyennes and Arapahoes by the Colorado Volunteers, and wrote of the plight of the Northern Cheyennes who fled the Indian Territory under Dull Knife and Little Wolf. For another interesting Ponca article, see H.H. [Jackson], "What Can Be the Difference between Poncas and Winnebagoes?" *Advertiser*, March 6, 1880, 2.

62. Untitled news item, *Tribune*, January 6, 1880, 8.

63. "Views from the Platform," *New York Times*, January 17, 1880, 5 (quotes); "Justice to the Indians," *Tribune*, January 17, 1880, 2.

64. "Bright Eyes," *Advertiser*, February 14, 1880, 1.

65. "The Poncas," *Niobrara Pioneer*, September 28, 1880, 1.

66. "Mr. Schurz's Report," *Advertiser*, December 3, 1880, 2. For additional accounts see "Secretary Schurz's Report," *Tribune*, December 2, 1880, 1; "The Wards of the Nation," *New York Times*, December 2, 1880, 4. For acting Indian Commissioner Marble's report, see "Condition of the Indians," *Tribune*, November 22, 1880, 2.

67. "The Poncas: Boston's Sympathy for Their Outrages and Wrongs," *Advertiser,* December 4, 1880, 1 (description of audience, meeting length, and Long speech), 4 (description of Phillips). A lengthy speech by Phillips was described in a small news item on page 2 of the same issue of the *Advertiser.* Delano A. Goddard and William H. Lincoln invited Dawes to attend; see Goddard to Dawes, November 29, 1880, and Lincoln to Dawes, November 30, 1880, Dawes Papers, box 24, Library of Congress. Dawes sent a letter, which was read to the audience. Kemble took offense at Long's address and wrote a lengthy rebuttal on December 8, 1880. This letter was reproduced in U.S. Senate, *Report of Special Commission,* 46–50.

68. "The Poncas: Boston's Sympathy for Their Outrages and Wrongs," 1 (Long quotes); Thomas Henry Tibbles, *Western Men Defended,* 6–7 (Tibbles quote). Part of Tibbles's speech is also reproduced in the December 4, 1880, issue of the *Advertiser,* 1.

69. Tibbles, *Western Men Defended,* 7–8.

PART TWO

Carl Schurz ranks as one of the more important interior secretaries in the nation's history.[1] A refugee from turmoil in Europe, where he actively participated in the movement for German unification, Schurz arrived in the United States in 1852. Appalled by the corruption evident in many areas of public life, he quickly became involved in American affairs. In 1856, while residing in Watertown, Wisconsin, he joined the new Republican Party, studied law, and became active in politics and the antislavery cause. In his capacity as a journalist, he started a German-language newspaper intended to bring German immigrants into the Republican Party. During the election year of 1860, he traveled over twenty thousand miles campaigning for Lincoln, focusing largely on gaining German voters; and during the Civil War, he commanded a division of Union troops.

After Lincoln's assassination and at President Andrew Johnson's request, Schurz toured the South to report on conditions. The president never acknowledged his report, but it was published by Congress. By the time he entered the Senate, having won a seat in the 1868 election, Schurz was half-owner and editor of a German-language newspaper published in St. Louis. As a United States senator from Missouri, he championed civil service reform, opposed President Grant, and became a leader in the Liberal Republican movement. He campaigned in 1872 for Horace Greeley, chiefly by criticizing the Grant administration. Thereafter, he voted for reform measures regardless of party and became known as a "Mugwump." Although he did not seek reelection in 1874, he supported Rutherford B. Hayes two years later because Hayes called for civil service reform and agreed with Schurz's views on reconstruction and sound money. The new president brought him into the cabinet as secretary of the interior.

Schurz administered a department that included the Bureau of Indian Affairs and supervised a quarter of a million Indians and millions of acres of reservation lands; public lands; hundreds of thousands of pensioners; the patent office; details of the government's land-grant railroads; the census; geological and geographical surveys; charitable institutions; and some of the public grounds and parks in Washington, D.C. No previous secretary had worked as assiduously as Schurz in seeking to master the business of the department. He concentrated his endeavors in three areas: administrative reform, conservation, and Indian affairs. He overhauled the personnel system by instituting competitive tests, defining the jurisdiction of bureau administrators, and establishing a board of inquiry to review individuals recommended for dismissal. Yet Schurz devoted comparatively little time to the administrative procedures that had engaged the energies of most of his predecessors.

The issues of conservation commanded much of his attention. He argued that the careless cutting of timber led to erosion and flooding and demanded federal intervention. He saw the need to establish guidelines for the sale of timber located on government lands, as well as to set aside such lands for homestead entry and preventing preemption. Over Schurz's vigorous objections, Congress enacted the Timber and Stone Act in 1878. He foresaw that the measure would be utilized by lumber companies to obtain extensive tracts of valuable timber at a low price. To protect these lands, Schurz employed agents to apprehend timber thieves. Although his actions aroused criticism, Schurz stood firm. He articulated the relation between deforestation, surface runoff, sedimentation, and erosion. "The rapidity with which this country is being stripped of its forests," he stated in his 1877 annual report, "must alarm every thinking man."[2] The federal government, he insisted, should retain title and strictly control private use of public lands. His concern for the conservation of natural resources and his questioning of the myth of inexhaustible resources marked him as an early leader in a field that attracted increasing national attention. In 1878, for example, he ordered the publication of John Wesley Powell's *Report on the Arid Region of the West*.

The secretary began his administration of Indian affairs by ordering a thorough investigation of the Indian Bureau, which he found to be irresponsible, lacking supervision, and rife with corruption. The Indians, he said, were systematically cheated. Schurz worked hard to bring order and efficiency to the bureau's administration. He adopted a strict code of regulations for the guidance of agents; he also thoroughly revised the office's system of keeping accounts. Under these new regulations, he managed to curtail, if not eliminate, the widespread swindling by agents and traders. In addition, he directed that supplies and amenities be distributed to heads of families, replacing the former recipients, the headmen and chiefs. He also established Indian police forces on various reservations. Under his new policy, he encouraged Indians to give up hunting and gathering and to apply themselves to the type of systematic labor common among Euroamericans. He also urged that agency farms be abandoned in order to persuade Indians to cultivate lands of their own. Moreover he directed that Indians be taught to do their own freighting, enabling them to purchase their own wagons and horses as well as to market their own crops.

Indian education also markedly changed during Schurz's tenure. He supervised the enrollment of Indian students at Hampton Institute, which had been established in Virginia for freedmen. This experiment served as the catalyst for the founding of the first federal Indian boarding schools, pioneered by two institutions, Carlisle Institute in Pennsylvania, established by Richard Henry Pratt, and what would later be known as Chemawa Institute in Forest Grove, Oregon. Pratt and his fellow enthusiasts aggressively countered the Indians' reluctance to seek education. Despite considerable native hostility to schooling, Schurz's administration changed the direction of federal involvement in Indian education.

During Schurz's tenure, the Department of War brought an end to Indian resistance in the Plains and Southwest. On the northern Plains, Sitting Bull returned from Canada, and the Lakotas moved onto reservations in Dakota Territory, where they were encouraged to shift from a culture of buffalo hunting to farming. On the southern Plains, the Battle of Palo Duro Canyon effectively ended the Red River War before Schurz assumed his cabinet post. By the end of his tenure, most military conflicts between Indians and the regular army had been resolved. In the southwestern borderlands, the Warm Springs Apache under Victorio presented the most serious disturbance, but Victorio's death in battle against Mexican troops in Chihuahua in October 1880 ended their resistance. In short, during Schurz's tenure the assimilation process had been forcibly moved forward among many western tribes.[3]

The case of the Poncas, however, was another story. It involved Schurz in a controversy that brought him unfavorable publicity, which he took very seriously. In his revealing letters of justification, Schurz insisted his behavior was honorable and beyond reproach. At times he responded emotionally or with sarcasm, indicating that his critics had penetrated his usual calm demeanor.[4]

Schurz's defenders were particularly critical of the behavior of Senator Henry Laurens Dawes of Massachusetts. They noted that Schurz's stance on the Poncas, which became clear in his annual reports of the late 1870s, did not elicit any commentary from Senator Dawes. Whatever the reason,

Dawes became involved in the Ponca affair only when he was appointed to the Senate committee investigating the matter.

During Schurz's tenure, Dawes was a relative newcomer to the Senate. Elected in 1874 to the seat of Charles Summer, who had died earlier in the year, Dawes already had served eighteen years in the House. He would serve another eighteen years in the Senate. For six years Dawes was a member of the Senate Committee on Indian Affairs and then became chairman for the next twelve years. He left the Senate in 1893 to chair a controversial body, known as the Dawes Commission, that would dissect the tribal affairs of the Five Civilized Tribes. He held this post until his death in 1903.[5]

A founder of the Massachusetts Republican Party, which elected him to the House of Representatives in 1856, Dawes remained faithful to the party though he frequently pursued a moderate and at times an independent path. During the Civil War as the floor leader of the House War Contracts Committee, Dawes aroused the ire of Radical Republicans and the president for dramatically revealing graft and corruption in such matters as shoddy blankets and rotten food furnished to the military.

In the postwar years, as chairman of the House Committee on Elections, he first called for a moderate congressional policy toward the South; later he supported all the major Reconstruction measures. In 1869 he became chairman of the House Committee on Appropriations and the Republican leader of the House. A powerful figure, he used his influence to counteract shoddy procedures and pressed for administrative reforms. He sponsored measures establishing Yellowstone National Park, the Fish Commission, and the Weather Bureau. He also favored increased funding for geological surveys and indicated an interest in Indian policy when he challenged the corrupt Indian Bureau and led the fight to halt treaty negotiations with American Indians in order that the House might have an equal voice in Indian affairs. Before Congress adjourned in 1871, it declared that "hereafter no Indian nation or tribe . . . shall be acknowledged or recognized as an independent nation, tribe, or power, with whom the United States may contract by treaty."[6] The net result of this measure was the end of the treaty era. Nonetheless, it was replaced by bilateral agreements, which were negotiated with Indian tribes, similar to treaties, but ratified by both houses of Congress. Old treaties remained in effect, however. Though Dawes was more concerned with economy and efficiency than with humanitarian reform, his actions were noted by influential reformers in his home state. Some of these reformers, searching for an alternative to abolition, saw Indian reform as a viable movement.

In 1870 Dawes's opposition to the graft and corruption rampant in the

Grant administration forced a reduction in expenditures and gave an impetus to the Liberal Republican movement. In his calls for administrative efficiency and fiscal retrenchment, Dawes reflected views that were not markedly different from those of Carl Schurz, who in 1870 was in his final years of service in office as the senior United States Senator from Missouri.

Like Schurz, Dawes at times could be alternately cool and impassioned, and even sarcastic in his remarks. But he was always earnest. Once he involved himself in an issue, he was a workhorse in his efforts to master its details. In control of his material, bolstered with quickness of wit and skill in debate, Dawes was a formidable opponent and a valuable ally. Adding to his potency as a senator was the fact that he faithfully represented the manufacturers of Massachusetts. When Dawes was challenged and his opponents were sure of success, those adversaries nevertheless found themselves in the minority when the General Assembly voted to select a senator. Dawes was chosen because too many powerful and prominent men depended on him for the security of their interests, and by 1880 he was assured of the safety of his Senate seat. Therefore, when the influential Massachusetts senator clashed with the secretary of the interior late in the presidency of Rutherford B. Hayes, it was a notable contest that drew widespread public attention.[7]

Notes

1. The literature on Carl Schurz is enormous. The most recent and best biography is by Trefousse, *Carl Schurz.*

2. U.S. House, *Report of the Secretary of the Interior,* H. Ex. Doc. 1, vol. 8, xvi.

3. For a general discussion of his views on Indians see "Schurz and the Indians," in Fuess, *Carl Schurz, Reformer,* 252–77. To the casual observer, all of these changes seem positive. They were, however, part of a master plan by reformers, designed to change the communal Indian way of life to that of a small self-sufficient farmer. Reformers concentrated on the children, sending them to distant boarding schools where they were not allowed to speak their native language or practice their religion. Boarding schools continued to be the focus of the government's educational program throughout the remainder of the nineteenth century. By the second decade of the new century, off-reservation schools were gradually phased out and more day schools built as government policy slowly moved from assimilation to Indian self-determination.

4. Fuess presents a strong case supporting Schurz's position regarding the Poncas. Shortly after leaving office, Schurz wrote a comprehensive reflective view; see his "Present Aspects of the Indian Problem." For an earlier, more defensive statement responding to an article by Indian Inspector E. C. Kemble, see Schurz, "The Removal of the Poncas," *Independent,* January 1, 1880, 1. A lengthy defense of his actions is

presented in his letter to Massachusetts Governor John D. Long on December 9, 1880, in the Carl Schurz Papers, container 184, Library of Congress.

5. Unlike research about Schurz, the literature on the career of Dawes is sparse. There is no complete biography. For a brief sketch see the entry by Claude M. Fuess in *The Dictionary of American Biography*, 3:149–50. For his early career see Nicklason, "The Early Career of Henry L. Dawes," available on microfilm by Xerox University Microfilm, Ann Arbor, Michigan.

6. Prucha, *American Indian Treaties: The History of a Political Anomaly*, 308; for a detailed discussion of the end of treaty making, see 289–310. See also Nicklason, "The Early Career of Henry L. Dawes," 371.

7. The Dawes Papers in the Library of Congress are spotty on many aspects of his senatorial career. There are very few of Dawes's outgoing letters. His interest in Indian reform is evident primarily from incoming correspondence. Therefore government documents comprise a basic source for his Indian policy.

CHAPTER SIX

Schurz Defines His Position
and Dawes Disagrees

When he took office, Carl Schurz had no previous connection to Indian affairs. There was no reason to suspect him of being prejudiced against the Poncas or any other Indian tribe, nor was there any indication that he favored any policy or specific reform. His previous experience both in Germany and the United States had never brought Indians to the center of his attention. Moreover, he did not originate the legislation for the Ponca removal. The 1868 treaty awarded the Ponca Reservation to the Lakotas, and Congress in August 1876 called for the Poncas' removal to the Indian Territory with their consent. The day before Schurz assumed office, two relevant pieces of legislation were signed into law. One appropriated additional funds for the Ponca removal; the other provided for the resettlement of the Brulé to the Ponca Reservation. In addition, by the end of January 1877, Colonel Edward C. Kemble, the Indian inspector in charge of the removal, reported he had secured Ponca approval. When Schurz became interior secretary in March, removal was initiated; the dispute had begun.

Schurz insisted that upon assuming office, his initial task was to become familiar with his new assignment; therefore, he accepted Kemble's report. He had no reason to question it or the policy launched by his predecessor. Of course, Schurz had been a severe critic of the Grant administration and as a prominent Liberal Republican, he was aware of the prevalent graft and corruption. Moreover, his claim that he had no immediate indication of opposition to removal for some months after he became secretary was challenged by several neighbors of the Poncas who had brought the matter to his attention.

However, before the year was out, Schurz, recognizing that a grave injustice had been perpetrated, acknowledged this situation in his December 1877 report and "urgently recommended that liberal provision be made to aid the [Poncas] in their new settlement."[1] In his two succeeding annual reports, Schurz called on Congress in stronger terms for "new legislation" to enable the Interior Department to atone for the injury inflicted upon these people. Schurz saw himself as a humane and concerned individual who had done all that he possibly could to call attention to a grievous wrong.

Once the Poncas were settled in the Indian Territory, Schurz, who had reached his last full year in office, insisted it would be an equally horrendous ordeal to return them to their northern homeland. Concluding that the Indians were both satisfied and pleased with their present location, he was disturbed by the criticism leveled at him by other concerned citizens and by members of Congress. He felt called upon to challenge the views of his critics, among whom the "Boston philanthropists" and Senator Dawes of Massachusetts were easily the most prominent.

Shortly before he left office, Schurz publicly defended his actions in print. In an August 22 interview on the subject of the Ponca Indians, the secretary expressed dismay at the criticism heaped upon his administration, which "when it came to power could do nothing but carry out laws previously enacted." He explained that he had noted in his annual reports the "wrong done" the Poncas and that everything was being done to "indemnify them for their losses and to make their situation as comfortable as possible." Cognizant of the reformers' demand that the tribe be returned to its old reservation, Schurz explained that the Interior Department had neither the legal authority nor the finances to do so. In addition, he personally feared that if Indians were encouraged to leave their reservations "and roam about as their fancy may suggest, the result would probably be general vagrancy and their being killed off in detail." Schurz's interview, which appeared in lengthy articles in many eastern newspapers, became his standard defense. He maintained he could not reverse the decisions of his predecessors and, although he was sympathetic to the Indians' predicament, everything possible under the law had been done to make the Poncas comfortable and contented.[2]

Schurz was not the only one on the defensive. In December 1879, Kemble published an article in the *Independent* refuting what he considered false statements made by Standing Bear and others in "awakening sympathy for unfortunate people." In justifying his actions, Kemble cited Schurz's reasons for removing the Poncas and stressed that in council the Indians agreed to surrender their lands and select a home in the Indian Territory. He also related in considerable detail the journey of their chiefs and what befell them.[3]

Among other things, Kemble mentioned "unscrupulous white men from a neighboring town" who advised the Poncas to resist the action of the government. He brought Schurz into his discussion when he said the secretary "received the Ponca delegation with respectful deference." While refusing to allow delegation members to return to their homeland, Schurz had "permitted them to do the next unwisest thing," which in Kemble's view was to "leave the Quapaw tract" for another location in the Indian Territory, where they would be exposed "to the worst effect of the change from a northern to a southern climate."[4]

In conclusion, Kemble, whose commission as inspector expired in February 1878, indicted Schurz. Kemble acknowledged that the secretary, in his annual report, had noted that the Poncas were "grievously wronged by their removal," but he perceived it as a wrong for which Schurz was "clearly responsible." The inspector cited an April 12, 1877, telegram in which the secretary urged him to "Press the removal!" Schurz also sanctioned the use of troops to coerce the Poncas into moving, if the need arose. Thus Kemble justified his actions by accusing Standing Bear of maligning him and holding Secretary Schurz immediately responsible for the removal of the Poncas from their homeland and for their additional move to an unsatisfactory location in the Indian Territory. As a good soldier, Kemble merely executed orders. His was a difficult assignment, one that he fulfilled despite his belief that removal was an arrant wrong.[5]

Carl Schurz quickly responded. In its first issue for 1880, the *Independent* published his rejoinder. While the Poncas were wronged, Schurz insisted he could not be blamed because at the time he was devoting his "whole attention" to "the vast and complicated machinery of the Interior Department" and was "little conversant with Indian affairs." He therefore relied on the judgment of his Indian commissioner, which was based on reports from Kemble himself. Schurz claimed he had never seen the dispatch attributed to him until he read it in Kemble's article. As evidence, Schurz cited telegrams of inquiry sent by Indian Commissioner John Quincy Smith to Kemble, to which Kemble had replied: "the Indians will go peacefully if you will telegraph decisively."[6]

As to his order to dispatch troops, Schurz insisted that Kemble had repeatedly and urgently demanded them. As to his removing the Poncas from the Quapaw tract, the Poncas had themselves requested the opportunity to select a new location. Schurz also noted that the Lakota chiefs Red Cloud and Spotted Tail refused to occupy the original Ponca lands, thereby refuting Kemble's insistence upon the urgency of Ponca renewal. Schurz further published the section of his first annual report that expressed his concern and argued that "the case of the Poncas seems entitled to a special consideration at the hands of Congress." Hence, Schurz supported the Senate's approval of a resolution to "investigate this whole Ponca business." The investigation would demonstrate that "the highly colored stories" about "brutal military force employed in compelling their removal" were "sensational fabrications" and not borne out by the facts in the official record. Thus, Schurz shrewdly shifted the blame to Kemble's shoulders and reiterated that a Senate committee would resolve the matter.[7]

Within a fortnight Kemble's rebuttal appeared. He presented further documents and related additional details of his activities in the Ponca removal. His primary thrust argued that Schurz's article, published in the *Independent*, was "mainly directed to the removal of the responsibility for their removal" from Schurz himself and to shifting it instead "to his subordinates and to the Indians themselves." The secretary, he said, "could have stopped the whole business, had he been so disposed." Schurz had enough information on Ponca opposition to removal to halt the process before it got underway. Indeed, Kemble himself had gone to Washington and reviewed the whole matter with Schurz, who informed him that it was the intention of the department to proceed. In short, Kemble concluded that Schurz's insistence that he had to rely on the judgment of the Indian commissioner simply could not be sustained. And neither, Kemble insisted, could Schurz provide documentation that he had repeatedly and urgently demanded troops.[8]

At the end of 1880, while the Senate Select Committee was investigating the status of the Poncas, Schurz reentered the public debate by responding to the remarks of Governor John D. Long of Massachusetts. Speaking before a Boston meeting on December 3, Long described the Ponca ordeal as a record of shame written against the administration, "a story of wanton and brutal outrage."[9]

In his seventeen-page public rebuttal, published in the form of a letter, Schurz reviewed the entire removal process. He reiterated that he relied on the advice and suggestions of agents familiar with the situation. He accepted Kemble's statement on the Poncas' consent, and he also noted the influence of friends of the Poncas who thought that under the circumstances removal was in the Indians' best interest. To bolster his position, the secretary mentioned that moving the tribe members back to their homeland would have allowed "a reckless, lawless, grasping element of adventurers" to usurp the lands the Poncas now occupied in the Indian Territory, thereby weakening "the position of the government defending them." Schurz also relied on the impact of the domino effect, arguing that if the Poncas returned to Dakota Territory, the Northern Cheyennes, the Nez Perces, and possibly the Pawnees would be "restless to follow their example."[10] In light of the fundamental mistake of ceding Ponca lands to the Lakotas, and the ordeal of the tribe's move to the Indian Territory and their suffering there, Schurz was not ready to consider another move. The Poncas, he asserted, "were more the victims of unfortunate circumstances than of evil designs on the part of anybody connected with the Interior Department."[11]

While several speakers at the Boston meeting in early December claimed that the wrong done the Poncas was just being "unearthed," Schurz claimed he had already noted the Indians' hardships and had called upon Congress to assist the tribe. He included in his letter the statement he had presented after meeting with the Poncas in November 1877 in Washington and an excerpt of Commissioner Hayt's 1878 report admitting the Poncas were wronged. But he also noted that Congress had failed to appropriate funds to alleviate their misery. Moreover, Schurz argued that the Poncas were beginning "to appreciate their real interests" and were willing to remain permanently in the Indian Territory.[12]

After a thirteen-page defense of his position, Schurz addressed the resolutions approved at the Boston meeting. The first "denounce[d] the wrong done the Poncas and demand[ed] reparations." The second deemed it unbecoming for "a free government to allow its agents to slander, prosecute and imprison those whose only offense lies in befriending the victims of that government's oppression." Schurz correctly noted that this resolution referred to the arrest of Tibbles in the Indian Territory by Agent William Whiting the previous summer. To justify Whiting's action, Schurz included a lengthy portion of the agent's report and sections of the Revised Statutes prohibiting persons from entering Indian lands with the purpose of disrupting the tranquility of a tribe.[13]

In responding to the second part of this resolution, which referred to the failure of "the highest officials" to deny a hearing "in our own courts to those who claim the protection of the laws," Schurz said that, according to the lawyers he had consulted, an Indian tribe could not sue the United States in federal courts. But, of course, Schurz understood that the censure in this resolution applied to the failure of the United States district attorney's brief for an appeal from Judge Dundy's habeas corpus decision. Unwilling to approve the principles upon which the argument of the brief was based, Schurz explained that he had advised the attorney general that the appeal should not go forward "but rather that Judge Dundy's decision should stand without question on the part of the government."[14]

This statement represented one of the very few times that Schurz moved beyond a rationalization of his inability to redress the injustices against the Poncas. By advising the attorney general to prevent an appeal and repeatedly calling on Congress to extend "the jurisdiction of the courts over Indian reservations," Schurz was following the premise of Chief Justice Roger B. Taney's opinion in the Dred Scott decision of 1857. Taney's ruling, which declared that blacks were not citizens of the United States, was later abrogated by the Fourteenth Amendment to the Constitution. By blocking an appeal of Dundy's decision, Schurz in effect was agreeing with Taney that cases in federal courts would have to involve disputes between citizens. Since Schurz understood the implications of an appeal, he chose to assert his authority, thereby helping to ensure that his position on the removal of the Poncas and the status of Indians in general would not be disturbed. Dundy's decision, therefore, would be contained.[15]

The third resolution of the Boston meeting called upon the president to use his power "to rectify the injuries done." Schurz cavalierly disposed of this request by noting that the president executed the laws and could not utilize funds without a congressional appropriation. Despite their differences, Schurz informed the governor they were in accord on two things: a great wrong was done the Poncas and reparation was due them. In both instances, he reminded the governor that he had pointed out these things long before the Boston philanthropists had done so. He differed from them only because of his responsibility for managing the affairs of all Indian tribes, of whom the Poncas formed "but a small part."[16]

Finally, Schurz reiterated his tireless efforts to better the condition of all tribes. He deemed himself "entitled to something better than scurrilous abuse or injurious insinuations from decent men." He repeated the important measures his department had accomplished on behalf of the Indians. In conclusion, he noted that "needless disagreements, preventing the cooperation for a good end of those who ought to work together, I should especially deplore in a community whose enlightened public spirit and active philanthropy have served so many noble causes, and whose good opinion I therefore particularly value."[17]

If Schurz thought his letter would clarify his position and resolve the concerns of the Boston Indian Committee, he was sadly mistaken. A rebuttal dated December 20, 1880, appeared in pamphlet form early the following year.[18] While the committee acknowledged that Schurz had presented a plausible letter, they concluded it was neither "a fair nor a candid statement." The misapprehensions of law, "and in some cases of fact," were considered "almost painful." Then in twenty-one pages the rebuttal restated the case of the Poncas, relying on the premise "that the Department of the Interior, with you at its head, responsible for its conduct, and kept informed of its proceedings, drove seven hundred Poncas from homes and lands to which you knew that their title was beyond the shadow of a question; and that you did this against their consent, in violation of the law of Congress and the dictates of humanity, employing for the purpose a company of soldiers, and, as you now add, four companies of cavalry."[19]

The rebuttal dissected Schurz's arguments, indicating among other things that the Poncas never signed any paper agreeing to move to the Indian Territory. Indeed, they had not known in 1875 that there was any such place, and moreover, Schurz had received ample notice from prominent missionaries and others living among them that the Poncas were opposed to removal. Since the act of Congress required their consent, the outrage of forced removal was not in the law, as Schurz contended, but in the manner of executing it. In conclusion the rebuttal presented three points regarding Schurz's handling of the situation. The first was a question asking, "Did you commit a cruel and unlawful outrage against the Ponca Indians, in robbing them of their homes?" The committee, which cast the questions in a most unfavorable way, said that Schurz in effect answered yes. He freely admitted a grievous wrong had been committed.[20]

The second charge indicated that Schurz at no time "lifted a finger" to restore the tribe to its homeland. In the third, the committee asked the secretary to offer the Poncas residing in the Indian Territory the opportunity to rejoin tribal members living on their former Niobrara lands. Although the committee engaged in harsh criticism, its members insisted that it sought to attack the injustice rather than to chastise Schurz. And they said that if out of this controversy there was awakened "a livelier popular sense of the rights of the Indians, of the injustice hitherto done them, and of the duty of this nation to them in the way of their education, and of guaranteeing to them citizenship and titles to their land, we shall have nothing to regret."[21]

Schurz, no doubt, could agree with much of the Boston committee's clarion call for reform; but he did not choose to respond to what it called the misrepresentations of his letter. Rather, in the closing months of the Hayes administration Schurz believed he had an opportunity to resolve the Ponca controversy in a most satisfactory manner. In the interim, however, he would have to contend with his most serious antagonist, Senator Dawes.

On February 11, 1880, the Senate Select Committee began taking evidence to ascertain the circumstances of the Ponca removal and whether the Indians were entitled to restoration of their former reservation. In addition, Senate Bill 1298, providing for the relief of the Poncas, was referred to the committee. Meeting intermittently between February 11 and May 31, the senators interviewed every conceivable witness who could provide information, from Standing Bear to Carl Schurz, from Thomas Tibbles to Edward C. Kemble. Interpreters, agents, several Ponca chiefs, including White Eagle and Stand-

ing Buffalo, Susette La Flesche, missionaries, and other individuals associated in one way or another with the controversy presented testimony.[22]

The chairman of the committee, Samuel Jordan Kirkwood, was a former
governor of Iowa (1860–64). He was elected as a Republican to the United
States Senate to fill a vacancy caused by the resignation of James Harlan,
who left to become Andrew Johnson's secretary of the interior. In 1867, after
completing Harlan's term, Kirkwood returned to Iowa, resumed the practice of law, briefly served as a railroad president, and again was elected
governor, serving from January 1876 to February 1877. When duly elected
to the Senate in November 1876, he returned to Washington and was selected by the chairman of the Committee on Indian Affairs, Richard Coke
of Texas, to chair the Select Committee.[23]

Other members aside from Dawes were Preston B. Plumb of Kansas, John
Tyler Morgan of Alabama, and James Edward Bailey of Tennessee. All were
freshman senators. Bailey and Morgan had served as Confederate officers,
while Plumb, long active in Kansas public life and one of the founders of
Emporia, rose to the rank of lieutenant colonel in the Kansas Infantry during the Civil War. In 1868 he served as speaker of the Kansas House of
Representatives. But it was Dawes, with his long legislative experience, who
dominated the hearings. He spent more time questioning witnesses than had
the other senators combined. And it was Dawes who prepared the majority report.[24]

Through his key role in the hearings, Dawes had made himself a master
of Ponca history, including the tribe's removal to the Indian Territory. In his
report Dawes noted that while Secretary Schurz and Commissioner Hayt
agreed that "a blunder" was made in the Sioux treaty of 1868, neither was
able to inform the committee "whether it was a blunder in policy or a mistake in boundaries." Either way, it was committed "without any notice to
the Poncas," and so far as the committee could determine, "without any
desire on the part of the Sioux [Lakotas]" to occupy the Ponca reservation.
Moreover, Dawes reported that the government's wish to award their reservation to the Lakotas was not made known to the Poncas "for several years
after it had been done."[25]

In his discussion of the 1875 negotiations, wherein the Ponca chiefs purportedly indicated their willingness to remove to the Indian Territory, Dawes
mentioned the conflict over the interpretation of the paper they had signed.
All that the document indicated was that they agreed to seek a new home
among the Omahas, who had expressed willingness to accept them "under
circumstances promising a beneficial result to both." Dawes viewed this
entire transaction as indicative of the difficulty involved in securing "a clear

and definite understanding" during negotiations between English-speaking government agents and Indians who had little or no mastery of English. This reality necessitated reliance upon interpreters, who sometimes were "ignorant and unable to clearly communicate or interpret," or took sides and as a consequence gave the coloring of "bias" to their interpretations.[26]

Confusion was compounded through divergent assessments of the situation by two branches of the federal government. The Indian Bureau moved first, approving removal of the Poncas to the Omaha Reserve. In 1876 Congress ignored this request and inserted a provision in the Indian appropriation allowing the interior secretary to expend twenty-five thousand dollars "for the removal of the Poncas to the Indian Territory, and provid[e] them a home therein, with the consent of said band."[27]

Thereafter in his report Dawes focused attention on the removal process. He first examined the role of Kemble, making much of the fact that the inspector claimed he had two sets of orders: written instructions and "a verbal understanding which he had with the Commissioner of Indian Affairs and the Secretary of the Interior." The report concluded that any departure Kemble made from his written instructions "arose from an utter failure on his part" to comprehend his power under the law authorizing removal, under the written instructions he received, and over the Indians with whom he had to deal. Moreover, Kemble's actions in procuring the removal of the Poncas, Dawes wrote, "were of an extraordinary character" and should have "excited the attention" of the department. It was a matter worthy of "the earnest consideration in all its details of the head of the department."[28]

The senator now shifted his attention to the Department of the Interior. Kemble, he said, at various times had informed his superiors that the Poncas were not willing to leave. Dawes concluded that "with this most important matter in the hands of a person totally unfitted for the work devolved upon him, accompanied by indifference and lack of knowledge upon the part of his superiors," what followed was "not only not surprising," it was inevitable. It led the government to violate "in the most flagrant manner" the property rights of the Poncas, while disregarding their appeals "to the honor and justice of the United States and the dictates of humanity." Dawes then reviewed the details of the journey of the ten chiefs who traveled to the Indian Territory with Kemble and then of the one hundred seventy Poncas who went with him, claiming that at no time was it possible "to construe" their consent to removal.[29]

His report next delved into the conditions the Poncas experienced in the Indian Territory, where they were settled without any prior arrangement for a permanent location. Forcibly removed from land they held by a grant from the United States, and oppressed by the indignity of the unjust treatment done them, many Poncas became ill and were consequently unable to cope with either the climatic changes or the other conditions they were forced to endure. He noted that Tibbles testified that when he visited in the Indian Territory in the summer of 1879, of the reported 760 Indians removed, there were only 428 remaining. Dawes also mentioned the murder of Standing Bear's brother, Big Snake, by soldiers at Fort Reno, and its impact upon the Poncas and their feelings toward their agent and the government.[30]

After reviewing the "great wrongs" perpetrated on the Poncas, Dawes confessed that the nature of redress posed "a question of some difficulty." Nevertheless, he asked "why should they not be restored to their old home, under the same conditions, as near as possible, which existed at the time of the removal?" This query represented the view of the majority of the Select Committee and of the reformers in Omaha, Boston, and elsewhere. Dawes went further by considering objections to this premise. First, it would involve trouble with the Lakotas. These Indians, he noted, had remained about six months at the old Ponca Agency and then moved themselves some two hundred miles from the Missouri River. The agency had remained unoccupied since their departure. The Lakotas thought they should be paid for yielding the Ponca lands. Dawes agreed and saw no reason "why the Poncas should be any longer held out of their own [land] without compensation."[31]

Another objection to the measure calling for Ponca restoration (Senate Bill 1298) was the expense involved. The bill provided an appropriation of $50,000 for assisting the tribe members on their return to their 96,000-acre reservation and restoring their dilapidated homes. In the Indian Territory, the Poncas resided on a tract of almost 100,000 acres belonging to the Cherokee Nation, which had agreed to sell it to the United States "for occupancy by other Indians at an agreed price of forty-seven cents an acre." On the score of expense, Dawes said, "quite as much will be involved in procuring for them a new home as in taking them back to the old one which belongs to them."[32]

But the most serious objection, one that Secretary Schurz raised repeatedly, was the concern that restoring the Poncas to their old home would create "uneasiness and discontent" among other tribes in the Indian Territory. They could also insist on a similar arrangement. To this concern Dawes responded, "If any other tribe there has suffered like treatment with the Poncas, restitution can not be made too soon." The committee, however, was of the opinion that nothing could strengthen the government in a just policy to the Indian as much as a demonstration of its willingness to do justice wherever it had "inflicted a wrong upon a weak and trusting tribe."

Indeed, the majority could find no valid objection to restoring the Poncas, as far as possible, "in precisely the condition they were in when E. C. Kemble undertook, without authority of law, to force them from their homes into the Indian Territory." The committee reported back to the Senate the bill to provide funds for Ponca restoration with the recommendation that it be approved.[33]

Senator Kirkwood, the lone dissenting member, presented a lengthy minority report. He reviewed the same testimony that Dawes had studied, but Kirkwood arrived at a different conclusion. He placed greater responsibility "for the wrongs done to and the injuries suffered by the Poncas" upon the Senate because of its approval of the 1868 treaty. Neither the Indian Bureau nor the Department of the Interior, Kirkwood insisted, "could properly undertake to set aside or disregard the treaty made with the Sioux in 1868." All the bureau or the department could do was what Schurz had done to no avail, namely, to call to the attention of Congress the wrongs done the Poncas and to recommend reparations.[34]

Kirkwood devoted several paragraphs to "the vexed and troublesome" Indian question evident since the formation of the United States. Relations between Indians and whites involved a history in which "the few have given way before the many, savagery has gone down before civilization." When he focused on the removal of the Poncas, Kirkwood too was "not prepared to approve all that was done by Kemble . . . nor all that was done by the Interior Department in authorizing his acts." But he made much of the fact that the Poncas had given their consent to abandon their reservation and make their home with the Omahas. Kirkwood noted that Kemble, with his knowledge of the Lakota treaty, which "had remained some eight years undisturbed," was aware of the congressional appropriation for removal, as well as the fact that his superiors desired it, and had therefore gone ahead with the removal.[35] To do Kemble justice, Kirkwood insisted "we must view his acts in the light of these facts." With the majority report in mind, he added, "a scapegoat is at times a very convenient thing to have." Kemble impressed Kirkwood as an "upright, honest, intelligent and earnest man" whose dealing with the Poncas might have been tempered "with a greater amount of suavity than he seemed to possess."[36]

Throughout his dissenting statement, Kirkwood noted the tendency among "a portion of our people" to consider Indians as a rule to be "peaceable, quiet, and truthful" whereas "our own citizens are violent, brutal, and false" in their dealings with Indians. Kirkwood believed the reverse. Misunderstanding arose because of the inability of Indians and officials to comprehend fully their respective languages in large part because, as a rule, Indians were "wholly uneducated" and could not read or write. But he conceded it was "clearly shown" that the Poncas did not give "unconditional consent" to removal. His review did not differ markedly from the majority report, though he was more understanding of Kemble's role. Like his colleagues on the committee, he too was critical of the caliber of most Indian agents. But in almost every instance, he gave the government the benefit of the doubt. Nonetheless, his conclusion was the same: a great wrong had been done the Poncas.[37]

Disagreement occurred as to how that wrong could be righted. And here Kirkwood could not agree with the majority of the committee. All the objections to returning the Poncas to their old reservation, to which Dawes had responded, Kirkwood raised and found almost insurmountable. Restoring Ponca lands would "break faith" with the Lakotas unless they agreed to the restoration. He emphasized this point, elaborating on it in some detail.[38]

Finally, in effect, he offered his own solution to the problem, calling for schools to educate Indians in reading, writing, and arithmetic so that they could "speak and read and write our language." And if Indians could begin to engage in agricultural pursuits, shifting from hunting to herding and then to husbandry, progress toward resolving Indian problems would follow. In offering what was becoming conventional wisdom and by not recognizing that the Lakotas were uninterested in the old Ponca lands, Kirkwood concluded "these people should be made secure in the title to their new home." He could not concur with the majority and recommended that the testimony and the report of the Senate Select Committee be referred to the Committee on Indian Affairs.[39]

The Senate report, among other things, suggested that Schurz would have a strong supporter in Kirkwood, even though the secretary had reason to disagree with the senator's evaluation of Kemble's role in the removal. For Dawes, the hearings determined his career as a United States senator. Where his predecessor, Charles Sumner, had made himself the champion of blacks, both as slaves and freed people, so Dawes would follow in his footsteps and champion the cause of Indians. The active role he pursued in the hearing on Ponca removal immersed him in the details of the controversy and led him to play a leading role advocating melioration.

The published version of the Senate testimony, complete with an index, comprised 534 pages; the majority report drafted by Dawes and the dissent by Kirkwood added another 28 pages. Throughout the hearings, as noted, Dawes served as the leading interrogator, and at one point he secured testimony and data indicating that Schurz had received urgent pleas from prominent citizens calling for a halt or at least a delay in the removal. Although

Schurz had heard the pleas of Solomon Draper, who had spoken with him in three separate interviews, the secretary accepted the word of the "authorized agents," who argued that the Poncas were willing to move, and ordered removal to proceed.[40]

In addition to Draper, other protesters had brought the situation to Schurz's attention. Calls for delay had come from knowledgeable and responsible individuals living among the Indians, not from eastern reformers and sentimentalists. Yet Schurz had taken no cognizance of their pleas, claiming that he had no option but to endorse the views of Indian Commissioner Ezra A. Hayt and Inspector Kemble. He admitted only the mistake of the 1868 treaty, but he had never validated the consent prerequisite in the law, enacted late in the Grant administration, which provided funds to remove the Poncas to the Indian Territory. He merely accepted Kemble's word. Later in the course of the hearings, responding to a question by Dawes, Schurz said, "Had I understood Indian Affairs then as I do now I should have opposed the removal." He never again repeated that statement.[41]

Dawes also questioned Inspector William J. Pollock, the agent in charge of moving the Lakotas from the old Ponca Reservation in July 1878 to a new location on the Little White River in Dakota Territory. The Lakotas, Pollock said, had moved to the Ponca Reservation in large part against their will; and they were aware of "the promise of the President" that they could depart "as soon as the grass started in the spring." Dawes's questioning revealed that the Lakotas arrived in November and December 1879, more than half a year after the Poncas were removed, indicating that there clearly was ample time for Schurz to reconsider the situation. Yet Schurz had never seen fit to do so.[42]

Schurz testified on May 15, 1880, shortly before the hearings concluded. Insisting that removing the Poncas from the Indian Territory could be "a very dangerous thing," he discussed his visit to the Indian Territory in the fall of 1879, where he spoke with agency employees who claimed that the Indians would "have gone to work more vigorously" if they had not been disturbed by outside agitators. The secretary was referring to Thomas Henry Tibbles, who, at the behest of the Omaha Ponca Relief Committee, had visited the Indian Territory the previous summer to assist any Poncas who wished to return to their former home. Tibbles had been arrested and ejected by Agent William Whiting and was consequently unable to accomplish his mission.[43]

Otherwise Schurz had only positive things to say about the Poncas. He found them located on good agricultural land that was well watered and well timbered. Their dwellings, he said, were "far superior to those which they had occupied on their old reservation." Under questioning by Dawes, however, Schurz admitted that most of the houses were unoccupied and that all lacked stoves. Indians, he said, habitually lived in tepees and some preferred to live in these dwellings in the summer. But Schurz made no mention of the fact that after two and a half years in the Indian Territory, the Poncas were still living in tents and that disease and death continued to exact a frightful toll. However, he did admit under questioning that Whiteman had been removed for his inefficiency.[44]

Dawes, who took the lead in questioning Schurz, brought to his attention the testimony of Indian Inspector William J. Pollock, who had visited the Poncas the following winter. Refuting Schurz's optimistic remarks, Pollock stated that "only two houses were occupied or in a condition to be occupied." There were about seventy poorly constructed, unfinished houses that would not be ready for occupancy until the spring, thus the Poncas lived in their tents "in the bottoms, on the lowlands, in the timber near the river." By bringing Pollock's testimony to Schurz's attention, Dawes cast doubt on the positive tenor of his remarks. The secretary's testimony, which consumed the last day of the hearings, sparked no controversy with Dawes. Both questions and answers were politely phrased, though it was clear that Dawes and Schurz markedly disagreed.[45]

The secretary's testimony and the course of the hearings, however, aroused the ire of the president. Hayes stunned Senator George F. Hoar when he appeared at his rooming house. The junior senator from Massachusetts explained that "President Hayes was very much excited. He seemed to think that a great wrong had been done by the Secretary." Slamming his fist upon the table, the president indicated his intention of turning "Mr. Schurz out." Hoar, who considered Schurz an able man, expressed his hope that Hayes would reconsider. "His mistake," Hoar said, "is only that he has adhered obstinately to a preconceived opinion, and has been unwilling to take advice or receive suggestions after he has determined his course." The senator thought it would be "a great calamity" for the president to discredit one of his cabinet members. Hoar's remarks soothed Hayes, who, he believed, accepted their validity and concluded "that it was his duty to sustain the Secretary." However, before Hayes left office he might have found reason to regret his acceptance of Hoar's advice.[46]

The lengthy report, dated May 31, 1880, was issued shortly before the second session of the 46th Congress adjourned on June 16. It effectively presented the issue of Ponca removal, questioning whether it was justifiable and whether the Indians ought to be returned to their former Dakota homeland. Through his penetrating and persistent questioning, Dawes had illustrated the inequities of a system that treated the Poncas as a dependent nation. The government, acting through a handful of comparatively irresponsible and inept individuals, forged bonds of Indian dependency that public sentiment, slowly being aroused, was as yet incapable of seriously challenging.

Once Congress adjourned, Dawes devoted most of his attention to securing a second term as a United States senator. When Congress convened in December for the "lame duck" session of the 46th Congress, the tensions between Schurz and Dawes came to the fore as the controversy over Ponca removal was played out in the waning months of the presidency of Rutherford B. Hayes.

Notes

1. U.S. House, *Report of the Secretary of the Interior,* vol. 8, viii.

2. For Schurz's interview, see, for example, "A Talk with Secretary Schurz about the Ponca Indians," *Chicago Tribune,* August 23, 1879, 7; "Wrongs of the Poncas," *New York Times,* August 23, 1879, 2; "The Troubles of the Poncas," *Tribune,* August 23, 1879, 1; "The Trials of a Tribe: The Two Sides of the Ponca Indian Story," *Advertiser,* August 23, 1879, 1. See also "The Indian Problem: Further Statements in Regard to the Ponca Removal," *Advertiser,* August 25, 1879, 1; Coward, *The Newspaper Indian,* 211–12.

3. E. C. Kemble, "The Story of the Poncas," *Independent,* December 18, 1879, 4. See also the *Advertiser,* December 20, 1879, 2. William Justin Harsha, secretary of the Omaha Ponca Relief Committee, wrote to the editor of the *Independent* criticizing Kemble's article. See Harsha, "Col. Kemble and the Poncas," *Independent,* January 29, 1880, 5–6.

4. Kemble, "The Story of the Poncas," *Independent,* 5.

5. Ibid.

6. Carl Schurz, "The Removal of the Poncas," *Independent,* January 1, 1880, 1. A copy of this article, prepared on December 22, 1879, can be found in the Schurz Papers, container 184, Library of Congress. For the text of some of these telegrams see U.S. Senate, *Testimony Relating to Removal,* 436, 439.

7. Schurz, "The Removal of the Poncas," 1.

8. E. C. Kemble, "A Few Words with Mr. Schurz," *Independent,* January 15, 1880, 5–6.

9. For Long's address, see "The Ponca Infamy," *Hartford Courant,* December 6, 1880, 2.

10. Carl Schurz to John D. Long, December 9, 1880, in the Schurz Papers. The copy consulted was seventeen printed pages. See pages 4 and 6 for quotes. This letter can also be found in Schurz, *Speeches, Correspondence and Political Papers,* 4:50–78. See also "Wrongs of the Poncas," *Tribune,* December 13, 1880, 1; "Boston and

the Poncas," *New York Times,* December 17, 1880, 4. For a story critical of Schurz, see "The Wronged Poncas," *New York Herald,* December 14, 1880, 8.

11. Schurz to Long, December 9, 1880, Schurz Papers, 7.

12. Ibid., 7–8, 10.

13. Ibid., 13 (quotes), 13–14 (agent Whiting's report), 14 (Revised Statutes).

14. Ibid., 15. In a January 17, 1880, letter to Helen Hunt Jackson, with regard to the Dundy decision, Schurz said that he advised the attorney general to drop the appeal as he could not approve the principles upon which the argument was based. He never elaborated further except to say that had an appeal been prosecuted, the general principles involved in it would have affirmed Dundy's decision without any other practical effect than that already obtained. He never mentioned the issue of citizenship. See Schurz, *Speeches, Correspondence and Political Papers,* 3:496–99, and Jackson, *A Century of Dishonor,* 362.

15. Schurz to Long, December 6, 1880, Schurz Papers, 15.

16. Ibid., 15–16.

17. Ibid., 17.

18. William H. Lincoln was listed as secretary of the committee but it is not clear if he was the chief author.

19. *Secretary Schurz: Reply of the Boston Committee,* 3–4 (quotes). A copy of this pamphlet is available in the Beineke Library, Yale University, New Haven, Connecticut, and in the Western American Microfilm Collection, microfilm 313, reel 63, no. 613. The press indicated that Governor Long replied to Secretary Schurz, though the pamphlet lists him as chairman of the committee, not as the author. See "The Poncas Defended," *Tribune,* December 21, 1880, 1. The *Advertiser,* in "Mr. Schurz Answered," December 21, 1880, 1, reproduced the entire letter.

20. *Schurz: Reply of the Boston Committee,* 8, 20 (for the question).

21. Ibid., 21.

22. All testimonies can be found in U.S. Senate, *Testimony Relating to Removal.* For White Eagle's testimony see 191–221, and for Standing Buffalo see 221–38. See also "The Poncas' Lament," *Tribune,* March 3, 1880, 1, and "Torn from Their Homes," ibid., March 4, 1880. White Eagle was accompanied by several of his children who were going to the boarding school in Carlisle, Pennsylvania.

23. For a biography see D. Clark, *Samuel Jordan Kirkwood.*

24. See Connelley, *The Life of Preston B. Plumb,* and Fry, *John Taylor Morgan.* There is no biography of James Edward Bailey. There are informative entries on all committee members in the *Biographical Directory of the United States Congress, 1774–1989.*

25. "The Dawes Report," in U.S. Senate, *Testimony Relating to Removal,* v–vi. For press coverage see "Congress and the Poncas," *Tribune,* February 5, 1880, 4.

26. "The Dawes Report," in U.S. Senate, *Testimony Relating to Removal,* vii.

27. Ibid.

28. Ibid. For coverage of Kemble's testimony see "The Poncas' Complaints," *New*

York Times, February 15, 1880, 1; "The Troubles with the Poncas," ibid., February 17, 1880, 5; "The Removal of the Poncas," *Tribune*, February 17, 1880, 1.

29. "The Dawes Report," in U.S. Senate, *Testimony Relating to Removal*, viii–xiii.

30. Ibid., xiv–xvii. The circumstances of Big Snake's death are controversial. See "The Poncas," *Advertiser*, November 3, 1879, 4. See too, U.S. Senate, *Alleged Killing of Big Snake*, 1–15.

31. "The Dawes Report," in U.S. Senate, *Testimony Relating to Removal*, xviii.

32. Ibid., xviii–xix.

33. Ibid., xix.

34. "Views of the Minority," in U.S. Senate, *Testimony Relating to Removal*, xxii. See also "A Picayune Indian Policy," *Tribune*, December 8, 1880, 1, for a discussion of Kirkwood's view on the treatment of the Poncas.

35. "Views of the Minority," in U.S. Senate, *Testimony Relating to Removal*, xxii–xxiii.

36. Ibid., xxiii.

37. Ibid., xxiv.

38. Ibid., xxvi.

39. Ibid., xxvi–xxvii.

40. "Draper's Testimony," in U.S. Senate, *Testimony Relating to Removal*, 305–21. See especially p. 316, wherein Draper reviewed his meetings with Schurz. Draper testified on March 30, 1880.

41. "Alfred S. Riggs's Testimony," in U.S. Senate, *Testimony Relating to Removal*, 177–78, 428–29; see also 433–44 for the statement of H. Westerman, a merchant. For Schurz's statement see p. 366.

42. "William J. Pollock's Testimony," in U.S. Senate, *Testimony Relating to Removal*, 254–55.

43. For Tibbles's visit see "T. H. Tibbles's Testimony," in U.S. Senate, *Testimony Relating to Removal*, 40–47. Dawes did not ask any questions of Tibbles, who testified on February 13, 1880. On April 26, 1879, a presidential proclamation had warned individuals intending to move into the Indian Territory without permission that they would be "speedily and immediately" removed by force if necessary. See *United States Statutes at Large*, 46th Congress, vol. 21, p. 797.

44. "Remarks of Hon. Carl Schurz," in U.S. Senate, *Testimony Relating to Removal*, 368–69.

45. Ibid., 369, where Dawes quoted from Pollock's previous testimony. For Pollock's recollection of his four-week visit to the Ponca agency, beginning in December 1879, see 255–62. For Schurz's testimony see 358–78.

46. Hoar, *Autobiography of Seventy Years*, 2:30. Hoar was a member of the commission that resolved the disputed 1876 election in Hayes's favor. Hoar's biographer wrote that Hayes considered Hoar "the soundest Massachusetts man in Washington" and would seek Hoar's advice and carefully consider his recommendations and

suggestions. See Welch, *George Frisbie Hoar*, 73–74. Years later Hoar wrote to Birchard A. Hayes, the president's son, that his father "changed entirely his opinion as to the motive of the persons who criticized Mr. Schurz's conduct." He added, but did not offer details, that the president visited him "and spoke with great freedom in regard to it." See George Frisbie Hoar to Birchard A. Hayes, May 3, 1893, Rutherford B. Hayes Papers. Nan Card, an archivist at the library, brought this letter and others to our attention.

CHAPTER SEVEN

EXPANDING THE PARAMETERS

Early in December 1880, before the Ponca controversy flared up again in
Washington, an event occurred in the West that could have ended the matter if the government had deemed it worthwhile. Unfortunately, it did not.
In the United States Circuit Court for the District of Nebraska, the case of
the *Ponca Tribe of Indians v. Makh-pi-ah-lu-tah or Red Cloud in his own
behalf and in behalf of the Sioux Nation of Indians* was resolved. The United
States district attorney, under instructions, did not contest the case. His
action indicated that the decision, like Dundy's earlier decision in *United
States ex rel. Standing Bear v. Crook,* would stand.[1]

Acting on behalf of "the remnant of this tribe of Indians," who sought
in "the courts of justice of this white man's government" the opportunity
"to seek out their old homes and the burying grounds of their fathers,"
Andrew Jackson Poppleton and John Lee Webster submitted a brief
affirming title of the Poncas "to the fee and occupancy of their old reservation."[2] Hearing the case, Judge Elmer Dundy decided that the Ponca tribe
had "legal estate" in its reservation and was entitled to regain possession.
He assessed the Lakota nation one dollar for unlawfully keeping the Poncas
from their tribal lands. The Poncas, Dundy declared, could now recover all
of their lands within Nebraska and "all lands of the disputed reservation,"
including that portion in Dakota territory as well.[3]

The *New York Tribune,* which claimed to be the first newspaper to utter
a "protest against the illegality and dishonesty of such a despotic measure"
as the Ponca removal, strongly approved this decision. The *Tribune* proph-
esied that two years hence it would be considered incredible that Indians
should have been held "legally as serfs," unable to sell their property, or
defend their families, "liable to be transported, starved or shot at the irresponsible will of one or two officials."[4]

According to the *Advertiser*, this case was the first on record where one Indian tribe brought suit against another in United States courts. Even though there was widespread feeling about the wrongs inflicted upon the Poncas, Dundy's decision was not widely noted. It had no impact and was rarely mentioned in committee hearings, in congressional debate, or later in the report of the president's special commission headed by General George Crook. The president, likewise, did not mention it in his final messages to Congress.[5]

Dundy's decision was not even noted by the Select Committee when it reconvened on December 28, 1880. Dawes, now assured of a second term as a United States senator, was eager to pursue his questioning. But in winning reelection, Dawes did so at some cost. His principal opponent was Governor John Davis Long, the resolute leader of the Boston Indian Committee. Despite their other differences, both men continued to support the cause of the Poncas. In a letter to Long, who invited him to the December meeting of the committee at Tremont Temple, Dawes insisted "that justice and humanity, common honesty and solemn covenant" all commanded redress of an ordeal perpetrated by a "sheer blunder" made worse because "the despoiler has shut his own courts against the Ponca, and there is none other to which he can appeal." The letter indicates Dawes was aware that Dundy's recent decision, like his earlier one, would not go forward in part because Schurz opposed federal courts' defining Indian citizenship or questioning the validity of Indian removal.[6]

On this occasion the Select Committee met in the room of the commissioner of Indian affairs at the Interior Department. Moreover, a Ponca delegation led by White Eagle was on hand, accompanied by Inspector James M. Haworth and Agent William Whiting. And in an unusual turn of events, Secretary Schurz directly interjected himself in the proceedings by asking questions of the witnesses, thereby defying all protocol: a cabinet member did not involve himself in a hearing of the legislative branch. Among other matters, the committee focused considerable attention on Thomas Henry Tibbles's visit, arrest, and ejection from the Indian Territory in June 1880.[7]

Haworth, Whiting, and Frank La Flesche recounted details of Tibbles's visit, while affidavits of interested parties related their individual encounters with the journalist. None of the testimony presented differed markedly from the account Tibbles gave to the Omaha Ponca Relief Committee. However, when Dawes questioned Whiting, who had succeeded William H. Whiteman as Ponca agent the previous April, he disputed the agent's authority to arrest and remove the journalist.[8] Whiting was unable to cite any treaty or law that Tibbles had violated while he was in the act of encouraging tribal members to return to their Niobrara homeland. When asked who authorized the arrest, the agent responded that the man he arrested was on "what was called the Ponca reservation,"whereupon Dawes reminded him that it was still legally Cherokee land. Apparently Whiting, who earlier assisted the Ponca chiefs in drafting a proposal to purchase this land, was aware of this fact. Since the land belonged to the Cherokee Nation in fee simple title as well as by treaty agreement, Dawes again asked the agent to cite some law authorizing him to arrest a non-Indian for being there. Whiting claimed he knew nothing of the title to the land although he asserted that the United States had dominion over the territory. Dawes then concluded that "Tibbles may have gone down there under the assumption that he could go anywhere the owner of the land did not forbid."[9]

Tibbles, who was carefully interrogated, first reviewed his involvement with the Poncas and then explained the two-pronged approach sponsored by the Ponca Relief Committee. The first involved the efforts of Poppleton and Webster to obtain the return of former Ponca lands. Rather than depend upon the Interior Department to settle the controversy, the lawyers resolved instead to bring a writ of habeas corpus to the Supreme Court of the United States, the only court with jurisdiction in the Indian Territory. As neither Poppleton nor Webster received any compensation, they had to prepare the suit only when it did not interfere with their other business. They had intended to sue out the writ during the previous session of the Court, but unfortunately Poppleton, who represented the Union Pacific Railroad Company, had to attend to cases in St. Louis. By the time he completed his work, the Supreme Court had adjourned.[10]

The second prong, in which Tibbles played a major role, centered on the activities of the Ponca Relief Committee, which, after Standing Bear's release, was organized to help the Poncas secure legal rights to their lands. The lawyers maintained that the Indians were held illegally in the Indian Territory, that they were taken there in direct violation of an act of Congress and two treaties, and that their legal reservation was in Dakota Territory. It was essential to assure the Poncas that they were illegally held in the Indian Territory, and that they could go home if they wished to do so. However, no state court had jurisdiction in the territory.[11]

The Ponca Relief Committee therefore asked Tibbles to inform the Poncas that if they crossed over into Kansas they would be under the jurisdiction of a state court and the committee would provide legal assistance. With this information as background, Tibbles recounted his experiences, which at times differed from the accounts of earlier witnesses. When asked why he did not report to the agent, Tibbles responded, "I have lived in the West all my life; I have been on Indian agencies hundreds of times and never went to the agent to report myself . . . , and never knew anybody else to do so unless he had business with the agent." Since he had no business with Agent Whiting, he only sought out tribal members to discuss his mission.[12]

Asked about his trip by the committee chairman, Samuel Kirkwood, Tibbles testified that instead of using cash he wrote checks, some $150 worth, to pay his expenses in Arkansas City, on the Kansas side of the border with the Indian Territory. At times Secretary Schurz interposed questions. But in no instance were committee members able to jar Tibbles's testimony, as Dawes had impaired Whiting's. More important, Tibbles placed on the record clearly and succinctly the strategy used by the Omaha reformers to return the Poncas to their former home. It was his second appearance before the committee, and he utilized the opportunity to the maximum extent.[13]

But Carl Schurz was not interested in the details of Tibbles's trip. He now had reason to believe that the Poncas were willing to stay in the Indian Territory if the price was right. In a letter dated May 3, 1880, Chief Standing Buffalo wrote the secretary, "I would rather stay here than anywhere else." Earlier he thought that only a few of the Poncas would be willing to remain, but now the chief claimed that twenty wagons and "money due us for damages committed by the Sioux" would ensure that his people stay where they were.[14]

Under close questioning by Dawes, Standing Buffalo conceded that for three years the Poncas had been waiting to return to their own land. Convinced that no help would be forthcoming, he concluded "we were tired." His people had abandoned all hope.[15] It was "like climbing up a wall . . . [with] nothing to take hold of."[16]

Schurz interjected himself in the questioning and persuaded Standing Buffalo to agree that many of his tribe now wanted to remain in the Indian Territory, that they "found the land was good," that they were "without sickness," and that "they wanted the white people to let them alone." These points had been called to the secretary's attention in an October 25, 1880, letter from the chief. This letter, which was reiterated in the hearing, provided Schurz with a long-desired opportunity. Instead of defending his behavior and actions, he now took the high ground and claimed that, despite the Indians' ordeal, the Poncas now enjoyed a markedly improved situation that showed every sign of continuing to improve with further federal assistance. Dawes, however, focused on past conditions, while seeking to determine what caused Standing Buffalo and other chiefs to change their minds.[17]

Schurz strengthened his position when White Eagle, endorsing Standing Buffalo, said that the October letter was agreed to by "the principal men." The secretary said that in his conversations with the Ponca chiefs (present at the hearing), all were in accord. They wanted to stay, and they wanted to be left alone. When Dawes inquired about Standing Bear and those Poncas residing in Dakota, White Eagle replied that "we hope to take them back, but they walk according to their own hearts."[18]

Schurz indicated that he was sensitive about the Ponca deaths in the Indian Territory, which Tibbles estimated to be about one-third of the 746 or 747 Poncas. The secretary, however, claimed that there were 683 Poncas remaining; 544 at the agency, 130 in Dakota, eight at Carlisle, and "one married to a Kaw woman," considerably more than Tibbles's estimate. The journalist accepted Schurz's number, but he reminded the secretary that numerous children had been born in the Indian Territory. Schurz replied that many who died had moved to their present location "without the knowledge or consent of the agent, without provisions and without accommodations, and camped upon bottom lands," implying that the responsibility for the large number of Ponca deaths could not be charged against the agent or the Indian Office, or ultimately be placed upon his shoulders.[19]

Schurz also emphasized that Antoine LeRoy, an interpreter with the Poncas, had letters from friends in Dakota indicating that they wanted to return to the Indian Territory, if they could obtain money to do so. Then the secretary, in another unusual move, interjected lengthy remarks into the questioning to refute the view that the Indian Territory Poncas were not permitted to have outside contacts. He informed the committee that they did their own freighting to and from the railroad terminus in Arkansas City, Kansas, and on Christmas Day, a Ponca delegation came to his home to meet his children and some friends. Schurz added that he had no "desire to put any obstruction in the way of anybody" who wished to visit them.[20]

Throughout the course of these hearings, Schurz took advantage of every opportunity to present the view that the Poncas in the Indian Territory wished to remain there. By the same token, Dawes sought to elicit information to the contrary. But he met with little success. Clearly the initiative had passed to Schurz, who was no longer defending or rationalizing his actions relative to the removal of the tribe. Once the Indian Territory Poncas indicated their desire to remain, Schurz, by way of proclaiming the validity of his course of action, actively participated in questioning witnesses and at times offered relevant information to clarify matters under discussion. Thus far, all of the testimony occurred on December 28, 1880. When the Select Committee reconvened on January 29, 1881, the situation and the nature of the questioning changed markedly.

Meanwhile the two Massachusetts senators had been informing President Hayes more fully about the Poncas. Hoar wrote to him in late November, enclosing an extract from the proceedings of a meeting of the tour group in Worcester. He felt strongly that any redress for the Ponca wrong "should come from [Hayes], not from a Senator or from Congress." Hoar believed it essential that Hayes's administration take "its place in history as the purest and freest from stain since the inauguration of Washington."[21] Several days later the president responded to a letter from Dawes, assuring him that he would be cautious and "see that nothing unfair or inconsiderate is done." Hayes further informed Dawes that since this was the first time the senator had called the subject to his attention, he "would be glad to know what" he advised. The information and advice he received from the Massachusetts senators prompted action.[22]

On December 18, 1880, President Rutherford B. Hayes appointed a four-man commission to confer with the Ponca Indians in the Indian Territory and, if deemed advisable, in Dakota "to ascertain the facts" pertaining to their removal and current condition and to determine "what justice and humanity" should be enacted by the federal government.[23] Commission members included George Crook and Nelson A. Miles, brigadier generals in the army; William Stickney of the District of Columbia, a member of the Board of Indian Commissioners; and Walter Allen of Massachusetts, a member of the Boston Indian Committee.

The creation of the commission immediately posed a financial dilemma for President Hayes. He could not provide for the expenses of any individual who was not in the army or in the Interior Department. Initially he wanted to select George W. Manypenny, former Indian commissioner (1853–57), early advocate for individual land allotment, and author of a newly published volume entitled *Our Indian Wards* (1880). In 1876, after the defeat of Custer at the Little Bighorn, Manypenny chaired a commission seeking to convince the Lakotas that they would receive no further subsistence unless they relinquished a portion of their reservation land that included the Black Hills. His final public service on behalf of the Indians was his appointment by Hayes in 1880 to head a commission to arrange for a survey of Ute lands prior to their being allotted in severalty. In both these instances funding was provided by congressional enactment. Hayes informed Senator Hoar, whom he had been consulting about these appointments, that "a man fit to be President is fit to be trusted with a contingent fund."[24]

In place of Manypenny, Hayes now suggested General Crook and William Stickney, who were already on the federal payroll, "or some other member of the Indian Board." Then he added in his December 16 letter to Hoar, "Of course I will name no one not approved by you and the Boston Committee"; however the committee "must provide for the expenses of those named by them." The president's only concern was that the investigation "be thorough and fair, to the end that complete justice may be done to the Poncas for the wrongs they have suffered preferring rather to go beyond than to fall behind full redress." When the commission was announced, Walter Allen was the choice of the Boston Indian Committee.[25]

John Gregory Bourke, Crook's aide-de-camp, jotted down an evaluation of the commission members in his diary. He described General Miles as "a man of considerable natural capacity and some merit." But he considered him "almost illiterate, owing to lack of early education." While calling Miles "brave, energetic and ambitious," Bourke, no doubt reflecting Crook's view of his rival, found the general to be "selfish, conceited and inordinately vain." Nevertheless, he recorded that Miles was "very courteous to him."[26]

Bourke was more charitable in his evaluation of William Stickney, whom he considered "a well-meaning, psalm-singing Christian—one of that class whose religion has given them the heart-burn." He noted that Stickney "traveled a great deal in foreign countries, especially in the Holy Land." And one evening Bourke was entertained by "a very bright description" of Stickney's visit there. Of William Allen, he was much more complimentary. He found the correspondent of the *Boston Advertiser* "a gentlemen of great mental cultivation, a little bit too inclined to the humanitarian side of the Indian question." This made Allen "perhaps too much disposed to detect dishonesty in Mr. Schurz's every act." Overall, however, he found Allen "a very intelligent, clear-headed, hard working and valuable member of the Commission."[27]

In pursuance of its charge, the commission visited the Poncas in both locations. A minority report by Walter Allen was appended to that of the majority along with the testimony gathered by the commission. In addition, Hayes noted that on December 27, 1880, a delegation of Ponca chiefs presented him with a declaration asserting their desire to remain in the Indian Territory and "to relinquish all their right and interest" in the lands they formerly occupied. They requested only compensation for their former homeland and for the injuries done them by removal. The president acknowledged that while the report of the commission, chaired by General Crook, added little to previous official reports by both the secretary of the interior and the Senate Select Committee, their recommendations suggested "measures of redress, which the Government of the United States ought now to adopt."[28]

The evidence, Hayes said, clearly showed that the Poncas in the Indian Territory were "healthy, comfortable, and contented." The fragment of the tribe in Dakota and Nebraska, numbering about one hundred fifty, likewise preferred to remain on their old reservation. With these findings in mind, the president recommended legislation authorizing the secretary of the interior "to secure to the individual members of the Ponca tribe, in severalty, sufficient land for their support inalienable for a term of years." Moreover, Hayes recommended that "ample time and opportunity" be afforded tribal members to freely select their allotments, "either on their old or new reservations." The president further called for full compensation for all lands ceded and for losses incurred by Lakota depredations and by removal. He considered it his "particular duty and earnest desire" to provide the Poncas "that measure of redress which is required alike by justice and by humanity."[29]

The Crook Commission Report vindicated the position held by Dawes and all friends of the Poncas when it declared that the tribe was moved "without lawful authority," and that the law requiring their consent "was overlooked or wholly disregarded." Since the Poncas had violated no condition of the treaty defining their reservation, their claim still existed "in full force and effect, not withstanding all acts done by the government of the United States." Most of the remaining portions of the report merely amplified the points the president made in submitting it. They specified that an allotment of one hundred sixty acres be issued to "each man, woman and child . . . said lands to be selected by them on their old reservation in Dakota" or in the Indian Territory "within one year from the passage of an act of Congress granting such tracts of land." For 30 years the land should be secured to them by patent free of encumbrances of any kind or until such time as the president might remove the restrictions.[30]

The report further recommended that the government continue its annual appropriations of not less than $53,000 for five years after the approval of an allotment act, and that $25,000 be immediately appropriated to secure seed, stock, and agricultural implements. Of this sum $5,000 would be for the "exclusive benefit" of the Poncas in Dakota and Nebraska; the balance then would be divided among the families of the whole tribe "in full satisfaction" for Lakota depredations and property losses sustained during removal. A further sum of not less than $5,000 would be utilized in the construction "of comfortable dwellings" and not more than $5,000 for the construction of a schoolhouse on the old reservation. The last recommendation required that responsible individuals be employed by the government to provide "instruction in religious, educational and industrial development, and to superintend, care for and protect all [the Poncas'] interests." In its conclusion the Crook Commission Report reinforced but failed to mention directly Judge Dundy's decisions by affirming that it was of "the utmost importance" that "all Indians should have the opportunity of appealing to the courts for the protection and vindication of their rights and property."

In this way they would be "relieved from the uncertainties and oppression frequently attending subjection to arbitrary personal authority."[31]

Dawes, no doubt, took great satisfaction from this report. It supported the views of the majority of the Select Committee and seemingly ensured that some recompense would be offered the Poncas. Schurz, on the other hand, could find little satisfaction in it. Contrary to his acceptance of the premise that the Poncas agreed to their removal and that their lands had been ceded to the Lakotas, the report proclaimed otherwise and, more important, challenged his effort to prevent further judicial evaluation of the Dundy decision. However, the majority signing the Crook Commission Report neither criticized nor assigned blame to individuals in their two-page statement. Such was not the case in the seven-page dissent offered by Walter Allen.

Allen agreed with the premises presented by his colleagues. He differed, however, in his view that it was the duty of the commission to present both the facts and reasons leading to their conclusions and recommendations. In detail and at times naming Schurz, he presented a withering denunciation of the circumstances affecting Ponca removal and relocation. Although Allen severely criticized the government for inadequately protecting the Poncas prior to 1877, most of his comments focused on Schurz's tenure. Allen reiterated the point brought out by Dawes that Schurz and the commissioner of Indian affairs were repeatedly informed by "persons of established, honorable reputation" that the Poncas did not consent to their removal in ample time "to prevent the removal and its lamentable consequences."[32]

In reviewing the consequences, Allen twisted Schurz's claim that "a grievous wrong" was committed in removing the Poncas, an action for which he was not responsible, into a wrong for which the secretary "gave credence to false reports and misleading advice." On point after point he challenged Schurz's claims: that if returned to Dakota, the Poncas would again suffer from Lakotas attacks; and that the removal of the Poncas from the Indian Territory would prompt other tribes to demand their own return. Allen concluded that "if the government had violated no obligations to the Indians, none would challenge its good faith as to the Indian Territory."[33]

When he turned his attention to the Poncas in the Indian Territory, Allen inquired how their recent decision to remain there permanently could be regarded as free determination. Certainly they were provided with no opportunity to make a choice; they had no option in the matter. For three and a half years they had received no assistance although their plight was called to national attention, and they "seemed unable to make their interest effective against the indifference of the majority and the taunts of men in high places." Though the question of their rights had been submitted to the courts, judgment was slow. And most Poncas, if they were aware of the recent Dundy decision, did not see its relevance to their plight. They knew that some of their numbers had "escaped" and returned home where they were treated as outcasts without "any consideration or help" by the government.[34]

Allen further noted that one of their chiefs, Big Snake, a brother of Standing Bear, had been killed "under circumstances which made them fearful for their fate if they put themselves in a position to be charged with insubordination." At the same time they saw one of their few friends, Thomas Henry Tibbles, who understood their sufferings and their hopes, arrested and forced to leave under guard when he came to visit and confer with them. In short, Allen concluded, "their resolution gave way"; their spirit was broken and they ceased to contend against a purpose they could not change. They decided to remain in the Indian Territory. Allen said their consent was "extorted by despair" and achieved "under duress." It could hardly be claimed as confirmation "of the wisdom of the government's course" toward the tribe and as a condemnation of those who desired and urged the restoration of the Poncas to their old home. Allen could see no great reason why any significance should be granted to recent letters and agreements as purporting to be a solution to the Ponca question and as an indication that justice and humanity had prevailed. Finally, in the last pages of his statement, he argued that the terms offered the tribe as outlined in the majority report were inadequate with regard to both groups of Poncas. Between seventy and eighty Poncas and possibly more in the north and about two hundred in the Indian Territory were no longer residing on tribal lands.[35]

The remaining pages of the Crook Commission Report consisted of the hearings conducted by its members. On January 5, 1881, in the presence of a large Ponca delegation, the commission assembled in the schoolhouse at the Ponca Agency in the Indian Territory. With the Reverends J. Owen Dorsey and Alfred L. Riggs interpreting, White Eagle and Standing Buffalo served as the major informants. The proceedings at the Ponca Agency continued on the following day. Four days later, on January 10, the members convened in a meeting room at the Naylor House in Canton, Dakota Territory, where Reverend Dorsey, who had served as a missionary among the Poncas from May 1871 to August 1873, answered questions.[36]

However, before the formalities began, an official party had visited Standing Bear's camp. The twenty-eight families there, numbering about one hundred fifteen people, lived on an island near the west bank of the Niobrara River. Lieutenant John Gregory Bourke described their village as "consisting both of tipis and log houses." Surveying the scene, he saw "ponies, wagons, cattle, hogs, hay and wood in piles and other indications of thrift and increasing comfort." Already they had cultivated over one hundred acres in corn. All of their efforts, Bourke noted, had been accomplished independent of outside help, except for "some little assistance from sympathizing friends in Boston and Omaha." As he watched, blankets from Omaha were distributed among the women and children. At one point Bourke met Standing Bear's wife. Estimating her age at about thirty-five, he described her as "tall, stout, comely and well-formed . . . with a good face and presenting a neat appearance."[37]

The next day the commission reassembled in the Academy of Music at Niobrara City. In addition to the four commissioners and several interpreters, there was a full delegation from Standing Bear's band, local residents eager to witness the proceedings, and three Poncas from the Indian Territory. Over the course of two days, Standing Bear and other residents of the old reservation testified. At one point, Standing Bear plaintively informed the commissioners that he had never sold the land and would not sell it today for a million dollars. He wished to become an old man, "to die in this land." On the second day of the proceedings, Standing Bear remarked that his "children have been exterminated; [and his] brother had been killed," but he refused to be scared because "I have come back to my own land." He did not want an agent assigned because agents took from the Indians and made them suffer. Instead he much preferred a teacher or a minister.[38]

On January 25, 1881, the Crook Commission Report, complete with an appendix comprising documents gathered by the commission, was placed before the president. On February 2, 1881, it was referred to the Senate Select Committee and printed as an Executive Document.[39] Meanwhile the Select Committee, which had held an extensive hearing at the end of December, reconvened on January 29, 1881. At this date much of what would be included in the Crook Commission Report was already known; the commission's members were in Washington and some were called to testify. The hearing focused largely on the report and gave Schurz, who again interjected himself into the questioning of witnesses, a further opportunity to present his decision that the Poncas should remain in the Indian Territory.

The first witness was William Stickney, a commission member. Schurz's questions allowed Stickney to assert how positive the Poncas were in their desire to remain in the Indian Territory, standing and showing "by their action as well as by their voice, that they were unanimous in that decision." Both Schurz and Dawes also heard from Stickney that Standing Bear and his followers wished to remain on their former reservation and "did not admit the right of others to sell" it.[40] Dawes learned from Stickney that White

Eagle, Standing Buffalo, and other chiefs agreed to remain in the Indian Territory because they were tired of wandering and wanted to settle down. Dawes sought to elicit information regarding negative aspects of their situation—inadequate housing, ill health, and the like—while Schurz sought answers of a more positive tone wherein the Poncas indicated satisfaction and contentment with their lot. The October 25 letter of Standing Buffalo to Schurz had marked the turning point. Thereafter the Poncas in the Indian Territory never wavered in their desire to remain. To reinforce this point Schurz asked Stickney if there was any evidence that pressure was brought upon the chiefs to send that letter. The answer, "that they had deliberately come to this conclusion themselves," no doubt pleased Schurz as did the further response that the Poncas had come to that conclusion before the October 25 letter was drafted.[41]

A clear indication that the initiative again had passed to Schurz lies in the fact that the secretary, who was not a member of the Senate Select Committee, asked more questions of Stickney than did Dawes. Most of these queries secured the response Schurz desired, namely that the Indians wanted to remain in the Indian Territory. In many instances his questions were much longer than the brief answers they prompted.

Walter Allen, author of the minority report, followed Stickney as the next witness. His testimony covered the same ground but in responding to questions from Dawes, Allen suggested that the enthusiasm manifested at the meeting in the Indian Territory might not have been as strong as previously reported. While questioning Allen, Schurz read from the Crook Commission Report. When Dawes inquired if he would be kind enough to let his colleagues see a copy of the report, Schurz responded that what he possessed were "extracts from the testimony" he had taken to refresh his memory. No senator questioned his use of a document unavailable to other committee members. Allen, therefore, had no opportunity to refresh his memory as to the testimony Schurz was referring to. Nevertheless Allen deflated Schurz when he said "the Indians in the Indian Territory did not strike me as nearly so energetic or hopeful or cheerful in temper as the Indians we saw in Dakota, although it was unquestioned that they were much better off."[42]

Responding to a question by Schurz, Allen reiterated the view presented in his minority report that the spirit of the Poncas in the Indian Territory was broken. They had enjoyed no opportunity to exercise a free option to return to their reservation. Schurz, however, persuaded Allen that his remarks were based upon "philosophical reasons" rather than upon actual information. Schurz then read portions of testimony in the Crook Commission Report wherein White Eagle, Standing Buffalo, and others expressed satisfaction with their lot.[43] The secretary relentlessly challenged Allen's premise that the Poncas were intimidated. But Allen held his own, describing the behavior of Agent William Whiting, who had threatened to shoot any Indian who cut down a tree near the agency and who had ordered Big Snake's arrest by the military, as an example of an arbitrary exercise of authority. Allen also responded to Schurz's question about the creation of a Ponca police force. He expressed concern that an agent could make pawns of unscrupulous officers, rewarding them for reporting Indians who disagreed with his view of how things should be run. The secretary in turn led Allen to admit to his inexperience in Indian matters. Though Schurz again dominated the questioning, he received little satisfaction from the answers offered by Walter Allen.[44]

General Nelson A. Miles was sworn in and testified on February 26. Responding to Dawes, the general described the Poncas living in the Indian Territory as having finally resigned themselves to "remain there permanently" since all attempts to move back to their old reservation had failed. In return, they were now "receiving quite large supplies of annuities—very liberal supplies—much more liberal than was given to the neighboring tribes." Miles noted that while the Nez Perces received appropriations of only $15,000, the Poncas received in excess of $63,000.[45]

Miles informed Dawes that the Poncas' decision to remain was reached only after they "had exhausted all efforts known to them to get back to their country." The title to their Dakota land, they believed, was "disregarded by the government" and was "absolutely worthless." Since they had lost most of their possessions—cattle, farming equipment, furniture—they feared being moved again and desired to secure "a strong paper" to the land they currently occupied. Reinforcing Allen's explanation of Ponca acquiescence, Miles had no doubt that these reasons had induced them to agree to remain. After Tibbles informed tribal members they could go back "by stealing away at night" a few lodges at a time, Miles said the Poncas had accepted the best terms they could get. They concluded that the government would not permit their return, despite the presidential commission's recommendation that they have a year to decide where they wished to make their home. "The mere fact," the general told the senators, "that they had consented to remain in that country under the circumstances which they did consent, did not convince me that it was necessary to cut them off as to time at once." Throughout the questioning of General Miles, Schurz was not on hand to cross-examine him.[46]

Dawes further elicited from Miles the general's perception that the dignity of the government would not be impaired, nor would its claim to the Indian Territory or its ability to hold it against encroachments by non-Indians be seriously damaged, if Poncas returned to their homelands. In contradistinction to Schurz's view, Miles believed that retaining the Poncas or any tribe in the Indian Territory to prevent encroachment by white invaders was "without justification and not a fair excuse."[47]

During an earlier session, Schurz had remarked that the government was not preventing the Poncas from trading or communicating with others. Several days later both Dawes and Kirkwood elicited testimony from Miles refuting this fact. The general observed that the Poncas engaged in trading expeditions to Arkansas City or other points in Kansas could do so only with a permit from the agent, who granted it "to certain privileged parties." That privilege, Miles added, "could be cut off at any time by the arbitrary act of the agent."[48]

In a final exchange, Miles cast further doubt on Schurz's claim about the enthusiasm exhibited by the Poncas. When Dawes inquired whether tribal members approved the action of their chiefs, Miles responded that they did not appear to be enthusiastic. He explained that when first asked, a number of men held up their hands. Whereupon White Eagle stood up and called upon the audience to raise their hands. Thereafter "men, women and children, and some very small children" complied. The response, Miles said, "was a call from their head man amounting almost to a demand." It was usual for Indians to endorse the desires of their leaders, who exerted "a very decided influence." Thus when the Senate Select Committee concluded its testimony in this round of hearings, the perceptions that Schurz had worked so hard to establish through his questioning of earlier witnesses were thrown into doubt by General Miles's responses to questions presented by Dawes.[49]

With the completion of these hearings and the report of the Crook Commission and the favorable reception of its recommendations, it appeared that the controversy over the Ponca removal had finally concluded with all parties claiming a measure of satisfaction. The Senate hearings ended on January 29, 1881. The Crook Commission Report was dated February 2, 1881. Within three weeks a new president would be inaugurated. And after March 4, Schurz would launch the next phase of his remarkable career, as an editor of the *New York Evening Post*. However, the tensions between Schurz and Dawes, evident throughout the extensive hearings, did not abate. No direct flare-up between the senator and the secretary had occurred, but this would change during the dwindling days of the 46th Congress and the Hayes administration.

The nation's press devoted considerable attention to the extensive hearings. Both Schurz and the Poncas had their supporters and their detractors. One of the more incisive editorials to illuminate the situation appeared in the *Springfield (Massachusetts) Daily Republican.* The writer believed that the hearings ought to make "a deep impression" on the nation's Indian policy. He expressed the view that henceforth the removal of a peaceful tribe from its homeland "should never be attempted without the most imperative reasons and with the most careful effort to preserve all rights of property." Moreover, tacitly accepting the premise of the Ponca Relief Committee and reflecting the impact of Judge Dundy's decisions, neither of which was mentioned in the editorial, the writer forthrightly stated that "there should be opened to the Indian the right of appearing in the United States and territorial courts, not merely as an accused person, but as a party to civil actions." The editorial also endorsed the concept of severalty, which encompassed the gradual division of portions of common property among heads of families, to be held in fee simple, unalienable for at least a generation, a proposal that Schurz personally endorsed. The editorial pointed the way toward what many Americans considered meaningful Indian reform.[50] But the Ponca controversy itself was not yet over. The final phase would play itself out in the chamber of the United States Senate.

Notes

1. The case began with the filing of petitions on April 3 (*Ponca Tribe of Indians vs. Makh-pi-ah-lu-tah or Red Cloud*) and May 18, 1880 (*Ponca Tribe of Indians vs. the Sioux Nation of Indians*), to recover possession and establish title to former Ponca lands. For mention of other suits filed in Dakota Territory during May 1880, see Jackson, *A Century of Dishonor,* 373. The summons, issued on April 5 to Red Cloud and the others, was not served by Deputy U.S. Marshal H. S. Moody until May 22. First Moody was arrested and removed from the Sioux reservation; then he was unable to board the steamboat carrying Red Cloud and the others on their return trip from Washington, D.C. He finally met the boat when it landed in Nebraska to take on wood. See "The Indian Exiles," *Advertiser,* May 28, 1880, 2. In late May, William H. Lincoln informed Dawes that "a writ has just been served on Red Cloud & Spotted Tail, so we will now get into Court"; Lincoln to Dawes, May 28, 1880, Dawes Papers, box 24, Library of Congress.

2. "The Poncas Vindicated," *Advertiser,* December 4, 1880, 1. See also "Justice at Last," *Omaha Daily Herald,* December 4, 1880, 8, a copy of which John Bourke pasted into his diary, 25:106–8; "The Ponca Case," *Tribune,* December 6, 1880, 4; and *Christian Union,* December 8, 1880, 489. See petition, *Ponca Tribe of Indians v. Makh-pi-ah-lu-tah or Red Cloud,* submitted by Poppleton and Webster to the U.S. Circuit Court for the District of Nebraska on April 3, 1880, in the National Archives, Central Plains Region, Kansas City, Missouri. For Webster and Poppleton's report to the Ponca Relief Committee see Jackson *A Century of Dishonor,* 372–74; see also Lake, "Standing Bear! Who?" 481–82.

3. "The Poncas Vindicated," 1; see too Dundy's judgment in *Ponca Tribe of Indians vs. Makh-pi-ah-lu-tah Red Cloud,* December 3, 1880, for the U.S. Circuit Court, District of Nebraska (*Omaha Journal,* vol. F, p. 573), National Archives, Central Plains Region.

4. "The Ponca Case," 4.

5. "The Poncas Vindicated," 1. The press story is more comprehensive than the archival files. Senator Kirkwood was one of the few individuals in Washington who noted Dundy's decision. He thought, as a result of it, that "we must go to war with the Sioux"; "A Picayune Indian Policy," *Tribune,* December 8, 1880, 1.

6. Dawes's letter to Long, dated December 1, 1880, was published along with the resolutions and speeches delivered at the Boston meeting in "The Poncas. Boston's Sympathy for Their Outrages and Wrongs," *Advertiser,* December 4, 1880, 1.

7. For news accounts of Haworth, Whiting, Tibbles, and White Eagle see "The Wrongs of the Poncas," *Tribune,* December 29, 1880, 1, and "The Ponca Wrongs," *Advertiser,* December 29, 1880, 1.

8. U.S. Senate, *Testimony before the Select Senate Committee . . . as to the Removal and Situation of the Ponca Indian,* S. Misc. Doc. 49 (hereafter cited as *Testimony before the Select Senate Committee*), 5–8 (Haworth's testimony), 15–25 (Whiting's remarks), 25–28 (La Flesche's account). See "The Wrongs of the Poncas," *Tribune,* December 29, 1880, 1, for an account of the first day of these hearings, on December 28, 1880.

9. "William Whiting's Testimony," in U.S. Senate, *Testimony before the Select Senate Committee,* 15–25; Dawes quote, 24.

10. "T. H. Tibbles's Testimony," in U.S. Senate, *Testimony before the Select Senate Committee,* 36–37. Dawes asked Tibbles only one question at the outset that allowed him to place the controversy in broad perspective. See also "The Ponca Wrongs," *Advertiser,* December 29, 1880, 1, for an account of Tibble's testimony and that of others.

11. "T. H. Tibbles's Testimony," in U.S. Senate, *Testimony before the Select Senate Committee,* 37.

12. Ibid., 39 (quote).

13. Ibid., 39–46; 44 (Kirkwood's questions), 46 (Schurz's questioning of Tibbles). Tibbles's full testimony covers pages 36–46.

14. "Standing Buffalo's Testimony," in U.S. Senate, *Testimony before the Select Senate Committee,* 31 (letter to Schurz).

15. Ibid., 32–33.

16. "The Wrongs of the Poncas," *Tribune,* December 29, 1880, 1; see also "The Ponca Wrongs," *Advertiser,* December 29, 1880, 1.

17. "Standing Buffalo's and White Eagle's Testimony," in U.S. Senate, *Testimony before the Select Senate Committee,* 33 (Schurz's questions of Standing Buffalo), 33–34 (Dawes questioning of White Eagle). See also "The Wrongs of the Poncas," *Tribune,* December 29, 1880, 1, for an overall discussion of the first day's testimony.

18. "White Eagle's Testimony," in U.S. Senate, *Testimony before the Select Sen-*

ate Committee, 35–36. For a press account favorable to Schurz's position see "Our Washington Letter," *Springfield (Massachusetts) Daily Republican,* January 6, 1881, 4. For a critical account see "Mr. Schurz and the Poncas," *New York Times,* January 10, 1881, 5.

19. "T. H. Tibbles's Testimony," in U.S. Senate, *Testimony before the Select Senate Committee,* 46.

20. "Antoine LeRoy's Testimony," in U.S. Senate, *Testimony before the Select Senate Committee,* 50–53.

21. Hayes, *Diary and Letters,* 3:626. Hoar's letter was dated November 20, 1880.

22. Ibid. Hayes's letter was dated November 27, 1880.

23. The president's message and the commission report are available in U.S. Senate, *Report of Special Commission.* There was a variety of press comments on the Crook Commission: see news item in the *Hartford Daily Courant,* January 22, 1881, 2, for rumored discussions among members; "Justice for the Wronged Poncas," *Tribune,* January 27, 1881, 1, and "The Ponca Wrongs," *Advertiser,* January 27, 1881, 1, for the commission report. Editorial comment was generally critical of Schurz, and most editors thought the report marked the end of the controversy.

24. Rutherford B. Hayes to George Frisbee Hoar, December 16, 1880, Hayes Papers, Hayes Presidential Center. This letter was published in Hayes, *Diary and Letters,* 3:631. For Manypenny's service as Indian commissioner see Kvasnicka and Viola, eds., *The Commissioners of Indian Affairs,* 57–67.

25. Hayes to Hoar, December 16, 1880. Years later, writing to the president's son, Hoar said that "he had already changed his opinion as to the character of the persons in Boston who were criticizing Mr. Schurz, and that he had become satisfied that the Poncas had suffered great wrong, and given to the Boston Committee the fullest liberty to suggest the Commission who were to investigate it." Hoar to Birchard Hayes, May 19, 1893. Both letters are in the Hayes Papers, Hayes Presidential Center.

26. Bourke diary, 38:953–54.

27. Ibid., 954–55.

28. "Message from the President of the United States," in U.S. Senate, *Report of Special Commission,* 3. For press accounts see "The Wrongs of the Poncas," *New York Times,* February 6, 1881, 2; "The President and the Indians," ibid., 4; "Congress and the Poncas," *Tribune,* February 6, 1881, 6.

29. "Message from the President of the United States," in U.S. Senate, *Report of Special Commission,* 3–4.

30. "Report of Special Commission to the Poncas," in U.S. Senate, *Report of Special Commission,* 5–6.

31. Ibid., 6.

32. "Minority Report," in U.S. Senate, *Report of Special Commission,* 7–8.

33. Ibid., 8–9.

34. Ibid., 9–10.

35. Ibid., 10–13. See also "The Cowardly Assassination of Big Snake," *Advertiser,* February 1, 1881, 4

36. "Proceedings of the Ponca Commission," in U.S. Senate, *Report of Special Commission,* 21–30.

37. Bourke diary, 38:979–80; for the description of Standing Bear's wife, see 1014.

38. "Proceedings of the Ponca Commission," in U.S. Senate, *Report of Special Commission,* 39–40. For a press account of the Niobrara meeting see "Ponca Princes," *Niobrara Pioneer,* January 14, 1881, 4.

39. For the complete report, see "Proceedings of the Ponca Commission," in U.S. Senate, *Report of Special Commission,* 13–53.

40. "William Stickney's Testimony," in U.S. Senate, *Testimony before the Select Senate Committee,* 58–59.

41. Ibid., 53–71 (Stickney's entire testimony); quote, 65.

42. "Walter Allen's Testimony," in U.S. Senate, *Testimony before the Select Senate Committee,* 74 (Allen's suggestion); 75–76 (Schurz's utilizing an extract of the commission report not yet officially released); 78 (remarks about the outlook of Northern Poncas).

43. Ibid., 80–81.

44. Ibid., 84–85.

45. "Nelson A. Miles's Testimony," in U.S. Senate, *Testimony before the Select Senate Committee,* 90.

46. Ibid., 91–94; quote, 92.

47. Ibid., 94. For a story on these hearings favorable to Schurz, see *Chicago Tribune,* January 30, 1881, 2, and January 31, 1881, 1, under the heading "The Poncas."

48. "Nelson A. Miles's Testimony," in U.S. Senate, *Testimony before the Select Senate Committee,* 97–98.

49. Ibid., 99–100.

50. "The Raw Side of the Indian Question," *Springfield (Massachusetts) Daily Republican,* January 14, 1881, 4.

CHAPTER EIGHT

CONCLUDED BUT NOT RESOLVED

The tensions that divided Schurz and Dawes were reflected in the press and in meetings that helped arouse public awareness. By 1881 concerned citizens recognized that the nation's Indian policy comprised a series of wrongs and blunders. "Next to slavery," *Harper's Weekly* proclaimed, "the Indian chapter of our history is probably one of the most unworthy of our national character and principles."[1]

The Ponca controversy excited much attention and led to the condemnation of the Interior Department. Secretary Schurz in his annual reports candidly explained the situation, but he also responded to outbursts leveled against him at public meetings. In frank statements, Schurz reiterated his connection to the removal of the Poncas in a manner that many considered both conscientious and defensible. However, citizens who heard or read the speeches of Standing Bear and the people accompanying him on his tours were not that easily impressed with the secretary's devotion to the welfare of the Indians. Among his most articulate and prominent critics were members of the Boston Indian Citizenship Committee. Proper Bostonians by the end of 1880 were in close contact with Dawes, their senior senator. His views and theirs were in accord. Although Schurz did not lack prominent and powerful supporters, the barrage of criticism emanating from Boston and spreading to other urban areas in the East alerted him to the need for sensitivity to public opinion.

Early in January Dawes spoke briefly to a reporter before departing for Washington after a holiday respite. The Poncas, he explained, had been harshly dealt with and had been led to understand that they would be treated most liberally if they consented to remain in the Indian Territory. In this way their objections had been overcome with the assistance of a new agent who "managed the government side of the case with great skill." Dawes indicated that Schurz persuaded the Indians to sign a paper expressing their willingness to give up all rights to the Dakota reservation "for a good sum of money." If the Crook Commission in its soon-to-be-released report concluded that, everything considered, it was best for the Poncas to remain in the Indian Territory, Dawes said, "then nothing would seem to be left for their friends except to accept it and see that the Indians are amply compensated for the property they have lost." It was a sad and sordid tale, one that "a government can [not] be very proud of."[2]

Dawes informed the reporter that "Mr. Schurz, . . . indignant at the course the friends of the Poncas have taken," had described their activities as "New England sentimentalism." What remained, Dawes said, was for Schurz "to run the gauntlet of Congress in order to obtain the $440,000 appropriation" to fulfill his agreement with the Poncas. If the tribe had remained in Dakota Territory, the government would have saved that sum and the expenses involved in moving them. "On the score of economy the whole business is a failure," Dawes said, "to say nothing of the inhumanity involved." Though the Poncas were "but a handful," the wrong inflicted upon them was "a disgrace to the government and a blot upon the fair name" of the Hayes administration. Dawes's remarks indicated that, like Schurz, he was indignant.[3]

Though there was little that Dawes could do to change the parameters of the Ponca settlement during the last weeks of the 46th Congress, a petition forwarded to him from Alfred L. Riggs, the principal of the Santee Normal Training School in Nebraska, suggested there were things he could do to ensure a more equitable settlement. The petition was prepared at the behest of Standing Bear and some one hundred twenty Indians on their old reservation. Riggs claimed that additional tribal members were "scattered around among the Yankton & Santee Sioux and among the Omahas," raising the number of Poncas not residing in the Indian Territory up to "two hundred by count." Thus at least one-third of the tribe was not involved in the settlement praised by Schurz.[4]

More than any other official, Riggs was intimately aware of the condition of these Poncas. He had been distributing food and other items to them for months. To supplement these meager supplies, the Indians sold wood and their horses. Sometimes they worked as day laborers for local whites.[5] Riggs trusted that Dawes would defend their right to the old lands and make sure that any who wished "to follow their inclinations and return from Indian Territory" be allowed to do so. These suggestions, some to be incorporated in the report of the Crook Commission, were in accord with Dawes's concern for justice.[6]

By the end of January 1881 the conclusions and recommendations reached by the Crook Commission were made available to the public and received widespread attention. They provided a basis for ending the Ponca controversy. The reputations of Generals Crook and Miles, leading members of the commission, were enough to dispel any suspicion of sentimentalism toward Indians. Those who had vented their sarcasm and invective on the Boston philanthropists, as well as on Susette La Flesche, Helen Hunt Jackson, and Thomas Henry Tibbles, could not assault noted Indian fighters of the regular army in the same way. Certainly Dawes had good reason to find satisfaction with the report, and its recommendations, and particularly with Allen's additional reflections.

On the other hand, the report by implication, if not by direct assertion, was a crushing condemnation of Secretary Schurz's official action. Comparing the commission report with the Senate hearings and stories emanating from Washington during the visit of the Ponca chiefs, one could conclude that some accounts of their newfound desire to remain in the Indian Territory "did not fairly represent the truth." Therefore it was possible to ascertain that the secretary "was too confiding in his agents and was deceived in a way which made him a party to a gross and utterly indefensible piece of injustice to a friendly and helpless tribe," thus tarnishing the creditable record of the Hayes administration as the president prepared to leave office.[7]

Schurz, of course, was not lacking supporters. In a special dispatch to the *Chicago Tribune,* one reporter called the "persistent attack" on Secretary Schurz a "most unfair, unjust, and unfounded" assault. The story presented once again Schurz's familiar rationalization as to how he was the victim of circumstances over which he had no control. Although wrongs were perpetrated on the tribe, Congress had ignored his pleas to reimburse them, but now the Poncas were content and their lot markedly improved.[8]

Dawes quickly challenged this dispatch and the report by the secretary upon which it was based. The senator commented upon Schurz's questioning of Crook Commission members before the Select Committee on January 29 and his utilizing the only copy then available of the testimony taken by the commission in the Indian Territory. The proceeding was entirely outside of Dawes's previous experience regarding the conduct of a congressional investigation.[9] Aroused by what he considered the arrogant behavior of the secretary, Dawes continued his attack on the Senate floor, criticizing Schurz for taking ten months to respond to a resolution calling for all available information relative to the killing of the Ponca chief Big Snake. "I have deemed it due to all concerned," noted Dawes, "that the true character of this occurrence be entered upon the permanent records of the country that whoever may read the history of our dealings with the weak and defenseless may have the material from which to judge those who dip their hands in innocent blood."[10]

That a transaction so grave as the death of Big Snake "at the hands of the government itself should not be permitted to escape its just place in history, and when those who caused it do not choose, even on request, to put it there" forced Dawes to beg the attention "of the Senate for a few moments." The few moments consumed more than two pages in the *Congressional Record*. In emotionally charged remarks, Dawes examined the circumstances surrounding the killing of Big Snake. He admitted that he was unable to disabuse his mind "of a feeling that our dealings with the weak who come under our power should be characterized by a scrupulous regard to justice and humanity." Then, attacking Schurz without mentioning his name, Dawes remarked that the "treatment of these weak and defenseless people" employed methods that bore "too striking a resemblance to the modes of an imperial government carried on by espionage and arbitrary power."[11]

To balance what he considered the capricious and autocratic treatment of the Poncas in the Indian Territory, culminating with the death of Big Snake, Dawes turned his attention to the murdered man's brother, Standing Bear, "an exile in his own land." He presented a petition from the Northern Poncas protesting the desire of their brethren in the Indian Territory to sell their old reservation. Standing Bear's followers wished to reside there and hoped to share in whatever assistance the government bestowed upon the tribe and specifically asked that a teacher be assigned to them.[12]

When challenged about his barbed criticisms of the secretary of the interior, Dawes made it clear that in all other matters he had never disparaged the general policy of "the Indian Department, or its head." It was "a mystery" that the Interior Department appeared willing "to go into history" without any effort "to remove a stain upon the record of this Government toward one of the most peaceable and honorable tribes" that lived under its flag. Although he complained of the injustice inflicted upon the Poncas, the senator insisted he had not charged the head of the department "with the commission of these wrongs." Rather he claimed to have entreated Schurz to disapprove of them. Thus Dawes was disillusioned when after a ten-month delay the Senate was informed that the secretary in effect did not deem it worthwhile to express an opinion on the requested information. Schurz regretted only the delay in forwarding the information. For his part, Dawes regretted the secretary's failure to hold those responsible for the removal of the Poncas "accountable to the laws of justice and humanity."[13]

Several colleagues refuted some of Dawes's remarks. And Samuel Kirkwood separated himself from Dawes by claiming that he, Kirkwood, was not an advocate but a judge. For his part, Dawes sought to assuage his critics. He agreed with comments complimentary to the secretary's management of the Department of the Interior. His only stipulation pertained to the circumstances affecting the Poncas. In all, Dawes discussed the Ponca situation over the course of two days. Heretofore, Senate discussion of removal of the Poncas had been confined to committee hearings. Now Dawes introduced a bill to execute the recommendations of the Crook Commission. At the time he spoke, senators were discussing a proposal that would allocate Indians land in severalty.[14]

While Dawes was criticizing Schurz's behavior, President Hayes, endorsing the report of his appointed commission, remarked that "the time has come when the policy should be to place the Indians as rapidly as possible on the same footing with the other permanent inhabitants of our country." The president did not undertake to apportion blame for the injustice done the Poncas. Indeed, possibly recalling his earlier desire to sack Schurz, he believed some of the responsibility rested on his presidential shoulders. But redress, "required alike by justice and by humanity," was now his chief concern.[15]

Carl Schurz was not of the same mind. His stubborn inflexibility became increasingly evident to a larger public as the president's message, Dawes's Senate remarks, and especially the report of the Crook Commission were disseminated through the press. In this report, the commissioners—the first white people friendly to the Poncas to be admitted within their reservation—gave tribal members not only a year to decide where they permanently wished to reside but a chance to regain their property. The Poncas' ordeal began and ended with the Hayes administration. But in the last weeks of its tenure, the tensions and outright antipathy between the secretary and the senator erupted in a clash that enlivened the controversy through its final days.

Dawes's Senate speech concerning the murder of Big Snake, for example, was well received by Governor Long and the members of the Boston Indian Committee. To William H. Lincoln, the secretary of the committee, Schurz's role in examining Allen and in manipulating newspaper correspondents was "worse than Machiavellian." But even in Boston Schurz had supporters, most notably the *Herald,* which consistently lauded his performance.[16]

One week after Dawes's Senate remarks, on February 7, 1881, Secretary Schurz wrote an open letter to the senator and had it placed on the desk of every member. Not having access to the Senate floor, Schurz responded to Dawes's attack in this manner because it relieved him of "those considerations of official restraint which otherwise would control [his] language."

The secretary argued that he had been "exposed to so much misrepresentation and obloquy in connection with the Ponca business" that he thought it "time to call things by their right name." He would utilize this last opportunity as interior secretary to present his side of the controversy. First Schurz reviewed the facts pertaining to the killing of Big Snake and attacked Dawes's perception that his department's treatment of the Poncas reflected "the tyranny of the government." He asserted that Dawes's remarks were "coolly and carefully prepared" to convey the impression that the murder of Big Snake was "a concerted and prearranged act, designed to rid the department of a troublesome opponent of its policy." He further claimed that Dawes's remarks had been distributed to newspapers throughout Massachusetts several days before he delivered them.[17]

But the depth of Schurz's bitterness and animosity became evident in his response to the brief paragraph in Dawes's speech where he talked about methods "not American in their origin" and bearing "resemblance to the modes of an imperial government." Schurz rose to the occasion and claimed in colorful language that he was being attacked because he was a German-born American citizen. Schurz insisted Dawes sought to discredit him and slanted his remarks to do so.[18]

In recounting his concern for the Poncas, Schurz made the telling point that he was "the first man, in 1877, to lay the hardships suffered by the Poncas frankly and without disguise before Congress and the public." Not a word was heard from Dawes until his constituents began to hold meetings and made it worth his while to take an interest in the Poncas. In this comment he was partially correct. Dawes, as a member of the committee on Indian Affairs, had his first opportunity in May 1880 to involve himself when the Select Committee began to investigate the circumstances of the Ponca removal.[19]

Schurz further emphasized that in October 1880 the Poncas in the Indian Territory signified their desire to remain there. Schurz now had shifted some of his criticism away from Dawes and toward portions of the Crook Commission testimony that indicated the dissatisfaction of Poncas in the Indian Territory. He then sharply attacked Dawes for his press statement criticizing his (Schurz's) cross-examination of Walter Allen. He feared that Dawes had "somewhat over-reached himself."[20]

According to Schurz, Dawes overreached himself because there were voices "making themselves heard among your constituents which show that fair play has its friends among them as well as elsewhere." He included a lengthy excerpt lauding his kindly and humane treatment of Indians that appeared in the *Boston Journal* and he noted that the *Boston Herald* and other newspapers had spoken in the same vein. "Sober and candid minds," Schurz believed, were recognizing the significance of what he had accomplished. A wrong had been committed against the Poncas. He was the first to acknowledge it and, "charged with the responsibility of the conduct of all Indian affairs," he proposed a remedy that provided "substantial justice" and at the same time avoided "other and greater difficulties concerning the peace, safety, and interest of other numerous tribes of Indians." Although vilified as the "cruel oppressor of the Poncas," Schurz proclaimed that they now confessed themselves "comfortable and contented," with bright prospects. And, taking the high road, in a final appeal he said, "Senator, let these Indians at last have rest."[21]

Thus in his last full statement on the Ponca controversy, Schurz, in a plausible way, achieved his goal of denouncing Dawes and justifying once again his policy toward the Poncas. The February 7, 1881, letter also revealed traits characteristic of his responses to criticism. When any proposal of his was disputed or any conduct criticized, his tendency was to resort to subterfuge. Those most concerned about the Ponca removal concluded that he was sacrificing public interest for the sake of wounded vanity.

When Schurz asked Dawes to "let these Indians at last have rest," he also requested they receive the indemnity "they justly ask for and which I asked for them three years ago." Here again were the seeds of another controversy: the president had endorsed the recommendation of the Crook Commission to appropriate $165,000 with the addition of $25,000 for the Poncas on the old reservation. Dawes soon introduced a bill to that effect. Schurz, knowing he could not directly counter or refute these provisions, ingeniously contrived to subvert them. A measure prepared at the Interior Department included a provision that Poncas in the Indian Territory select their land there, while those in Dakota and Nebraska select their lands on the old reservation. Excess lands would be relinquished, along with all rights and titles that would revert to the government. This part of the bill directly repudiated the recommendation of the president, who specified in his special message that "ample time and opportunity should be given to the members of the tribe freely to choose their allotments either on their old or the new reservation." Schurz in effect still refused to concede, despite abundant evidence to the contrary, that the removal of the Poncas was ordered by his department in violation of law and against the will of the tribe.[22]

The measure, sent to the Capitol at the time Schurz's letter was laid on each senator's desk, was not offered in the Senate to be printed and then referred. Instead it was sent directly to the Committee on Indian Affairs with a copy to the Senate Select Committee. This ploy, a further effort at subterfuge by Schurz, would expose his proposal to a minimum of public scrutiny, especially if it could emerge as a new draft of a bill that would thwart the recommendations of the Crook Commission and the president.[23]

There was little chance at this late date that Schurz's proposal would be enacted into law or that Dawes's bill would be approved; if the Poncas were to secure justice, the bill would have to be introduced by the Garfield administration. To further this effort, William H. Lincoln, chairman of the Boston Indian Committee, invited Tibbles and Susette La Flesche to a meeting reviewing what had been accomplished and what yet needed to be done, while thanking "our friends in and out of Congress" for their support. He intended that at such a meeting, once again there would be detailed discussion of the wrongs done the Indians "and the hypocrisy of the Secretary."[24]

Dawes, however, was not going to await another Boston meeting to spell out Schurz's perfidy. The secretary's fourteen-page letter was on the desk of each senator on February 10. The following day Dawes requested the attention of his colleagues "for a few moments to a matter, which, in some aspects, is somewhat personal to myself." He acknowledged that he had reread his remarks that had prompted Schurz's letter and found nothing in them that he desired "to qualify or withdraw." He asked the indulgence of the Senate for a few moments "to go once and for all to the bottom of the Ponca business."[25]

While all involved in this controversy admitted a great wrong was done, Dawes claimed that the key to the wrong resided in the appropriation bill that called for the expenditure of $25,000 for the removal of the Poncas to the Indian Territory "with the consent of said band." Only because the Poncas were removed without their consent was a wrong perpetrated. The basic question he wished to call to his colleagues attention was "who is responsible for that wrong?" Dawes proposed to show through records available in the Department of the Interior and the Senate that not only was the secretary conversant with every step taken but that "with full knowledge of it all laid before him he ordered it to be done."[26]

When Schurz had assumed his secretarial position on March 5, 1877, "every Ponca Indian was in his home in the Territory of Dakota and on his reservation, for which he had an indefeasible title, then and there protesting his desire to remain in his home." Every step thereafter, Dawes said, was brought to the attention of the department, chiefly to the commissioner of Indian affairs, until the situation attracted the attention of nearby white inhabitants among whom the tribe had made their home. Once this happened these individuals made their representations known directly to the secretary of the interior in April. Dawes mentioned some of these individuals and their letters, which he included as part of his remarks. He inserted other items, including a lengthy letter submitted by Inspector Kemble and one written by Alfred Riggs, of the Dakota Mission, likewise indicating that the Poncas were opposed to moving. He mentioned the April 1877 visit of Solomon Draper to Washington to intercede with the secretary, and he pointedly inserted Draper's testimony. Nebraska Senator Algernon Paddock, who had accompanied Draper, corroborated the fact that Draper had asked the secretary to stay "this inhuman proceeding" long enough to send a delegation to investigate. Nebraska's other senator, Alvin Saunders, also had appeared before the secretary explaining "that the Poncas desired to stay in their old home" and that their white neighbors likewise wanted them to stay.[27]

If the Poncas had given their consent, Dawes insisted, there would have been no "outrage." But that had not been the case; consequently "an outrage admitted by the Secretary of the Interior was committed." The Poncas had been removed, and Dawes, using various documents citing the Nebraska senators remarks, tried "to impress upon the Senate" that Schurz was aware of all of the facts. He then inserted a portion of Kemble's testimony pertaining to his visit when the secretary ordered that "the Poncas would be removed, and that if necessary, troops would be called upon to enforce the removal." The outrage, Dawes said, had to be laid at the door of "the man who ordered it."[28]

"This unlawful enforced removal" carried along with it "all the unlawful outrages that have followed." Out of it, Dawes remarked, came the imprisonment of Standing Bear and Big Snake in Dakota; the seizure of Standing Bear and his followers after they fled the Indian Territory; the imprisonment, arrest, and murder of Big Snake; the arrest and removal of Tibbles from the Indian Territory; and an effort to obtain from Congress legislation that would keep the Poncas in the Indian Territory. Dawes concluded this portion of his remarks by alluding to the Crook Commission and the president's message, both of which urged redress of grievances by allowing the Poncas time to choose where they wished to reside.[29]

Further, he mentioned Schurz's attempt to inculpate members of the Crook Commission before the Senate Select Committee because they had recommended that tribal members seek their home where they wished. Dawes mentioned Schurz's most recent endeavor, the bill he had prepared providing that no funding be given the Poncas in any measure calling for free choice. Dawes concluded his remarks by affirming that Schurz bore responsibility for the wrong and now stood in the way of redress. "He is the last man to arraign a Senator in his place for the discharge of his official duty," Dawes noted. In manifesting his anger, Dawes succinctly responded to the secretary's rambling and disconnected open letter. This last confrontation between Dawes and Schurz reinforced the emergence of Dawes as the leading and most effective friend of the Indians in Congress.[30]

Dawes's allies in Boston were delighted. Since Schurz's "inconsistency and deceit" had been exposed, friends in Boston hoped that an opportunity might arise with the support of a more friendly secretary of the interior to test the validity of the 1879 Dundy decision in the Supreme Court. In addition to Dawes's male friends, many local women took up the Ponca cause. One of them described "meek Boston women, laden with Ponca tracts; and antagonistic Boston women, armed with arguments; and logical Boston women, laden with petitions miles long" all "going" for the secretary of the interior and "ready to descend on him at any moment in righteous chastisement for his sins, real and imagined," but primarily for "the cruel and unjust order that removed the Ponca Indians."[31]

Notes

1. "Secretary Schurz and the Poncas," *Harper's Weekly,* January, 1, 1881, 2. *Harper's Weekly,* the *Nation,* and *Evening Post,* all published in New York City, were strong supporters of the secretary.

2. "Interview with Senator Dawes," *Springfield (Massachusetts) Daily Republican,* January 4, 1881, 8.

3. Ibid.

4. Alfred L. Riggs to Henry Laurens Dawes, January 18, 1881, Dawes Papers, box 24, Library of Congress. Several days earlier Riggs had made the same suggestion to the Crook Commission.

5. "Proceedings of the Ponca Commission," in U.S. Senate, *Report of Special Commission,* 36.

6. Riggs to Dawes, January 18, 1881, Dawes Papers.

7. "The Poncas Vindicated," *Hartford Daily Courant,* January 28, 1881, 2 (quotes). See also "A Verdict for the Poncas," *Tribune,* January 27, 1881, 4, and "Justice for the Wronged Poncas," ibid., 1.

8. "The Poncas: Secretary Schurz's Part in Their Removal," *Chicago Tribune,* January 31, 1881, 1; "This Week," *Nation,* February 3, 1881, 67.

9. "The Poncas: Secretary Schurz's Part in Their Removal," and "A Card from Senator Dawes," *Chicago Tribune,* January 31, 1881, 1. Walter Allen's letter, also protesting Schurz's activities, preceded Dawes's card. Dawes's statement can also be found in "The Ponca Indian Investigation," *Springfield (Massachusetts) Daily Republican,* January 31, 1881, 1. A lengthy discussion of Schurz's interrogation of Crook Commission members Allen and Stickney can be found in "The Poncas: Mr. Schurz Makes the Commission Say Its Catechism," *Chicago Tribune,* January 30, 1881, 2; see also "Mr. Schurz's Position," *Advertiser,* February 1, 1881, 2.

10. *Congressional Record,* January 31, 1881, 1057. For a news account of Big Snake's murder, see "Indian Grievances: The Cowardly Assassination of 'Big Snake,'" *Advertiser,* February 1, 1881, 1.

11. *Congressional Record,* January 31, 1881, 1058.

12. Ibid.

13. Ibid., 1059.

14. Ibid., and February 1, 1881, 1095–96. On January 28, 1881, Dawes introduced a bill (S. No. 2113) to establish the rights of the Poncas. It was not enacted during this session of Congress.

15. Richardson, ed., *Messages and Papers of the Presidents,* 7:630–34. A complete copy of Hayes's February 1, 1881, message on the Ponca controversy can also be found in Speeches and Messages, Hayes Papers, Hayes Presidential Center. See also "The Wrongs of the Poncas," *New York Times,* February 3, 1881, 2, and "The President and the Indians," ibid., 4. The latter article is reprinted in Hays, *A Race at Bay,* 248–50.

16. William H. Lincoln to Dawes, February 4, 1881, Dawes Papers, box 24.

17. Carl Schurz to Henry L. Dawes, February 7, 1881, Schurz Papers, container 184, Library of Congress (quotes, 1–3). The letter also can be found in Schurz, *Speeches, Correspondence and Political Papers,* 4:91–113.

18. Schurz to Dawes, February 7, 1881, Schurz Papers, 4.

19. Ibid., 6.

20. Ibid., 9–13 (quote, 13).

21. Ibid., 13–14. The *Nation,* a strong supporter of the secretary, said that even though provoked by Dawes, who implicated him in the killing of Big Snake, Schurz responded "in a tone which everyone must regret." However, its editorial was more critical of Dawes than of Schurz. See "This Week," *Nation,* February 17, 1881, 103. For editorial comment critical of Schurz see "Sec. Schurz's Letter to Mr. Dawes," *Boston Transcript,* February 10, 1881, 4. This letter suggested "an unflattering familiarity . . . with fighting tactics of a small pattern and low order." The editorial noted Schurz's animus toward anyone presuming to advocate the cause of the Poncas while "posing as the first and only true friend of the Poncas par excellence."

22. "A New Ponca Bill," *Tribune,* February 11, 1881, 1.

23. Editorial comment in *Tribune,* February 14, 1881, 4.

24. Lincoln to Dawes, February 10, 1881, Dawes Papers, box 24.

25. *Congressional Record,* February 11, 1881, 1147. See also "Senator Dawes's Rejoinder to Secretary Schurz," *Advertiser,* February 12, 1881, 2; "Dawes: His Reply to Schurz," *Chicago Tribune,* February 12, 1881, 1; and "This Week," *Nation,* February 17, 1881, 103–04.

26. *Congressional Record,* February 11, 1881, 1147–48.

27. Ibid., 1148–49.

28. ibid., 1150.

29. Ibid.

30. Ibid.

31. Lincoln to Dawes, February 14, 1881, Dawes Papers, box 24 (first quote); Mary Clemmer, "A Woman's Letter from Washington," *Independent*, February 17, 1881, 3 (remaining quotes; complete letter on 3–5). A strong letter endorsing Dawes by William H. Lincoln was published as "Secretary Schurz and Fair Play," *Boston Evening Transcript*, February 23, 1881.

CHAPTER NINE

Seeking a Better Way

When it was learned that Interior Secretary Carl Schurz would be feted at a reception and dinner in Boston upon his retirement, Dawes's friends proposed a small affair honoring the senator on his reelection. Fifty to seventy-five "prominent Massachusetts men" would be in attendance. Meanwhile, in Washington, Schurz's friends rallied to his support, including Senator John Logan of Illinois, who informed the secretary that the attack waged against him was a "damned outrage." Marian Adams noted that Dawes inspired "wild contempt" in the circles in which she and her husband socialized. Dawes and his wife introduced themselves to Marian and her husband, Henry Adams, at a reception hosted by Secretary of State William Maxwell Evarts. Mrs. Adams informed her father "we were not gushing to their unsought advances." She reported that several days later when Schurz was visiting with John A. Logan in the Senate, Dawes got up from his desk and held out his hand as he approached Schurz. The secretary responded by holding out his hand, at which point the Illinois senator burst out laughing. Whether this was a conciliatory gesture or an indication that sentiment in Boston was shifting, Mrs. Adams did not say.[1]

While Dawes indicated to Schurz, by proffering his hand, that the issue dividing them transcended personality, eminent Bostonians continued their plans for the secretary's congratulatory dinner. Dawes supporters did "not propose to sit quiet" and allow this last hurrah on behalf of Schurz to go unchallenged. They intended to "rally to meet this last attack—for such it is," noted William H. Lincoln in a February 28, 1881, letter to Dawes. Lincoln informed the senator that Governor Long had drafted a paper that would be signed by "principal officials of the State and City," and a public meeting honoring both of the state's senators would be called "to show that the sense of Massachusetts is not on the side of Mr. Schurz,—but with you."

Lincoln accused Schurz of having "a hand in [his own] testimonial," which was urged by those whom he described as "blue bloods."[2]

Lincoln, who spearheaded the drive to honor Dawes and George F. Hoar, was highly critical of Schurz. In a lengthy letter to the editor of the *Boston Evening Transcript*, he claimed that, although Schurz's February 7 open letter was addressed to Dawes, it was "intended for all those who have been instrumental in creating the unusual public interest upon the Indian question." He wondered if it were proper to honor Schurz when the secretary "so wilfully violated the principles of justice," and when his administration had "been characterized by such acts of inhumanity and oppression." He concluded by warning that those reformers interested in the "just cause" of the Poncas would not remain quiet.[3]

By early March, Lincoln had "secured at least 300 good names" and expected those of several hundred more who would support a celebration for Dawes. He made it evident that Dawes in no way was responsible for what he and his associates were planning. Delano A. Goddard, editor of the *Boston Daily Advertiser,* wrote the letter of invitation, which was approved by Governor Long and Lincoln. Prominent citizens signed either the letter calling for a meeting to recognize the two senators or the one supporting a gathering to honor Schurz. The Schurz letter, Lincoln said, "approved all the acts of his administration." The other invitation, in honor of the senators, declared that such a statement was not in accord with public sentiment throughout the commonwealth as was evident by the names appended to it. The names crossed party lines and indicated pervasive support for Dawes's role in the Ponca controversy "among the influential men of the state." Adding to the enthusiasm generated for this meeting was the fact that the 46th Congress, during its last moments, agreed to the passage of a bill for the relief of the Poncas. Indeed, Lincoln, unaware of the controversy surrounding its passage, was convinced that Dawes "and Senator Hoar [would] receive an ovation that [had] not been accorded to any Senators since the time of Webster." He believed that now that justice had triumphed in behalf of the Poncas, a new era "full of hope and promise for the poor Indians is about to dawn upon them."[4]

The Ponca controversy thus came to an end through a provision in the Deficiency Appropriation Bill passed in early March 1881. This provision, presented in the House too late for passage, had become an amendment to the bill in the Senate. It allotted $165,000 to the tribe "to secure to them lands in severalty on either the old or new reservations." Brought to the Senate floor in the waning hours of the 46th Congress, the amendment provoked brief but sharp debate. Dawes denounced it as a "cruel act" because the Senate wanted to fix the status quo and not allow the Poncas the right to settle on the reservation of their choice despite the recommendations of the Crook Commission and the approval of President Hayes. Therefore Dawes, George F. Hoar, and Senator John Tyler Morgan of Alabama endorsed an amendment to the amendment that would allow the Poncas to make a final determination within six months whether "to be one of the old tribe or the new." But Samuel Kirkwood, who chaired the Select Committee, manifested his antipathy to the dominant role Dawes played throughout its proceedings. "I have no doubt whatever that the best thing that can be done for the Poncas is to recognize the exact state of affairs as it exists today," noted Kirkwood. He reflected Schurz's sentiment by stating that the judgment of the Crook Commission and the president was not binding upon his colleagues.[5]

Senator Morgan remarked that denying the Poncas the option of choice as free agents after they had been "sent south, in fraud of their treaty rights," and then kept there "in fraud of their treaty rights," would indicate that the Indians had no rights. The amendment to the amendment would make evident, Morgan argued, that Indians had some rights "that our people are bound to recognize." If they had no rights, "they would not be persons in the meaning of the Constitution." The Dawes amendment would grant them a basic right to determine their own destiny.[6]

When a division was called for, there were thirteen ayes and twenty-three nays, indicating a lack of a quorum. Dawes then withdrew his amendment whereupon the Senate, now with a majority present, approved the amendment as presented by the Committee on Appropriations. Thus ended the Ponca controversy. It was a stinging blow to Dawes, humiliated by too few senators bothering to vote, let alone by his being on the short side of the final vote. Schurz had reason to be jubilant. His point of view had prevailed. Furthermore he found a forceful spokesman in Samuel Kirkwood. And the fact that Kirkwood would succeed him as secretary of the interior in the Garfield administration meant that any attempt to revive the matter in the next Congress would not be favorably viewed.[7]

Despite the action in the Senate at the end of the session, the Indian committee in Boston went ahead with plans to honor Hoar and Dawes. Indeed the *Advertiser,* not recognizing Dawes's humiliation, commented that the outcome came "nearer the requirements of justice than it was feared would be possible." On March 11, one week into the Garfield administration, a letter was presented to the Massachusetts senators, asking that they designate a time to address a public meeting "to consider what justice, humanity and wise public policy require of the nation in its treatment of the Indians." The letter was signed by the governor and lieutenant governor, the secretary of state, seven of the eight members of the executive council, numerous members of the legislature including the president of the Senate and speaker of the House, the mayor of Boston, and over four hundred other concerned citizens.[8]

The impressive list of signatures was deemed necessary because other "eminent citizens" had publicly expressed approval of Secretary Schurz's tenure. In the judgment of the more than four hundred individuals who signed the letter to the senators, the supporters of Schurz did not "represent the sentiment of Massachusetts." Hoar and Dawes, of course, had no option but to comply with the request to speak. They would set a time once the current special session of the Senate was over.[9]

Meanwhile, a number of "Boston gentlemen of the best standing, both socially and politically," went ahead with their plans for a tribute to the services and character of the recently retired secretary. The historian Francis Parkman, one of its organizers, explained that it was intended as "a kind of silent protest against the reckless bestowal of abuse on one whose honorable past ought to have secured for him candid consideration." While Parkman recognized that government had much to answer for in its relations with the Indians, he was convinced "that some signs of compunction" were at last appearing. He thought it "hardly fair" to scapegoat "one of our best citizens" by making him "bear the burden of our iniquities." Though Parkman was the logical choice to chair the dinner honoring Schurz, he announced that the state of his health would not permit him to be on hand. Instead he asked Charles R. Codman, a prominent lawyer and businessman who, like Parkman, was an early advocate of civil service reform, to take his place.[10]

The reception for Schurz was held at the Hotel Vendome during the afternoon of March 22, 1881. That morning William H. Lincoln wrote Dawes that "a coterie of ambitious and disappointed politicians will have an opportunity of displaying their oratorical powers," adding that "Harvard College will do homage to the 'great reformer' but the sentiment of the people is not in accord." He cited a recent article in the *Philadelphia American* that was highly critical of Schurz and his role in the Ponca controversy. It indicated to Lincoln that organizing the public meeting honoring Dawes and Hoar was important "as a counter movement." He told Dawes that the governor remained firm; "nothing disturbs him or shakes his convictions." In a postscript he added, "We are thinking of forming a permanent organization."[11]

The Schurz reception at the Hotel Vendome was followed by a gala dinner. Over two hundred fifty of the commonwealth's most distinguished citizens were on hand. The Reverend James Freeman Clarke and President

Charles W. Eliot of Harvard were among the prominent speakers. Charles Codman chaired both gatherings. Schurz spoke at the reception and, of course, at the dinner. In both instances he mentioned the Poncas, noting that they were satisfied, that the government was satisfied, that the American public at large seemed to be satisfied, and that soon there would be general satisfaction, and "that honest philanthropy will find for this unity of purpose . . . more harmony of action." That evening Schurz reviewed his conduct of Indian affairs. Throughout, his remarks were greeted with applause. If Schurz needed further vindication for his role in the Ponca controversy, his reception provided it.[12]

But the Boston reformers had hopes of countering Schurz's reception with the proposed public meeting and addresses by their two senators. Early in May, Lincoln wrote Dawes that now that the Ponca situation seemingly was resolved, the committee members could attack remaining problems. They had in mind "the elevation and enfranchisement of a race" but thought a conference with both senators would be necessary before a course of action could be determined. Among the issues they hoped to discuss were legal suits they had in hand "to determine the status of the Indians." Neither the meeting nor the suits ever came to fruition.[13]

While the Boston philanthropists were seeking to broaden their reform efforts, the destitution of Standing Bear and his band of Poncas had not yet been relieved with the infusion of funds appropriated to them in the closing days of the 46th Congress. At the end of June, Tibbles informed Governor Long that Standing Bear had not been paid, and to further aggravate the Poncas' economic situation, those in the Indian Territory were running away "one by one" back to their Niobrara homeland. As a warning, Tibbles noted that "if Standing Bear is driven out, it will make it easier for Senator Alvin Saunders to steal that large slice from the Lakotas, which he wants to annex to Nebraska." Senator Saunders eventually succeeded in transferring a section of the Sioux reservation, as well as the Ponca lands, from Dakota Territory to Nebraska. It would take time before the Indian commissioner, Hiram Price, resolved the transfer of funds to Standing Bear's band of penurious Poncas.[14]

As the Poncas' situation receded from public view, Carl Schurz, basking in the afterglow of his Boston triumph, published his final judgment on the Indian problem in the *North American Review.* It was essentially a rationale for his behavior as interior secretary, though he never discussed the Poncas. To readers who were aware of the controversy, one of the most revealing and hypocritical sentences appeared in the second paragraph. Schurz wrote that "still less would I justify some high-handed proceedings on the part of the government in moving peaceable Indians from place to place without their consent, trying to rectify old blunders by new acts of injustice."[15]

Schurz again discussed his broad program of preparing Indians "for the habits and occupations of civilized life, by work and education" by allotting them lands in severalty "to individualize them in the possession and appreciation of property." But he went further in his hypocrisy when he wrote that Indians "should certainly have that standing in the courts which is necessary for their protection." The ultimate goal was full citizenship. But the task he had assigned himself as interior secretary was "to fit them for it" through "the protecting and guiding care of the government during the dangerous period of transition from savage to civilized life." Everything, Schurz declared, "depended upon the wisdom and justice of that guidance."[16]

The only time he mentioned the Poncas was when he included them among "the so-called wild tribes": the Shoshones, Lakotas, Cheyennes, Arapahoes, and others. In general, the article presented an overview of his dealings with and approach to resolving the Indian problem. Readers unfamiliar with the Ponca controversy could only be impressed with Schurz's humane concern for "the civilization and welfare of the red man, and the general interests of the country."[17]

A month after Schurz's article was published, there occurred a most unusual and impressive gathering at the Indian Office. Present were the new interior secretary, Samuel J. Kirkwood, Indian Commissioner Hiram Price, twelve Lakota chiefs and headmen, and representatives from the Ponca tribe. At this meeting the Lakotas formally ceded a portion of their reservation for the settlement of Standing Bear and about 175 of his followers currently residing on or near the old Ponca reservation. The agreement provided 640 acres for each head of family and unmarried men ages twenty-one and older. Other Poncas, male or female, not connected with a family, would be eligible to receive 80 acres. Title to the land would be in fee simple, not subject to lease, alienation, or encumbrance. In addition, the land would be free from taxation for twenty years. While the arrangement needed to be ratified by a three-fourths vote of the heads of Lakota families, its approval was considered a foregone conclusion by all present.[18]

In allotting this land, which included about twenty-five thousand acres, to the Poncas, White Thunder, the successor of Spotted Tail, spoke for the Lakota delegation with forcible gestures and eloquence. He said the Lakotas would allow the Poncas to have the land and he assured Schurz's successor, Samuel Kirkwood, that he did not expect the government to give anything to them in return. With ratification assured, the Ponca controversy could be considered definitely but not equitably resolved. Nonetheless, this resolution suggested the outline for Indian reform Dawes would capitalize on several years later.[19]

One immediate response to Schurz's article was written by William Justin Harsha. Describing the Ponca removal as "sheer robbery—an unblushing outrage," Harsha focused on the subject "Law for the Indians," a theme Schurz had briefly mentioned when commenting that those advocates of the movement to secure law for the Indians were "philanthropists" who paid no regard to "surrounding circumstances." Harsha disagreed. To him, law as the solution to the Indian problem was a self-evident proposition. Harsha was aware that Schurz was instrumental in preventing the federal attorney in Omaha from appealing Judge Dundy's decision to a higher court. Indeed in his public letter to Governor Long, Schurz openly took credit for this action. As previously noted, this was the only decision in the Ponca affair for which Schurz assumed responsibility and his action was decisive.[20]

In critiquing Schurz's article, Harsha cited the reports of various agents indicating that as long as the Indian had no legal protection "by which his life, his possessions, his permanent residence in a particular locality, shall be assured to him," there could be no resolution to the Indian problem.[21] On the other hand, Schurz had long asserted with regard to the Poncas that Indians had no rights under the law, and that no attorney, unless authorized by the Indian Department, had the right to represent them. Thus Standing Bear had no legal redress or rights that would be of concern to an American citizen. Harsha countered "by declaring that the Indian is a person before the law as the first and all important thing." Once the Indian was secure in his possessions, his labor could become meaningful and profitable. Education for both himself and his children would become desirable if not imperative, and the granting of land in severalty "something more than a pretentious form." In short, Schurz's reform program could be efficaciously achieved and Indians would have good reason to say, as did Standing Bear when released by Judge Dundy, "We have found a better way."[22]

Harsha effectively voiced one of the most significant themes to emerge from the Ponca controversy. His premise was succinctly stated by President Chester A. Arthur in his lengthy and little-noted first annual message to Congress. In a brief paragraph, the president said "the Indian should receive the protection of the law. He should be allowed to maintain in court his rights of person and property." Exercising these rights would be invaluable to Indians "in their progress towards civilization."[23]

In the last days of the 46th Congress, during a Senate discussion about granting lands in severalty to reservation Indians, several senators ventured one step further and called for awarding citizenship rights to Indians, thus repeating the pattern of the Fourteenth Amendment. Dawes's colleague George F. Hoar proposed a constitutional amendment stipulating that Indians "are hereby declared to have become citizens of the United States and entitled as such to the full protection of the Constitution and laws." By placing Indians upon land in severalty and removing them entirely from tribal jurisdiction, they then would be subjected to all the laws, civil and criminal, of the state or territory in which they resided. They would be bound to all the restraints and obligations of citizenship without enjoying its privileges. Hoar's amendment was designed to remedy this situation by awarding citizenship to Indians receiving title to lands in severalty.[24]

His Senate colleague from Alabama, John Tyler Morgan, expressed similar views. Senator Joseph E. Brown, former Confederate governor of Georgia, was inclined "very strongly to think that the Indian who has settled himself upon a homestead is a citizen already, under the fourteenth constitutional amendment." However, if he was not, Brown was "prepared to vote to make him one whenever he takes his land in severalty, and to give him the rights of a citizen if he lacks anything." Brown's remarks, which consumed over three pages in the *Congressional Record,* elaborated on the theme of permitting Indians to enjoy the same rights as other citizens. Although these arguments went nowhere, they indicated that a small number of public officials envisioned awarding citizenship with lands in severalty as a sensible approach for the government to pursue in its Indian policy.[25]

The theme was more forcefully stated by Susette La Flesche in an introduction to an 1881 novel, *Ploughed Under: The Story of an Indian Chief.* She wrote, "Allow an Indian to suggest that the solution to the vexed 'Indian Question' is citizenship." Granting citizenship would allow Indians to seek judicial redress when deprived of their liberty or property; it would "provide them opportunities to make something of themselves in common with other citizens." By recognizing the Indian "as a person and a citizen," by giving him "title to his lands," and by placing him "within the jurisdiction of the courts as an individual," Le Flesche agreed with President Arthur, the Omaha and Boston reformers, Judge Dundy, Standing Bear, and numerous others who believed that maintaining in court their rights to person and property offered a meaningful solution to the Indians' growing problem.[26]

It remained for Andrew Jackson Poppleton and John Lee Webster to argue the case for citizenship before the Supreme Court. Successful in their arguments on behalf of Standing Bear and the Poncas, Poppleton and Webster would receive no historical attention as pioneers battling for the same rights for Indians that former slaves gained as a result of the Civil War–era amendments to the Constitution. The Indians received no recognition because the court, with only two justices dissenting, in the case of *Elk v. Wilkins* decided that an Indian—even one voluntarily separated from his tribe who "fully and completely surrendered himself to the jurisdiction of the United States" and who resided in Omaha—was not, despite the claim of his attorneys to the contrary, a citizen as defined by the first section of the Fourteenth Amendment. Arguing for the defendant was Genio Madison Lamberton, the United States district attorney for Nebraska, who previously appeared before Judge Dundy against Standing Bear.[27]

Elk v. Wilkins thus shut down the fight for the rights of Indians as citizens. On into the next century a vast number of American Indians remained in a situation outlined in the 1857 Dred Scott decision by Chief Justice Roger B. Taney. As with the antebellum African American, most Indians were not, nor were they ever intended to be, citizens of the United States. With this decision Carl Schurz, otherwise a humane reformer and civil service advocate, won his greatest victory over the Indians, one that outdistanced his triumph over the Poncas. Indians were destined to remain a dependent people with whatever rights and privileges the federal government saw fit to grant or reformers and possibly Indians themselves could secure.

It is worthwhile noting that the dissenting opinion in *Elk v. Wilkins* was written by John Marshall Harlan, who twelve years later in *Plessy v. Ferguson* presented the most famous dissenting opinion in American history on behalf of racial justice.[28] In *Plessy* the defendant was seeking to maintain the rights and privileges of citizenship, something that John Elk, a Winnebago Indian, had hoped to obtain, namely a certificate of full membership in American society and a minimum of social dignity. In the struggle for citizenship, Judge Dundy had sought to break down barriers to recognition of non-reservation Indians rather than encouraging aspiration to civic participation. This was the thrust of the developing movement for citizenship launched by Tibbles, Poppleton and Webster, and the Omaha Ponca Relief Committee and forcefully articulated in *Standing Bear v. Crook*. *Elk v. Wilkins* meant that Indians would remain a dependent people.

When the decision in the case of *Elk v. Wilkins* was rendered on November 3, 1884, it was promptly challenged by the Board of Indian Commissioners in its annual report. "The solution of the Indian problem is citizenship," it noted, further stating "we believe that the time has come to declare by an act of Congress that every Indian born within the territorial limits of the United States is a citizen of the United States and subject to the jurisdiction thereof." The report argued that many Indians already had adopted "the habits of civilized life"; they paid taxes, were self supporting, and had achieved favorable recognition in all walks of American life. Yet, the commissioners observed, "there is no way by which even these educated, self-supporting Indians can gain a title to the rights, privileges and immunities of citizens."[29]

At the end of its 1884 report, the board pointed to the 1866 Civil Rights Act, which stated that "all persons born in the United States and not subject to any foreign power, excluding Indians not taxed, are hereby declared to be citizens of the United States." By excluding Indians not taxed, the law thereby sustained the view that one of its purposes was to confer "national citizenship upon a part of the Indian race" in the United States.[30]

The commissioners also examined in detail the situation with regard to Indians in the territory ceded to the United States in the Treaty of Guadalupe Hidalgo. Under the Mexican constitution, Indians were citizens. After reviewing court decisions emanating from the 1848 treaty, the commissioners could see "no escape from the conclusion that the Indians of all the Territories ceded by Mexico are citizens of the United States." They conceded that some Indians were in a state of hostility and were not included in its provisions. But there could be no doubt among the commissioners that the Treaty of Guadalupe Hidalgo was intended to secure the rights of all peaceful Indians residing in the ceded territory.[31]

What brought the 1884 report back to the unstated Dundy decision and the Ponca controversy was the inclusion of a lengthy letter written by General George Crook, whose experience among the Indians, the commissioners said, entitled his opinion "to great weight." General Crook came right to the point, stating that what the Indian needed most was "protection under the law; the privilege of suing in the courts, which privilege must be founded upon the franchise to be of the slightest value." Crook asserted "most emphatically" that he considered the American Indian "the intellectual peer of most, if not all, the various nationalities we have assimilated to our laws, customs, and language." If awarded both the ballot and access to the courts, Crook was convinced that Indians would be fully able to protect themselves. The prevailing treatment indicated in *Elk v. Wilkins,* he said, served only to degrade Indians, making evident the discrepancy between their condition "and that of those about them." To make Indians self-supporting it would be necessary, Crook concluded, to provide them with "the privileges which have made labor honorable, respectable," and able to defend themselves if such privileges be withheld from them.[32]

Crook's letter, along with the recommendation of the Board of Indian Commissioners that Congress declare Indians to be citizens and that it promptly enact a general allotment bill, suggested that the decision rendered in *Elk v. Wilkins* would be challenged and that the battle waged by Standing Bear and his supporters might yet be resolved in some fashion.[33] His letter also served to reiterate the premise that a major impetus for Indian reform in the late nineteenth century had been sparked in the West, thanks to the efforts of Thomas Henry Tibbles, who served as a catalyst for the incidents leading to Judge Elmer Dundy's 1879 decision in the case of *Standing Bear v. Crook*. The impetus would receive some resolution when Senator Dawes bundled all the reform suggestions together in a piece of legislation that Congress approved and the president signed in 1887.

Notes

1. Herbert E. Hill to Dawes, February 21, 1881, Dawes Papers, box 24, Library of Congress; Marian Adams to Robert W. Hooper, February 23, 1881, and February 27, 1881, in Adams, *Letters of Mrs. Henry Adams,* 270–71.

2. Lincoln to Dawes, February 28, 1881, Dawes Papers, box 24.

3. "Secretary Schurz and Fair Play," *Boston Evening Transcript,* February 23, 1881.

4. Lincoln to Dawes, March 3, 5, and 8, 1881 (Lincoln quotes, March 8), and D. W. Gooch to Anna Dawes, March 3, 1881, Dawes Papers, box 24. Anna was the senator's daughter.

5. *Congressional Record,* March 3, 1881, 2381–82.

6. Ibid., 2384.

7. Ibid., 2385.

8. *Boston Daily Advertiser,* quoted in "The Week," *Nation,* March 10, 1881, 159 (first quote); "The Treatment of the Indians," *Tribune,* March 12, 1881, 1 (second quote).

9. "The Treatment of the Indians," 1.

10. Francis Parkman to George William Curtis, March 15, 1881, and Parkman to Charles R. Codman, March 21, 1881, in Parkman, *Letters of Francis Parkman,* 2:143–44.

11. Lincoln to Dawes, March 22, 1881, Dawes Papers, box 24. The Boston Indian Committee, organized in November 1879, actively supported the Ponca cause until it was resolved. It continued its efforts on behalf of American Indians into the early decades of the twentieth century.

12. "Ex-Secretary Schurz at Boston," *Tribune,* March 23, 1881, 1; "The Schurz Dinner," *Advertiser,* March 23, 1881, 2; "Carl Schurz: The Reception and Dinner Last Evening," ibid., 1. See also a pamphlet entitled *Visit of the Hon. Carl Schurz to Boston,* and "Dinner Given by Citizens of Massachusetts," *Boston Morning Journal,* March 23, 1881, 1, both in the Carl Schurz Papers, container 184, Library of Congress.

13. Lincoln to Dawes, May 3, 1881, Dawes Papers, box 25. In September, Goddard was still inquiring about a meeting. See Goddard to Dawes, September 17, 1881, Dawes Papers, box 25.

14. Tibbles to John D. Long, June 22, 1881, Dawes Papers, box 25. On May 4 Reverend Harsha had written to Lincoln about the destitute condition of Standing Bear and his band. This letter was forwarded to Goddard at the *Advertiser,* who in turn wrote to Commissioner Hiram Price. On May 31 Price informed Goddard that orders had been given to the Santee Agent to make payments of ten thousand dollars per capita. See Hiram Price to Delano A. Goddard, May 31, 1881, Dawes Papers, box 25.

By February 1882 the situation still had not been resolved. The Indian land that Senator Saunders wanted granted to Nebraska contained the old Ponca reservation where Standing Bear was now located. While funds allocated to the Indians had been received, nothing was done about building a schoolhouse, something Standing Bear ardently desired. See Alfred L. Riggs to Dawes, February 11, 1882, Dawes Papers, box 25.

15. Schurz, "Present Aspects of the Indian Problem," 2.

16. Ibid., 8.

17. Ibid., 12, 24. In August, one of Schurz's assistant secretaries now serving in the same capacity under his successor, Samuel Kirkwood, wrote, "Our Indian policy is substantially yours. In fact, I see no desire anywhere to depart from the wise plans laid down by you." He also rejoiced "that the Ponca war was at last ended." See Alonzo Bell to Schurz, August 5, 1881, in Schurz, *Speeches, Correspondence and Political Papers,* 4:147–48.

18. "A New Home for the Poncas," *Advertiser,* August 19, 1881, 1; "The Ponca Settlement," ibid., August 22, 1881, 2. See also "Poncas," in U.S. Department of the Interior, Office of Indian Affairs, *Annual Report of the Commissioner of Indian Affairs* (1881), xlviii.

19. "A New Home for the Poncas," 1.

20. Harsha, "Law for the Indians," 277 (quote); see also 272–74.

21. Ibid., 285 (quote); see also 281–89.

22. Ibid., 290–92.

23. *Messages and Papers of the Presidents,* 8:56.

24. *Congressional Record,* January 24, 1881, 875–76.

25. Ibid., 878–82; Parks, *Joseph E. Brown of Georgia,* 538–40. It is interesting to note that in 1895 President Grover Cleveland in a letter to his interior secretary, Hoke Smith, observed, "I still believe, as I have always believed, that the best interests of the Indians will be found in American citizenship, with all the rights and privileges which belong to that condition." Cleveland, *Letters of Grover Cleveland,* 389.

26. Inshta Theamba (Bright Eyes/Susette La Flesche), introduction, in Harsha, *Ploughed Under,* 4 (quotes); also see 3–6 for her complete introduction.

27. *Elk v. Wilkins* (112 U.S. 94) (1884) involved John Elk, who severed his tribal relation and surrendered himself to the jurisdiction of the United States. By virtue of the Fourteenth Amendment, he deemed himself a citizen entitled to the rights and privileges of an American citizen. But Charles Wilkins, registrar of voters in Omaha's

fifth ward, disagreed. See Deloria and Wilkins, *Tribes, Treaties, and Constitutional Tribulations*, 145–47; Bodayla, "'Can an Indian Vote?'" 372–80; Prucha, *American Indian Policy in Crisis*, 345–46; Shattack and Norgren, *Partial Justice*, 94–96; and Priest, *Uncle Sam's Stepchildren*, 206–8. Susette Tibbles in a letter to Dawes, November 12, 1884 (Dawes Papers, box 25), decried the decision in *Elk vs. Wilkins*. She thought that a citizenship bill might have to be brought before Congress. She was right. By congressional action in 1924 all Indians born within the territorial limits of the United States became citizens. However, some Indians, chiefly through treaties prior to 1924, had secured citizenship. See Cohen, *Handbook of Federal Indian Law*, 153–54, and M. Smith, "The History of Indian Citizenship," 25–35.

28. For more on that decision see *Plessy v. Ferguson* (163 US 537). In his dissent in the case of *Elk v. Wilkins*, Harlan was joined by William Woods. For a penetrating brief discussion of *Elk v. Wilkins* see Lee, "Indian Citizenship and the Fourteenth Amendment," 215–20. In examining Harlan's dissent, Lee carefully illustrates how Harlan seriously diminished the logic and the reasoning of the majority opinion. He notes too that Senator Dawes called the opinion "the strangest, if not the wickedest decision since the fugitive slave cases" (207).

29. *Report of the Board of Indian Commissioners* (1885), 7.

30. Ibid., 8.

31. Ibid., 9–10.

32. Ibid., 10 (all quotes). Crook's letter was inserted without a date, place of origin, or recipient, and without indicating whether or not it was requested. This letter was published in pamphlet form as *Letter from George Crook on Giving the Ballot to Indians*.

33. *Report of the Board of Indian Commissioners* (1885), 11. The commissioners had two further recommendations: one called for the organization of a government in the Indian Territory, the other for a large increase of the facilities for education.

CONCLUSION

When Standing Bear and a small band of followers fled the Indian Territory initially to bury his son, they accepted refuge among the Omaha tribe. His hope and the goal of his band was to resume their life within a farming community amidst friendly neighbors. Through a chance set of circumstances, such was not to be the case. First, the interior secretary, Carl Schurz, who had previously ordered their removal, in March 1879 ordered the "runaways" taken into custody at Fort Omaha and returned by the army to the Indian Territory. This would have occurred but for the intervention of the enigmatic, colorful Omaha journalist Thomas Henry Tibbles.

Tibbles is enigmatic because relatively little is known about him. His memoir, *Buckskin and Blanket Days,* published in 1957, fifty-two years after his death, relates exciting adventures in Bleeding Kansas where he served with John Brown's abolitionist band and thereafter lived among the Omaha Indians for a brief period, establishing himself as a firm friend of the Indians. When he came into contact with the Poncas, he was an editor on the *Omaha Herald.* The chief source of information remains his memoir; but scholars have observed that at times he was prone to exaggeration. Nevertheless, it was Tibbles who gathered the individuals who brought Standing Bear and the plight of his small band into federal court. This prompted a decision that launched a campaign for Indian rights culminating in 1887 with a law that one philanthropist called "the end of a century of dishonor."[1]

It was Tibbles who activated the concern of George Crook, the commandant at Fort Omaha whose assignment was to return the Poncas to the Indian Territory. Tibbles further aroused the interest of prominent clergymen and other citizens in Omaha, and he recruited two of the ablest lawyers in that city, who, without fee, agreed to seek a writ of habeas corpus and bring the case before Judge Elmer Scipio Dundy. They argued that the Poncas had been imprisoned illegally and restrained of their liberty. Dundy concluded that the Poncas could be considered as persons and he therefore ordered their release. Though he never used the word "citizen," Dundy asserted that Standing Bear and his band were free to enjoy the rights of any other person in the land.

The decision did not vitiate federal authority over Indians, and it also failed to recognize the importance of Indian cultural autonomy, let alone tribal sovereignty. But it was a beginning, and Tibbles encouraged the Omaha reformers to take advantage of it, thereby launching a western impulse for a change in Indian policy geared toward granting Indians the same rights the Fourteenth Amendment had granted to recently emancipated freedmen.

The committee in Omaha developed a three-part strategy with the ultimate goal of persuading the Supreme Court to consider Standing Bear's case. One part was immediately curtailed. At Schurz's urging, the federal attorney was barred from appealing Dundy's decision. Nevertheless, the committee hoped to reverse the decision, thereby immediately raising the question of Indian citizenship and bringing it to national attention. First, the committee sent Tibbles to Indian Territory to encourage Poncas wishing to return to their homeland to cross over into nearby Kansas where they would be beyond the jurisdiction of their agent. Once in a sovereign state, Tibbles could provide them with funds, transportation, and further assistance. This approach was a notable failure. But such was not the case with the lecture tour that started working its way east from Chicago. In Boston, tour members met their warmest reception. There they appealed to former abolitionists and other reform-minded citizens, who took up the cause and helped bring the removal of the Poncas to widespread public attention through mass meetings and extensive press coverage, themes repeated in New York and elsewhere in the East. Concerned citizens in Boston went further and organized an Indian committee that endured into the next century.

Carl Schurz soon found himself beleaguered, answering charges leveled in the press by former officials, by proper Bostonians, and by prominent citizens close to the Poncas who informed him that the Indians did not want to move. In one way or another these charges impugned his integrity and forced him to respond in articles and public letters. Schurz never admitted that he had made a mistake, but at times his responses indicated that the charges were undermining his calm, urbane demeanor.

So powerful was the impact of the tour that in the last year of the Hayes administration a Senate Select Committee, a presidential commission, and the president himself in a formal message to the Congress all reviewed the case of the Poncas. All sought to resolve the situation by allowing the Poncas in the Indian Territory to decide if they wished to remain in place or to move back to their homeland. Schurz opposed this premise, and in the last days of Hayes's presidency Congress affirmed Schurz's view and voted compensatory funding that made no provision for the Poncas to determine where they wished to reside. As the president learned more and more about Schurz's role, he became so annoyed that he seriously considered calling for his resignation.

Indeed, the controversy sparked by Judge Dundy's decision, the removal of the Poncas, the media coverage, and the Senate committee hearings served as catalysts for humanitarians and growing numbers of politicians to address issues affecting Native Americans. Many leaders recognized that the enhanced impact of technology on the trans-Mississippi West, which they deemed as progress and civilization, would overturn the forces of traditionalism. Most reformers believed peaceful coexistence could not occur as long as Native Americans maintained their traditional ways and culture. Influenced by theories of racial Dawinism, as well as by the evolutionary ideas of Lewis Henry Morgan, which viewed Indians in transit from savagery to civilization, they insisted that Indians embrace the ways of the Euroamerican invaders and adopt their traditions and culture or face extinction.[2] The playing out of this theme with regard to the Standing Bear removal is what made the Indians' plight so ironic.

Like the Cherokees and others before them, the Poncas were forced to leave their homeland, where already they had left their impression on the natural environment, developed an identity with the land, and created a cultural landscape. Like the Cherokees, the Poncas wished to possess and defend their homelands. But neither the Cherokees nor the Poncas could withstand the might of federal forces.

In their homeland along the Niobrara, the Poncas had lived in frame houses, most with wood-burning stoves. They farmed and sought to emulate and cooperate with their neighbors in peaceful coexistence. Standing Bear, once resettled in his homeland, asked if the government could build his people a schoolhouse. In the Indian Territory the Poncas complained that the housing slowly provided for them could not compare with what they enjoyed in Dakota Territory. They were a tribe that wished to conform and were well along on the road to assimilation. They paid a terrible price because of unfounded fear that they would be molested and killed by the Lakotas who were awarded the Poncas' lands through a treaty oversight. Slowly surrounded by the white population, even the Lakotas had trouble clinging to their traditional ways and culture, while the neighboring Poncas were embracing Anglo-American culture as yeoman farmers and developing a strong attachment to place. In effect, in the eyes of reformers, the Poncas were ceasing to be Indians and were completing the transition from savagery to civilization. Thus some reformers called for Indian citizenship so that the Native Americans could enjoy equality before the law and begin to break the dependency they had endured. Citizenship, its supporters believed, would be a major step in the right direction.

The fight for expanding Indian citizenship increased in tempo as a result of the Dundy decision and the Ponca controversy. Indeed, the entire controversy revealed an element of hypocrisy in the behavior of Carl Schurz, who, as secretary of the interior, always asserted that he was a warm friend of the Indians. His aim, he insisted, was to absorb them into American life since they had only two options: assimilation or extermination. Oddly, the reformers shared this belief with Schurz. Few of them were willing to accept and value the differences between their culture and that of the Indians. Instead the focus of the reform movement was to impose the dominant culture upon the Indians.

At the outset of Rutherford B. Hayes's presidency, the Reconstruction era officially came to an end. During the waning years of his administration, the plight of the Poncas came to national attention. Calls for change emanated from citizens throughout most of the country, through the echelons of power, reaching the White House itself. The controversy provided a catalyst for Indian reform. In creating the Crook Commission and endorsing its findings after becoming aware of the perfidy of his interior secretary, the president added to the luster of his administration.

But other changes were in the air during the Hayes presidency. The momentum for a separate woman-suffrage amendment got underway when Susan B. Anthony dedicated herself to the goal formally presented in a militant address at the Centennial Exhibition in Philadelphia in 1876. Four years later she began the compilation and publication of the multivolume *History of Woman Suffrage*. Then, in 1879, upper- and middle-class women in Philadelphia formed the Women's National Indian Association (WNIA) to protest the unauthorized intrusion of both railroads and settlers into the Indian Territory.[3] Through the process of petition gathering, these women, who quickly formed branches and auxiliaries throughout the country, actively worked on behalf of the Poncas and other tribes. In short, the ferment for freedom so evident in Jacksonian America surfaced in a much better organized form during the Hayes presidency. It is ironic that the most controversial figure in the Standing Bear controversy, Carl Schurz, was a leading champion of civil service reform.

It is worth reiterating that Standing Bear came to national attention during years of unprecedented urban and industrial growth accompanied by the quickened pace of western settlement. The world's most extensive railroad system furthered these developments and helped reformers of Indian affairs accept the validity of land in severalty, an allotment of one hundred sixty acres, as a viable solution to the Indian problem. Ironically, about the same time as the passage of the 1887 law bearing his name, Senator Dawes became active in promoting legislation to grant James J. Hill authority to construct railroad trackage through Indian reservations in Montana and Dakota Territories and to open these lands "to immediate settlement."[4]

The concept of lands in severalty was the Indian equivalent of the Reconstruction era's forty acres and a mule. In both instances the beneficiaries were not seriously consulted, and the outcome in each instance was disastrous. For the freedmen it came to involve a system of sharecropping, insurmountable debt, a life of unending toil, and devastating poverty. For the Indians, the purported beneficiaries of lands in severalty, the result was the same. The point to be mentioned here is that virtually every individual or group that took up the cause of Indian reform accepted lands in severalty as the most viable solution to the Indian problem.

As with previous reformers, proponents of Indian reform were largely but not exclusively located north of the Mason-Dixon line. Comparing the fate of Indians with that of the freedmen is instructive in several ways. The three Civil War amendments to the Constitution ended slavery, defined citizenship to include freedmen, and then guaranteed freedmen the right of suffrage. However, even before the removal of the Poncas to the Indian territory, these rights were slowly being eroded. Beginning with the Slaughterhouse Cases (1883), the Supreme Court began redefining the Fourteenth Amendment to include corporations. And southern states devised numerous ways, formal and informal, legal and illegal, to curb and virtually eliminate black suffrage.

So too did the Supreme Court thwart efforts of Indians to achieve equality under law. *Elk v. Wilkins* (1884) declared that Indians fully integrated into American society were not entitled to the franchise or any other rights accruing to American citizens. Then in 1903, in *Lone Wolf v. Hitchcock,* the court contended that Congress could overturn treaties through use of its plenary power.[5] By the turn of the century, despite the efforts of reformers, the plight of both the Indian and the freedman was bleak.

Before the reform impulse waned, both former slaves and certainly the Poncas earned the respect of top military officers, who valued them as worthy individuals regardless of skin color. General O. O. Howard and other officers associated with the Freedmen's Bureau valiantly assisted former slaves in launching their arduous journey toward freedom. In the case of the Poncas, Generals Nelson A. Miles and George Crook, seasoned Indian fighters, endorsed the desire of Standing Bear and others to choose where to make their permanent home. And Crook went on to champion the cause of Indian citizenship.

Notes

1. The quote introduces the text of the Dawes Act in Commager, ed., *Documents in American History,* Document 315, p. 574. No scholarly study on Tibbles is currently available; Howard Lamar's masterful *New Encyclopedia of the American West* (1998), for example, contains no entry for him; Tibbles is mentioned only briefly in a section on Susette La Flesche Tibbles in *Encyclopedia of the American West* (1996).

2. Morgan, the author in 1851 of *League of the Iroquois,* stressed three stages of societal development: savagery, barbarism, and civilization, and claimed that "all people could be placed at one of these levels." Hoxie, *A Final Promise,* 18.

3. For more details on the WNIA see Mathes, "Nineteenth-Century Women and Reform," 1–18.

4. D. Smith, "Procuring a Right-of-Way," 24, 27–31, 42 (quote). Thanks to W. Thomas White of the James J. Hill Library in St. Paul, Minnesota, for providing the authors with a copy of this important thesis.

5. For a detailed study see B. Clark, *Lone Wolf v. Hitchcock.*

EPILOGUE

What of the Poncas themselves? In Nebraska the Northern Poncas were fortunate to have land along the Niobrara River and Ponca Creek in broad and fertile valleys with good drainage. Lieutenant Bourke described the soil as rich and black and concluded it "ought to support them without trouble."[1]

It was expected that the Poncas would continue their former agrarian ways. But indigenous land holdings were historically communal, and to many reformers of Indian policy, individualized land allotment was the key to Indian assimilation. In his annual reports of 1881 and 1882, Hiram Price, Indian commissioner during President Grover Cleveland's first administration, clearly spelled out the advantage of individualized Indian land holdings when he wrote that allotment taught "the Indians habits of industry and frugality, and stimulate[d] them to look forward to a better and more useful life."[2] These sentiments, voiced by Carl Schurz and others for decades, became a reality with the 1887 passage of the General Allotment Act, or the Dawes Act. However, Standing Bear and the other Nebraska Poncas could not receive allotments until after the passage on March 2, 1889, of the Sioux bill, which divided the former Great Sioux Reservation into six small reservations and provided for Ponca allotment. Finally in August 1890, the Ponca reservation in Nebraska was allotted. The 217 Northern Poncas soon began to prosper, outstripping their Santee Sioux neighbors with better crops, larger acreage, greater thrift, "and more interest taken in everything that [was] done to promote their welfare."[3]

The same was not true of the 605 Southern Poncas living in the Indian Territory. Their agent in 1890, writing in his annual report, "found drunkenness, demoralization and a tendency to look with distrust on the words of the white man." Hot winds and dry weather made "the corn in August, with few exceptions, look as dry as in December, and no ears on the stalk." Their housing, which Secretary Schurz a decade earlier had claimed was satisfactory, had become "unfit for occupancy," affording insufficient protection from inclement weather. Agent William J. Pollock had made similar observations earlier.[4]

Less than two decades later, great progress was noted in the Indian Territory despite the presence of "a few confirmed old inebriates . . . [who] hung around the saloons and dives of Ponca and got drunk on every possible occasion." Of the 101,895.28 acres comprising the Ponca reservation, 75,249.37 acres had been allotted to 628 tribal members and 523.53 acres were set aside in 1894 for the agency, the school, and the cemetery. Some allotted lands had been sold, usually by the heirs of the original recipients. Crops were thriving, and the Poncas had built houses, barns, and granaries. The 1906 annual report indicated that the 570 Southern Poncas were "in a much better position to live upon and cultivate a portion of their allotments than ever before." Moreover, the Ponca Training School, with a capacity to serve 100 pupils, was flourishing with students engaged in animal husbandry and completing a water system that furnished both the school and the agency with an ample supply of spring water.[5]

In Nebraska, the Northern Poncas had come under the supervision of the superintendent in charge of the Santee Agency. Their subagency soon had warehouses, a blacksmith-carpenter shop, and houses. Ponca children were attending nearby public schools because there was no provision for their education in a reservation school. The agent further noted "a decided interest in the amount of rentals derived from the leasing of lands." Nearby white farmers sought leases on Indian allotments, but the agent also noted that "the sales of inherited lands have largely decreased during the year." More favorably he observed that "no serious crime has been committed on the reservation during the past year," and the standard of morality was "undoubtedly higher" than among tribes situated under similar conditions. In 1906 there were 263 Poncas in Nebraska. About a quarter of them were mixed-bloods.[6]

What of Standing Bear? During the eastern lecture tour, his name had continually appeared in newspapers, his every move closely chronicled by reporters. But after he joined his followers on an island near the west bank of the Niobrara River, accounts of his activities are few and far between.

The first such account appeared in the fall of 1881. Thomas Henry Tibbles and his wife, the former Susette La Flesche, agreed to escort a woman they had met in Boston in 1879 on a tour to visit tribes on the Northern Plains. Alice Cunningham Fletcher had been studying ethnology, visiting museums, and reading widely and now wanted to observe Indian life and customs. Armed with letters from cabinet members and men of science, she joined Tibbles and his wife in Omaha in September. They spent several months in the field, first among the Omahas. Years later, with the assistance of Francis La Flesche, Fletcher wrote a major anthropological study, *The Omaha Tribe*.

Following their sojourn among the Omahas, the threesome journeyed toward the Ponca Reservation, making their camp at the Niobrara River. Tibbles was surprised to see all the Nebraska Poncas, "men, women, and children, led by Standing Bear, a joyously happy throng," crossing the river to greet them. Invited to have dinner at Standing Bear's tent, the three visitors and the Poncas recrossed the Niobrara. Later that evening all the Poncas assembled to listen to Tibbles explain the latest information about their government settlement. Taking leave of Standing Bear, the three spent time among the tribes of the Sioux Nation. They received a friendly reception everywhere they went primarily because Tibbles was regarded as a friend to the Indians.[7]

Almost a decade passed before Standing Bear's name surfaced again. In 1889 he and "some 60 Poncas" had run away from their northern reserve and headed for the Indian Territory, arriving in April. According to Agent James E. Holms, Standing Bear, whom he described as "a shrewd, cunning savage" and married to two women, had encouraged these Poncas to join him. The agent also reported that they were displeased with the uncompleted allotment process at home.[8]

In the Indian Territory, Standing Bear expressed an earnest desire to remain and indicated that this was "the wish of all of his followers in Dakota." On May 20, 1890, Standing Bear, White Eagle, and other Indians held a council with Agent D. J. M. Wood, the agent in charge of the Indian Territory Poncas. Wood reported to the Indian commissioner, Thomas Jefferson Morgan, that Standing Bear "spoke very feelingly in reference to his people returning to Nebraska—said he would keep his promise to you and would go back alone as his people would not go with him." Because members of his party had relatives living in the Indian Territory, they wished to remain and did not care if they lost their land in Nebraska. Their petition to remain reminded Agent Wood "very much of the children of Israel in their troubles."[9]

While Standing Bear wished to remain in the Indian Territory, he had no intention of abandoning his land in Nebraska. Instead he wanted the Indian commissioner to sell his land and use the money "to see [that] the [Santee] Sioux reservation is separated from the Ponca in Nebraska." Furthermore, because some white people were living on Ponca lands, Standing Bear not only wanted them to pay for the land, but he requested that the commissioner "look over our farms." The Ponca leader was informed he would lose his land if he did not return. "Early in July they began to drift back, and late in July," Wood reported of the Indian Territory Poncas, "Standing Bear went back with all he could get to go with him." Agent Wood did not state how many Poncas returned to Nebraska, though he did note that "about twenty-five of those who came down" with Standing Bear remained.[10]

Standing Bear again came to public attention when Carl Schurz died in New York City on May 14, 1906. Later that month the *New York Times* printed an article with an Omaha dateline entitled "One Case Where Carl Schurz Was Not on the Side of Human Liberty." The Ponca chief, now "white-headed, old and decrepit," told the *Times* reporter that he remembered Carl Schurz and still blamed him for much of the ordeal his people had experienced. When informed of Schurz's death, Standing Bear "smoked a full minute before answering the one word of English which he ever uses: 'good.'"[11]

While Schurz was eulogized in the press throughout the country, the *Times* story, based heavily on Tibbles's account, recounted the tale of the Ponca removal, the return of Standing Bear, and Dundy's decision, which enabled Standing Bear to bring the body of his dead child "back to the hunting ground of his fathers" and to bury him with tribal honors."[12] The story, like the entire controversy, cast aspersions on the reputation of Carl Schurz, but it was soon lost amidst the notices lauding his career and contributions. Moreover, Schurz would have been pleased to learn that in the year of his death, the condition of the Poncas had improved considerably over the previous decade.

Standing Bear died two years later, in September 1908. He was buried on the allotment granted him in 1890. The burying ground contained the graves of his nearest relatives, possibly including his two wives. The site of his grave, purportedly on the west bank of the Niobrara River, is in doubt because the allotment, number 146, was sold in 1925 to a white farmer who plowed much of the land, including the graveyard. In 1937 the Poncas repurchased Standing Bear's allotment with federal funds provided under the terms of the Indian Reorganization Act.[13]

As for the friends of the Poncas, Henry Laurens Dawes for the remainder of his career worked to further the cause of Indian reform.[14] He served as chairman of the Committee on Indian Affairs until he retired on March 3, 1893. As chairman, Dawes visited reservations throughout the West, conferred with tribal delegations that came to Washington, conducted hearings, and in general became the best-informed person on Indian matters on Capitol Hill. His most enduring work was accomplished in 1887 when he became Senate sponsor of the General Allotment Act, quickly dubbed the Dawes Severalty Act, or simply the Dawes Act.

The act was the first systematic effort to provide for Indian welfare and marked a fundamental change in the handling of Indian affairs. Although considered a step toward progress, its unilateral implementation proved a disaster for the Indians, who were never consulted by its authors. Well-meaning reformers viewed the process as a means of promoting Indian economic advancement, but instead "it changed Indian farming and Indian life in ways that were not foreseen by the reformers" and, more important, led in large measure to "the failure of Indian farming in the early twentieth century."[15] Land speculators, including railroad promoters, and some members of Congress saw in the law an opportunity for profit with the opening of vast acreage for non-Indian settlement. Over ninety million acres or two-thirds of Indian Country ended up in private hands.

Humanitarian reformers who endorsed the act could point with pride to Section VI, which signified that upon completion of the allotment process, the issuance of patents, and a twenty-five-year trust period, Indians could not be denied equal protection of the law. Moreover, every Indian born within the territorial limits of the United States, including those who maintained a residence apart from any tribe and who "adopted the habits of civilized life," was declared to be a citizen of the United States and "entitled to all the rights, privileges, and immunities of such citizens."[16] While it broke tribal status by subjecting Indians to state laws, Section VI in effect partially reversed *Elk vs. Wilkins* and marked a victory for those who had taken up the cause of Standing Bear and argued for Indian citizenship as the culmination of Judge Elmer Dundy's 1879 decision. On the other hand, it mitigated against tribal communities and encouraged mainstream American concepts of individualism.

After eighteen years of service in the Senate, in 1895 Dawes traveled to the Indian Territory as the head of the Commission to the Five Civilized Tribes (also known as the Dawes Commission), mandated by Congress to secure the consent of the Indians to the abandonment of tribal relations through the allotment in severalty of their lands. He died in Pittsfield, Massachusetts, in 1903 at the age of eighty-seven, three years before the death of his erstwhile opponent Schurz.[17]

Dawes's colleague George Frisbie Hoar during his long tenure in the Senate only occasionally spoke on matters pertaining to Indians, but moral issues, comparable to his concern for the plight of the Poncas, quickly won his support. While many citizens of Massachusetts agreed with their senators in promoting reform of Indian policy, few agreed with Hoar in denouncing the anti-immigrant, anti-Catholic bigotry of the American Protective Association. As Hoar endorsed citizenship combined with severalty for Indians, so he encouraged "love of New England liberty and New England traditions" among the Irish Catholics of his native state.[18] As removing the Poncas against their will was an imperious move that was devastating to a small, peaceful tribe, so too was religious proscription tyrannical and defeating for Irish Catholics.

Just as he had opposed Schurz's handing of the Ponca removal and its aftermath, Hoar would also strenuously oppose his party's Philippine policy in his last years in the Senate. But for American military action on Luzon, Hoar believed a peaceful settlement—one that recognized Emilio Aquinaldo's provisional constitution—could have achieved a strong measure of justice and equity for the people of the Philippine Islands. As in the case of the Poncas, intervention brought dependence and subjugation. Views that Hoar articulated on the treatment of the Poncas reverberated at critical times during his long and distinguished career in the United States Senate. He was reelected in 1901 to a fourth term and died three years later, on September 30, 1904.[19]

John Davis Long, the leading figure in the Boston Indian Citizenship Committee, sought in the 1880s to succeed both Dawes and Hoar as a United States senator from Massachusetts. Although he failed to do so, he served three terms in the State House, once as lieutenant governor and twice as governor, from 1878 through 1882, and three terms in Congress, from 1883 to 1889. His career in the House revealed little interest in Indian affairs, while his later service as secretary of the navy during the McKinley administration precluded it. Upon retiring from government service, he returned to Massachusetts and resumed his law practice. Though in frail health, he rekindled his interest in Indian affairs. In 1912 he presided at a meeting of the Boston Indian Citizenship Committee where he noted some of the current grievances of the Indians and dwelt on the valuable work done by the committee when he was its leading figure at the time of its creation.[20]

While Long resumed an interest in the Indian at the end of his public career, such was not the case with Rutherford B. Hayes, who intimately involved himself with the plight of the Poncas in the waning months of his presidency. Their misfortune undoubtedly stimulated his growing concern for what he soon considered the intolerable oppression endured by large segments of the American people: freedmen, working people, and prisoners. He championed equality of rights but never specifically focused on Indians, though he attended at least two Lake Mohonk conferences.[21] At one meeting where Dawes was present, Hayes spoke of him in a most complimentary way. In his post-presidential years, Hayes became increasingly liberal, calling for curbing the excessive power of wealth and for a more equitable distribution of property. He valued manual labor and saw it as a way to reduce class tensions, if it were made universal through a program of education. Near the end of his life, Hayes defined his outlook, concluding, "I am a radical in thought (and principle) and a conservative in method (and conduct)."[22]

Unlike Hayes, Thomas Henry Tibbles and Susette La Flesche, who were married on June 29, 1881, at the Omaha Reservation, never abandoned their involvement in Indian affairs. Earlier, in 1880, while lecturing in the East during the Ponca controversy, Tibbles, using a pseudonym, wrote a book entitled *The Ponca Chiefs: An Account of the Trial of Standing Bear,* based on his articles in the *Omaha Daily Herald.* In the following year, under his own name, he published *Hidden Power,* a novel that purported to expose the intrigues and machinations of what he called "The Indian Ring." Meanwhile, Susette La Flesche was writing Indian stories and articles for several periodicals and also was developing an interest in painting.

The years 1882–83 found them lecturing in the East and lobbying Congress to enact legislation granting the Omaha tribe permanent individual allotments. This was achieved on August 7, 1882. In May 1886 they embarked on a yearlong lecture tour in England and Scotland in which they discussed the past, present, and future of American Indians.

After their marriage, they resided briefly in Omaha, Nebraska, before moving to the Omaha Agency. Here Tibbles built a sod house and started farming on their quarter section near Bancroft. In June 1888 he leased the farm to a tenant, sold all his livestock and equipment, and rejoined the staff of the *Omaha World Herald.* In 1890, he and Susette went to the Pine Ridge Agency to report on the disturbances culminating in the death of almost one hundred fifty Indians at Wounded Knee. While Tibbles covered the situation and sent lengthy dispatches to Omaha, Susette assisted wounded and frightened Indians in what Tibbles called the "War of 1890," the last major engagement between the army and Indians.

Thereafter Tibbles worked for several Nebraska newspapers: as a Washington correspondent for one, an editor for another, and the founder of the *Independent,* an organ of the Populist party. After Wounded Knee, he shifted his concern from Indians to the Populist party. He returned to the *World-Herald* in 1910 as an editorial and feature writer, a post he held until he retired shortly before his death on May 14, 1928.

Susette had joined her husband in his increasing involvement in the Populist movement. She also continued writing articles and painting. In 1898 she illustrated *Oo-Mah-Ha-Ta-Wa-Tha,* a book about the Omaha tribe, considered the first book ever illustrated by an American Indian. But her health became increasingly fragile. She died on May 26, 1903. Tibbles remarried in 1907. After Susette's death and following the presidential campaign of 1904, wherein Tibbles was the vice-presidential candidate on the Populist ticket, he wrote his autobiography, *Buckskin and Blanket Days,* in 1905. Half a century later, in 1957, the manuscript was published and generally well received. David Lavender in reviewing the volume aptly characterized Tibbles as "a reformer, a crusader, and a dreamer of the world as it ought to be." If *Buckskin and Blanket Days* serves as Tibbles's legacy, Susette trumped him. In 1954 she was inducted into the Nebraska Hall of Fame, joining Standing Bear, who had been inducted four years earlier.[23]

The forced removal of Standing Bear and his tribe changed the focus of Helen Hunt Jackson's literary career. Previously she had been primarily a poet and an author of travel essays, domestic essays, and novels. But her obsession with the mistreatment of the Poncas essentially transformed her into a muckraker who ferreted out bits and pieces to be used in her condemnation of the government's Indian policy. On a broader level, she can be viewed as a "cultural broker," who in a space of six short years stepped on many toes in a calculated measure "to gain public support and congressional action," and who, in the wake, "left a heritage of concern among other reformers." Jackson's "unusual brokering stance" was "more straightforward because she was not defending her own heritage." Thus she seldom compromised.[24]

Following the publication in 1881 of *A Century of Dishonor,* in which she challenged the 46th Congress "to cover itself with a lustre of glory, as the first to cut short our nation's record of cruelties and perjuries,"[25] she traveled to California to write articles for the *Century Magazine.* Here she discovered her next crusade, the former Mission Indians. She wrote articles, a government report in 1883 as a special agent to the Mission Indians, and finally *Ramona,* which she hoped would be the Indians' *Uncle Tom's Cabin.* Even after her death in 1885, her writings influenced members of the Women's National Indian Association, who carried on her work establishing the Ramona missionary field in Southern California. Jackson's final legacy was the creation of the California Mission Indian Commission in 1891, which implemented most of the recommendations in her government report, including the establishment of numerous small reservations that exist today.[26]

Standing Bear's impact was ever widening. For example, John Gregory Bourke's expertise in Indian matters, which came "to the attention of American anthropologists," was stimulated by the Ponca controversy. As a result of his service as recorder on the Crook Commission, Bourke composed more than four thousand pages of ethnological notes during eleven years working among various western tribes with General Crook.[27]

Another ripple of the Standing Bear episode was its impact upon the membership of the Women's National Indian Association. Although established the year of Standing Bear's escape, trial, and tour, the association was not organized to protest the treatment of the Poncas but to challenge the unauthorized encroachment into the Indian Territory. The initial WNIA reference to the "wrong to the Ponca Indians" occurred on March 17, 1881; then in June, Thomas Henry Tibbles spoke before the group. Although association records cite no specific reference to the Poncas, it can be presumed that Tibbles discussed their situation while also explaining the "legal helplessness" of Indians in general.[28]

By August 1881 the WNIA had expanded into twenty states. Two years later their Missionary Department was established to care for the needs of Indian women and children and to bring Christianity, education, domestic skills, and health care to tribes that had no resident missionary. At the suggestion of Inspector James M. Haworth, who had testified before Senator Dawes and members of the Senate Select Committee in December 1880, the WNIA established its first mission among the Poncas, Otos, and Pawnees of Indian Territory.[29] On August 15, 1884, Amelia Stone Quinton, general secretary of the association and later its longtime president, visited the WNIA mission among the Poncas in the Indian Territory. She described them as "a helpless looking hungry horde of men and women." The sight was sickening, she noted, "as much from the inhumanities of our Indian management thus revealed as from the starvation, abject helplessness, misery and degradation seen."[30]

Senator Dawes also worked closely with the WNIA. Its members believed that the solution to the Indian problem was to end the reservation system and to promote acculturation, education, allotment of land in severalty, and citizenship, all flavored with a dose of evangelical Christianity. To present their ideas to government officials, they used an annual petition drive. They personally presented their first petition, protesting white encroachment in the Indian Territory and signed by 13,000 individuals from fifteen states, to President Hayes at the White House in February 1880. Dawes presented their 1881 petition, with 50,000 signatures, and the 1882 petition, with 100,000 signatures, to the Senate. The day before Dawes delivered the 1881 petition, Helen Hunt Jackson gave each congressman a copy of *A Century of Dishonor,* which included a chapter on the Poncas. The 1882 petition called for a departure from the usual government treatment of the Indians, advocating maintenance of all treaties, establishment of schools, recognition of Indian legal rights, and the granting of one hundred sixty acres in severalty to reservation Indians—land that would be inalienable for twenty years. This petition prompted Dawes to remark that the government's new Indian policy "was born of and nursed by the Women's National Indian Association."[31] The Dawes Severalty Act of 1887 would include the concept of allotment in severalty promoted by the women of WNIA. The idea of individual land holdings, of course, was not original with the WNIA but their annual petitions drives pushing the concept made it more acceptable to reformers.

Like the WNIA, the male-dominated Indian Rights Association (IRA), founded in late 1882, initially had not been involved in the Ponca controversy. But its members too became interested in the Poncas' condition in subsequent years. In 1888 Charles Cornelius Painter, the organization's lobbyist, visited the Ponca Agency in Indian Territory on an investigative tour. During their conference with Painter, the Poncas presented him with a long list of grievances. They complained about the agency personnel but were especially critical of their children's school. After a personal visit to the school, Painter agreed, describing it as "very poor indeed."[32] Thus, despite the intensity of the reform movement on their behalf, improved living conditions for the Poncas were still long in coming.

A final legacy of Standing Bear was the publication of several Indian-related histories. In addition to books by Tibbles, several others were written by individuals who were involved with the Poncas. William Justin Harsha, pastor of the Omaha First Presbyterian Church and member of the Omaha Ponca Relief Committee, wrote two books. The first, *Ploughed Under: The Story of an Indian Chief* (1881), was severely criticized by Jackson, who noted that it was "a great pity that the first man who has undertaken to make a novel on the Indian question, should have made such a bad one."[33] Harsha's second book was *A Timid Brave: The Story of an Indian Uprising* (1886). In addition, *Omaha and Ponka Letters,* by James Owen Dorsey, an Episcopal minister, was published in 1891 as a bulletin of the Bureau of American Ethnology.[34] Dorsey spent two years among the Omahas working on a philological study of their language and, during the Ponca crisis, served as interpreter.

When the saga of the Poncas is told and when the tale of their friends and foes is recounted, all the incidents, events, and people involved relate in one way or another to one person, Standing Bear, and his efforts to seek "a better way." By the latter part of the twentieth century, memory outpaced history, and Standing Bear emerged as an enduring symbol of resistance against insurmountable odds. He is honored both in his native Nebraska and in the Indian Territory. A lake in Nebraska bears his name and a bust of him adorns the Nebraska Hall of Fame in the state capitol. The Standing Bear Bridge spans the Missouri River, adjacent to his homeland. A bronze statue of him, twenty-two feet tall and weighing four thousand pounds, was created by Oreland C. Joe, a Southern Ute–Navajo artist. It rises majestically over the sixty-three-acre Standing Bear Native American Memorial Park in Ponca City, Oklahoma. Ponca City is also the headquarters of the Standing Bear Native American Foundation, which has the lofty goal of educating all Americans about Native American heritage, promoting intercultural under-standing, and enhancing Native Americans' self-worth.

* * *

On September 5, 1962, Public Law 87-629 provided for the termination of federal supervision of the Ponca Tribe in Nebraska and for the division of all tribal assets. However, late in 1990 Congress reinstated its federal rela-tionship with the Nebraska Poncas.

Notes

1. Bourke diary, 38:979–80.
2. "Hiram Price: Allotment of Land in Severalty and a Permanent Land Title," in Prucha, ed., *Americanizing the American Indians,* 89.
3. "Ponca Agency," and "Ponca Subagency," in U.S. Department of the Interior, *59th Annual Report of the Commissioner of Indian Affairs* (1890), 146. For the Sioux bill see Lake, "Standing Bear! Who?" 487–88.
4. U.S. Department of the Interior, *59th Annual Report of the Commissioner of Indian Affairs,* 192.
5. U.S. Department of the Interior, *Annual Reports of the Department of the In-terior* (1906), 320–22.
6. Ibid., 266–67; the population figure is given on page 482. Standing Bear sup-posedly encouraged intermarriage to increase the population and thus strengthen the Poncas' claim to the land. See also Wishart, *An Unspeakable Sadness,* 214–15.
7. Tibbles, *Buckskin and Blanket Days,* 236–47 (quote, 239), and Mark, *A Stranger in Her Native Land,* 49–50; Fletcher and La Flesche coauthored *The Omaha Tribe.*
8. U.S. Department of the Interior, *59th Annual Report of the Commissioner of Indian Affairs,* 146.
9. D. J. M. Wood, Ponca, Pawnee, Otoe and Oakland Agency, Indian Territory to Hon. Thomas Jefferson Morgan, Commissioner of Indian Affairs, Washington, D.C. May 21, 1890, Oklahoma Historical Society, Pawnee Agency (PA 17), Letter-press Book—Ponca Agency, vol. 14, 282–83.

10. Interview with Standing Bear outlined in office letter dated June 21, 1890, and mailed to Washington, D.C. Sam Compton witnessed the interview and conveyed its contents to Agent Wood. Pawnee Agency (PA 17), Letterpress Book—Ponca Agency, vol. 14, 478–79; see also U.S. Department of the Interior, *59th Annual Report of the Commissioner of Indian Affairs*, 193.

11. "One Case Where Carl Schurz Was Not on the Side of Human Liberty," *New York Times*, May 27, 1906, part 3 of Sunday edition, 7.

12. Ibid.

13. Peter Le Claire to Marvin Kivett, December 11, 1951, and *Research Report on: Grave of Standing Bear*, February 15, 1952, both items in the Standing Bear File, Nebraska State Historical Society. For Standing Bear's obituary, see *New York Times*, September 6, 1908, 9. The Indian Reorganization Act, passed in 1934 during the administration of Franklin Delano Roosevelt, is often called the Indian New Deal. The legislation, among other provisions, provided for the end of allotment and the establishment of tribal governments.

14. Dawes worked closely with the recently established WNIA. In 1885, for example, after visiting Round Valley, California, he suggested that it establish one of its missions there. This was done. See Mathes, *Helen Hunt Jackson and Her Indian Reform Legacy*, 12, 17.

15. Carlson, *Indians, Bureaucrats, and Land*, 4.

16. "General Allotment Act," in Prucha, ed., *Documents of United States Indian Policy*, 174.

17. Although no biography or monograph examining Dawes's role as a leading figure in Indian affairs has yet been written, several books devote careful attention to his involvement with the Dawes Act. See for example, Otis, *The Dawes Act*. Otis provides a detailed account of the law, its effect, and the motives behind it. A careful perusal also indicates Dawes's shifting views on severalty and the legislation bearing his name. Otis's volume was first published in 1934 as a government document; Francis Paul Prucha edited the 1973 edition and wrote an explanatory introduction. For more of Prucha's analysis see "Allotment of Lands in Severalty," chapter 8 of his *American Indian Policy in Crisis*, and "Severalty, Law, and Citizenship," chapter 26 of his *The Great Father*, 659–86. See also Washburn, *The Assault on Indian Tribalism*. Washburn, in his lengthy introduction to that volume of documents, devotes attention to Dawes's shifting views on the question of allotment.

18. Welch, *George Frisbee Hoar*, 188.

19. For Hoar's interest in moral reform as a senator see his *Autobiography of Seventy Years*, vol. 2, chapters 29 and 33. See also Welch, *George Frisbee Hoar*.

20. See Long, *America of Yesterday*. The years in which he was active in the affairs of the Boston Indian Committee are the years in which, owing to the pressures of his office and the declining health of his wife, Long devoted no attention to maintaining his diary. For his revived interest see "Robbery of the Indian Charged," *Boston Herald*, February 22, 1912, 1. We thank Professor Henry Fritz for calling this news item to our attention.

21. Every autumn, beginning in 1883, "friends of the Indians" gathered at a resort hotel on Lake Mohonk, near New Paltz, New York, to discuss Indian reform. The conference host was Albert K. Smiley, a Quaker schoolteacher, who along with his brother Alfred purchased the lakefront property in 1869. Smiley, appointed to the Board of Indian Commissioners in 1879, believed that board meetings were too short and offered his resort for more lengthy discussion. Congressmen, reformers, philanthropists, government officials, clergymen, and editors of leading eastern newspapers, all carefully selected to unite the best minds, became a dominant force in formulating Indian policy for the next three decades. See Burgess, "The Lake Mohonk Conference on the Indian."

22. Hoogenboom, *Rutherford B. Hayes,* 540 (quote). Hogenboom's book is the best biography of Hayes. See chapters 27 and 28 and the afterword for Hayes's reform interests. Volumes 4 and 5 of Hayes, *Diary and Letters,* cover the postpresidential years.

23. A basic source for information about Tibbles and Susette after the Ponca controversy is his autobiography, beginning with chapter 25, "Guests of the Ponca Tribe." Francis Paul Prucha in his introduction to the Lakeside Classic edition, published in Chicago by R. R. Donnelley and Sons in 1985, reviewed Tibbles's career and the reception of his autobiography within a carefully documented historical perspective. The Lavender quote can be found on pp. 49–50. The publisher's 1957 preface to *Buckskin and Blanket Days* provides a succinct outline of Tibbles's career. It appears in the paperback edition, first published in 1969 by the University of Nebraska Press. For more on Susette see Mathes, "Iron Eye's Daughters," 135–52.

24. Szasz, ed., *Between Indian and White Worlds,* 138.

25. Jackson, *A Century of Dishonor,* 31.

26. Mathes, "The California Mission Indian Commission," 339–58.

27. Porter, *Paper Medicine Man,* 69. Another, more distant example was that of Elaine Goodale, teacher, author, and Indian school superintendent on the Sioux reservation. Although not directly influenced by Standing Bear and the Poncas, she was deeply affected by Jackson's *Ramona,* which she reviewed in 1885 as editor of the new Indian Department of the *Southern Workman,* the journal published by Hampton Normal and Industrial Institute. Goodale later married a Santee Sioux physician, Charles Eastman, whom she had met shortly after Wounded Knee, and collaborated with him on numerous Indian-related books. See Alexander, "Finding Oneself through a Cause," 13–14.

28. "Records of the Indian Treaty Keeping and Protective Association from Dec. 1880," Museum of the American Indian Library, Huntington Free Library and Reading Room, Bronx, New York, 13, 16. The association went through numerous name changes.

29. *Fourth Annual Report of the Women's National Indian Association* (Philadelphia, 1884), 33.

30. *The Indian's Friend* 10, no. 3 (November 1897): 2. *The Indian's Friend* was the association's monthly newsletter.

31. *The Indian's Friend* 9, no. 8 (April 1897): 2 (quote). For Jackson see *The Indian's Friend* 9, no. 2 (October 1896): 2.

32. Painter, *The Condition of Affairs,* 9. For a detailed history of the work of the IRA see Hagan, *The Indian Rights Association.*

33. A copy of this letter, written on February 11, 1881, to Joseph Benson Gilder, cofounder with his sister of the weekly *Critic,* can be found in Jackson, *The Indian Reform Letters,* 177–78.

34. These letters, dictated in the summer of 1879 by Omaha leaders, including Joseph La Flesche, and translated by Dorsey, were supportive of Tibbles's work on behalf of the Poncas. Dorsey became an ethnologist at the Bureau of Ethnology in 1879.

BIBLIOGRAPHY

Government Documents

Congressional Globe. 1866.

Congressional Record
  46th Congress, 3d Session, January 24, 1881
  46th Congress, 3d Session, January 31, 1881
  46th Congress, 3d Session, February 11, 1881
  46th Congress, 3d Session, March 3, 1881

Eleventh Annual Report of the Board of Indian Commissioners for the Year 1879. Washington, D.C.: Government Printing Office, 1880.

Howard, James H. *The Ponca Tribe.* Bureau of American Ethnology, Bulletin No. 195. Washington, D.C.: U.S. Government Printing Office, 1965.

Report of the Board of Indian Commissioners. Washington, D.C.: Government Printing Office, 1885.

United States. Congress. House of Representatives.
  Report [to Accompany Bill H.R. 6332]. 45th Cong., 3d sess., 1879. H. Rept. 107.
  Report of the Secretary of the Interior. 45th Cong., 2d sess., 1878. H. Rept. 1. Washington, D.C.: Government Printing Office, 1878.

United States. Congress. Senate.
  Alleged Killing by Soldiers of Big Snake, a Chief Man of the Poncas. 46th Cong., 3d sess., 1881. S. Ex. Doc. 14. Serial 1941.
  Report of Special Commission to the Poncas. 46th Cong., 3d sess., 1881. S. Ex. Doc. 30. Serial 1941.
  Testimony before the Select Senate Committee . . . as to the Removal and Situation of the Ponca Indian. 46th Cong., 3d sess., 1881. S. Misc. Doc. 49. Serial 1944.
  Testimony Relating to the Removal of the Ponca Indians. 46th Cong., 2d sess., 1880. S. Rept. 670. Serial 1898.

United States. Department of the Interior.

    Annual Report of the Secretary of the Interior. Washington, D.C.: Government Printing Office, 1876, 1877.

    Annual Reports of the Department of the Interior, 1906. Washington, D.C.: Government Printing Office, 1907.

    59th Annual Report of the Commissioner of Indian Affairs to the Secretary of the Interior for the year 1890. Washington, D.C.: Government Printing Office, 1890.

    Office of Indian Affairs. *Annual Report of the Commissioner of Indian Affairs to the Secretary of the Interior for the Year.* Washington, D.C.: Government Printing Office, 1876–1879, 1881, 1890.

    United States Statutes at Large.

Manuscript Collections and Archival Sources

Bourke, John Gregory. Diary. Library of the United States Military Academy, West Point, New York. (Microfilm consulted.)

Clarkson, Robert Harper. Diaries, 1846–84. Nebraska State Historical Society, Lincoln, Nebraska.

Dawes, Henry L. Papers. Library of Congress. Washington, D.C.

Dundy, Elmer. Papers. Nebraska State Historical Society, Lincoln, Nebraska.

Hayes, Rutherford B. Papers. Rutherford B. Hayes Presidential Center. Spiegel Grove, Fremont, Ohio.

Holmes, Oliver Wendell. Papers. Houghton Library, Harvard University, Cambridge, Massachusetts.

Jackson, Helen Hunt. Manuscripts. Huntington Library, San Marino, California.

Jackson, William Sharpless. Family Papers. Tutt Library, Colorado College, Colorado Springs.

Longfellow, Henry Wadsworth. Papers. Houghton Library, Harvard University, Cambridge, Massachusetts.

National Archives. Central Plains Region. Kansas City, Missouri.

Pawnee Agency (PA 17). Letterpress Book—Ponca Agency, Oklahoma Historical Society, Oklahoma City, Oklahoma.

Ponca Biographical File. Rutherford B. Hayes Presidential Center. Spiegel Grove, Fremont, Ohio.

Poppleton, Andrew J. "Reminiscences." Nebraska State Historical Society, Lincoln, Nebraska.

Schurz, Carl. Papers. Library of Congress. Washington, D.C.

Standing Bear File. Nebraska State Historical Society. Lincoln, Nebraska.

Warner, Charles Dudley. Collection. Watkinson Library, Trinity College, Hartford, Connecticut.

Newspapers

Boston Daily Advertiser. 1879–80
Chicago Tribune. 1879–81
Cincinnati Commercial. 1877
Colorado Springs Weekly Gazette. 1879
Hartford Daily Courant. 1879–81
New York Daily Tribune. 1879–81
New York Evening Post. 1879–81
New York Herald. 1880
New York Independent. 1879–81
New York Times. 1879–81
Niobrara Pioneer. 1877–81
Omaha Herald. 1879
Omaha Weekly Herald. 1879–80
Rocky Mountain News. 1879
Sioux City Daily Journal. 1877
Springfield Daily Republican. 1881
Yankton Daily Press and Dakotaian. 1879

Other Sources

Adams, Marian. *The Letters of Mrs. Henry Adams, 1865–1883.* Edited by Ward Thoron. Boston: Little, Brown, 1936.
Alexander, Ruth Ann. "Finding Oneself through a Cause: Elaine Goodale Eastman and Indian Reform in the 1880s." *South Dakota History* (Spring 1992): 1–37.
Andrist, Ralph K. *The Long Death: The Last Days of the Plains Indians.* New York: Macmillian, 1993.
Annual Meeting and Report of the Women's National Indian Association. Philadelphia, October 1883.
Armstrong, Virginia Irving, comp. *I Have Spoken: American History through the Voices of the Indians.* Chicago: Swallow Press, 1971.
Baird, W. David. *The Quapaw Indians: A History of the Downstream People.* Norman: University of Oklahoma Press, 1980.
Barrett, Jay Amos. "The Poncas." In *Proceedings and Collections of the Nebraska State Historical Society,* vol. 2, 12–25. Lincoln: State Journal Company Printers, 1989.
Berkhofer, Robert F., Jr. *The White Man's Indian: Images of the American Indian from Columbus to the Present.* New York: Knopf, 1978.
Billington, Ray Allen. *Land of Savagery, Land of Promise: The European Image of the American Frontier in the Nineteenth Century.* Norman: University of Oklahoma Press, 1981.
Biographical Dictionary of the United States Congress, 1774–1989. Washington, D.C.: Government Printing Office, 1989.

Bodayla, Stephen D. "'Can an Indian Vote?' Elk v. Wilkins, A Setback for Indian Citizenship." *Nebraska History* 67 (Winter 1986): 372–80.

Bourke, John Gregory. *On the Border with Crook.* Lincoln: University of Nebraska Press, 1971.

Brown, Thomas. "In Pursuit of Justice: The Ponca Indians in Indian Territory, 1877–1905." In *Oklahoma's Forgotten Indians,* edited by Robert E. Smith, 53–61. Oklahoma City: Oklahoma Historical Society, 1981.

Burgess, Larry Y. "The Lake Mohonk Conference on the Indian, 1883–1916." Ph.D. diss., Claremont Graduate School, 1972.

Burton, Jeffrey. *Indian Territory and the United States, 1866–1906.* Norman: University of Oklahoma Press, 1995.

Canfield, George F. "The Legal Position of the Indian." *American Law Review* 15 (1881): 21–37.

Carlson, Leonard A. *Indians, Bureaucrats, and Land: The Dawes Act and the Decline of Indian Farming.* Westport, Conn.: Greenwood, 1981.

Cash, Joseph, and Gerald W. Wolff. *The Ponca People.* Phoenix: Indian Tribal Series, 1975.

Clark, Blue. *Lone Wolf v. Hitchcock: Treaty Rights and Indian Law at the End of the Nineteenth Century.* Lincoln: University of Nebraska Press, 1994.

Clark, Dan E. *Samuel Jordan Kirkwood.* Iowa City: State Historical Society of Iowa, 1917.

Clark, J. Stanley. "The Killing of Big Snake." *Chronicles of Oklahoma* 49 (1971): 302–14.

———. "Ponca Publicity." *Mississippi Valley Historical Review* 29 (March 1943): 495–516.

Clark, Wahnne C. "An Indian Delegation to Washington." *Chronicles of Oklahoma* 66 (Summer 1988): 192–205.

Cleveland, Grover. *Letters of Grover Cleveland, 1850–1908.* Edited by Allan Nevins. Boston: Houghton Mifflin, 1933.

Cohen, Felix S. *Felix S. Cohen's Handbook of Federal Indian Law.* Albuquerque: University of New Mexico Press, [1971].

Commager, Henry Steele, ed. *Documents in American History.* New York: Appleton-Century-Croft, 1963.

Connelley, William E. *The Life of Preston B. Plumb.* Chicago: Browne and Howell, 1913.

The Council Fire. April, August, December, 1879.

Coward, John. "Creating the Ideal Indian: The Case of the Poncas." *Journalism History* 21 (Autumn 1995): 112–21.

———. *The Newspaper Indian: Native American Identity in the Press, 1830–1890.* Urbana: University of Illinois Press, 1999.

Cox, John E. "Soldiering in Dakota Territory in the Seventies: A Communication." *North Dakota Historical Quarterly* 6, no. 1 (October 1931): 63–65.

Crary, Margaret. *Susette La Flesche: Voice of the Omaha Indians.* New York: Hawthorne, 1973.

Davis, William T. *History of the Bench and Bar.* Vol. 1 of *Professional and Industrial History of Suffolk County, Massachusetts.* 3 vols. Boston: Boston History Company, 1894.

DeFrance, Charles Q. "Some Recollections of Thomas H. Tibbles." *Nebraska History Magazine* 13, no. 4 (1932): 239–47.

DeLoria, Vine, and David E. Wilkins. *Tribes, Treaties, and Constitutional Tribulations.* Austin: University of Texas Press, 1999.

Dictionary of America Biography. New York: Scribner's, 1930.

A Documentary History of the United States. Compiled by Richard D. Heffner. New York: New American Library, 1965.

Dorsey, James Owen. *Omaha and Ponka Letters.* Washington, D.C.: Smithsonian Institution, 1891.

Fritz, Henry E. *The Movement for Indian Assimilation, 1860–1890.* Westport, Conn.: Greenwood, 1963.

Fry, Joseph. *John Taylor Morgan and the Search for Southern Autonomy.* Knoxville: University of Tennessee Press, 1992.

Fuess, Claude M. *Carl Schurz, Reformer.* New York: Dodd, Mead, 1932.

Green, Norman Kidd. "Four Sisters: Daughters of Joseph La Flesche." *Nebraska History,* 45 (June 1964): 165–76.

———. *Iron Eye's Family: The Children of Joseph La Flesche.* Lincoln: Johnsen, 1969.

Hagan, William T. *The Indian Rights Association: The Herbert Welsh Years, 1882–1904.* Tucson: University of Arizona Press, 1985.

Harsha, William Justin. "Law for the Indians." *North American Review* 134 (March 1882): 272–92.

———. *Ploughed Under: The Story of an Indian Chief.* New York: Fords, Howard, and Hulbert, 1881.

Hayes, Rutherford Birchard. *Diary and Letters of Rutherford Birchard Hayes: Nineteenth President of the United States.* Edited by Charles Richard Williams. 5 vols. Columbus: Ohio State Archaeological and Historical Society, 1924–26.

Hays, Robert G. *A Race at Bay: New York Times Editorials on "The Indian Problem," 1860–1900.* Carbondale: Southern Illinois University Press, 1997.

Hayter, Earl. "The Ponca Removal." *North Dakota Historical Quarterly* 6 (July 1932): 263–75.

Hill, Edward E. *The Office of Indian Affairs, 1824–1880: Historical Sketches.* New York: Clearwater, 1974.

Hoar, George Frisbie. *Autobiography of Seventy Years.* 2 vols. New York: Scribner's, 1903.

Hoig, Stan. *The Sand Creek Massacre.* Norman: University of Oklahoma Press, 1961.

Hoogenboom, Ari. *Rutherford B. Hayes: Warrior and President.* Lawrence: University Press of Kansas, 1984.

Hoxie, Frederick E. *A Final Promise: The Campaign to Assimilate the Indians, 1880–1920.* Lincoln: University of Nebraska Press, 1984.

Hutton, Paul Andrew. *Phil Sheridan and His Army.* Lincoln: *University of Nebraska Press,* 1994.

The Indian Question: Report of the Committee Appointed by Hon. John D. Long. Boston: Frank Wood, 1880.

Jablow, Joseph. *Ponca Indians: Ethnology of the Ponca.* New York: Garland, 1974.

Jackson, Helen (H.H.). *A Century of Dishonor: A Sketch of the United States Government's Dealings with Some of the Indian Tribes.* Boston: Roberts, 1888. Rpt. Norman: University of Oklahoma Press, 1995.

———. *The Indian Reform Letters of Helen Hunt Jackson, 1879–1885.* Edited by Valerie Sherer Mathes. Norman: University of Oklahoma Press, 1998.

Jacobs, Kenneth. "A History of the Ponca Indians to 1882." Ph.D. diss., Texas Tech University, 1977.

James, Joseph B. *The Framing of the Fourteenth Amendment.* Urbana: University of Illinois Press, 1956.

Jefferson, Thomas. *The Writings of Thomas Jefferson.* Monticello Edition. Washington, D.C: Thomas Jefferson Memorial Association, 1904.

Jones, William A. "Toby Riddle, Catalyst: From Tragedy to Reform." *The Californians,* March/August 1989, 33–39.

Keller, Robert H., Jr. *American Protestantism and the United States Indian Policy, 1869–82.* Lincoln: University of Nebraska Press, 1983.

King, James. "'A Better Way': General George Crook and the Ponca Indians." *Nebraska History* 50 (Fall 1969): 239–56.

Kvasnicka, Robert, and Herman Viola, eds. *The Commissioners of Indian Affairs, 1824–1977.* Lincoln: University of Nebraska Press, 1979.

Lake, James A. "Standing Bear! Who?" *Nebraska Law Review* 60, no. 3 (1981): 451–503.

Lambertson, G. M. "Indian Citizenship." *American Law Review* 20 (1886): 183–93.

Larson, Robert W. *Red Cloud: Warrior-Statesman of the Lakota Sioux.* Norman: University of Oklahoma Press, 1997.

Lee, R. Alton. "Indian Citizenship and the Fourteenth Amendment." *South Dakota History* 4, no. 2 (Spring 1974): 208–11.

Letter from George Crook on Giving the Ballot to Indians. Philadelphia: Indian Rights Association, 1885.

Long, John Davis. *America of Yesterday as Reflected in the Journal of John Davis Long.* Edited by Lawrence Shaw Mayo. Boston: Atlantic Monthly Press, 1923.

Mardock, Robert Winston. *The Reformers and the American Indian.* Columbia: University of Missouri Press, 1971.

———. "Standing Bear and the Reformers." In *Indian Leaders: Oklahoma's First*

Statesmen, edited by H. Glenn Jordan and Thomas M. Holm, 101–13. Oklahoma City: Oklahoma Historical Society, 1979.

Mark, Joan. *A Stranger in Her Native Land: Alice Fletcher and the American Indians.* Lincoln: University of Nebraska Press, 1988.

Mathes, Valerie Sherer. "The California Mission Indian Commission of 1891: The Legacy of Helen Hunt Jackson." *California History* (Winter 1993/94): 339–58.

———. "Helen Hunt Jackson and the Campaign for Ponca Restitution, 1880–1881." *South Dakota History* 17 (Spring 1987): 23–42.

———. *Helen Hunt Jackson and Her Indian Reform Legacy.* Austin: University of Texas Press, 1990. Rpt., Norman: University of Oklahoma Press, 1997.

———. "Helen Hunt Jackson and the Ponca Controversy." *Montana, the Magazine of Western History* 39 (Winter 1989): 42–53.

———. "Iron Eye's Daughters: Susette and Susan La Flesche, Nineteenth-Century Indian Reformers." In *By Grit and Grace: Eleven Women Who Shaped the American West,* edited by Glenda Riley and Richard Etulain, 135–52. Golden, Colo.: Fulcrum, 1997.

———. "Nineteenth-Century Women and Reform: The Women's National Indian Association." *American Indian Quarterly* 14 (Winter 1990): 1–18.

———. "Ponca Chief Standing Bear: Catalyst for Indian Reform." *South Dakota History* 30 (Fall 2000): 249–76.

Milner, Clyde A., II. *With Good Intentions: Quaker Work among the Pawnees, Otos, and Omahas in the 1870s.* Lincoln: University of Nebraska Press, 1982.

Monnett, John H. *Tell Them We Are Going Home: The Odyssey of the Northern Cheyennes.* Norman: University of Oklahoma Press, 2001.

Morton, J. Sterling. *Illustrated History of Nebraska.* Vol. 2. Lincoln: Jacob North, 1906.

Mulhair, Charles. *Ponca Agency.* Niobrara, Neb.: Charles Mulhair, 1992.

Nichols, David A. *Lincoln and the Indians: Civil War Policy and Politics.* Urbana: University of Illinois Press, 2000.

Nicklason, Fred H. "The Early Career of Henry L. Dawes, 1816–1871." Ph.D. diss., Yale University, 1967.

Niobrara Centennial: 1856–1956. Niobrara, Neb.: Niobrara Bicentennial Committee, 1976.

Osborne, Newell Yost. *A Select School: The History of Mount Union College.* Alliance, Ohio: Mount Union College, 1967.

Otis, Delos Sacket. *The Dawes Act and the Allotment of Indian Lands.* Norman: University of Oklahoma Press, 1973.

Painter, Charles Cornelius. *The Condition of Affairs in Indian Territory and California* Philadelphia: Office of the Indian Rights Association, 1888.

Parkman, Francis. *Letters of Francis Parkman.* Edited by Wilbur R. Jacobs. Norman: University of Oklahoma Press, 1960.

Parks, Joseph Howard. *Joseph E. Brown of Georgia.* Baton Rouge: Louisiana State University Press, 1977.

Phillips, George H. "The Indian Ring in Dakota Territory, 1870–1890." *South Dakota History* 2 (Fall 1972): 345–76.

Porter, Joseph C. *Paper Medicine Man: John Gregory Bourke and the American West.* Norman: University of Oklahoma Press, 1986.

Price, David H. "The Public Life of Elmer S. Dundy, 1857–1896." M.A. thesis, University of Nebraska at Omaha, 1971.

Priest, Loring Benson. *Uncle Sam's Stepchildren: The Reformation of United States Indian Policy, 1865–1887.* Lincoln: University of Nebraska Press, 1969.

Prucha, Francis Paul. *American Indian Policy in Crisis: Christian Reformers and the Indian, 1865–1900.* Norman: University of Oklahoma Press, 1976.

———. *American Indian Treaties: The History of a Political Anomaly.* Berkeley: University of California Press, 1994.

———. *The Great Father: The United States Government and the American Indians.* 2 vols. Lincoln: University of Nebraska Press, 1984.

———. "Historical Introduction." In Thomas H. Tibbles, *Buckskin and Blanket Days,* xxiii–li. Classic Edition. Chicago: Lakeside Press, 1985.

———, ed. *Americanizing the American Indians: Writings by the "Friends of the Indians," 1880–1900.* Cambridge: Harvard University Press, 1973.

———. *Documents of United States Indian Policy.* Lincoln: University of Nebraska Press, 1990.

Richardson, James D., ed. *A Compilation of Messages and Papers of the Presidents.* Vols. 7–8. Washington, D.C.: Government Printing Office, 1898.

Robinson, Charles M., III. *General Crook and the Western Frontier.* Norman: University of Oklahoma Press, 2001.

Savage, James, and John Bell. *History of the City of Omaha, Nebraska.* New York: Mansells, 1894.

Schmitz, Neil. *White Robe's Dilemma: Tribal History in American Literature.* Amherst: University of Massachusetts Press, 2001.

Schurz, Carl. "Present Aspects of the Indian Problem." *North American Review* 133 (July 1881): 1–24.

———. *Speeches, Correspondence and Political Papers of Carl Schurz.* Edited by Frederic Bancroft. Vol. 3. New York: Putnam, 1913.

Secretary Schurz: Reply of the Boston Committee. Boston: Frank Wood, 1881.

Seymour, Flora Warren. *Indians Agents of the Old Frontier.* New York: D. Appleton Century, 1941.

Shattuck, Petra T., and Jill Nogren. *Partial Justice: Federal Indian Law in a Liberal Constitutional System.* Providence, R.I.: Berg, 1991.

Sheldon, Addison Erwin. *History of Nebraska.* Chicago: Lewis, 1931.

———. *Nebraska: The Land and the People.* Chicago: Lewis, 1931.

Smith, Dennis J. "Procuring a Right-of-Way: James J. Hill and Indian Reservations, 1886–1888." M.A. thesis, University of Montana, 1983.

Smith, Michael T. "The History of Indian Citizenship." *Great Plains Journal* (Fall 1970): 25–35.

Sorenson, Alfred. *The Story of Omaha from the Pioneer Days to the Present Time.* Omaha: National, 1923.

Szasz, Margaret Connell, ed. *Between Indian and White Worlds: The Cultural Broker.* Norman: University of Oklahoma Press, 1994.

Tibbles, Thomas Henry. "Anecdotes of Standing Bear." *Nebraska History Magazine* 13 (October–December 1932): 271–76.

———. *Buckskin and Blanket Days: Memoirs of a Friend of the Indians.* Lincoln: University of Nebraska Press, 1969.

———. *The Ponca Chiefs: An Account of the Trial of Standing Bear.* Lincoln: University of Nebraska Press, 1972.

———. *Western Men Defended: Speech of Mr. T. H. Tibbles.* Boston: Lockwood, Brooks, 1880.

Trefousse, Hans L. *Carl Schurz: A Biography.* Knoxville: University of Tennessee Press, 1982.

Utley, Robert M. "The Celebrated Peace Policy of General Grant." In *American Indian Past and Present,* edited by Roger L. Nichols and George R. Adams, 183–99. Waltham, Mass.: Xerox College Publishing, 1971.

———. *Frontier Regulars: The United States Army and the Indian, 1866–1891.* New York: Macmillan, 1973.

Viola, Herman J. *Diplomats in Buckskins: A History of Indian Delegations in Washington City.* Washington, D.C.: Smithsonian Institution Press, 1981.

Visit of the Hon. Carl Schurz to Boston: March 1881. Boston: John Wilson, 1881.

Wakeley, Arthur C., ed. *Omaha: The Gate City and Douglas County, Nebraska.* Vol. 2. Chicago: S. J. Clarke, 1917.

Washburn, Wilcomb E. *The Assault on Indian Tribalism: The General Allotment Law.* Philadelphia: Lippincott, 1975.

Weeks, Philip. "Humanity and Reform: Indian Policy and the Hayes Presidency." In *The American Indian Experience: A Profile, 1524 to the Present,* edited by Philip Weeks, 174–88. Arlington Heights, Ill.: Forum Press, 1988.

Welch, Richard E. *George Frisbie Hoar and the Half-Breed Republicans.* Cambridge, Mass.: Harvard University Press, 1971.

Williams, Charles Richard. *The Life of Rutherford Birchard Hayes.* Columbus: Ohio State Archeological and Historical Society, 1928.

Wilson, Dorothy Clarke. *Bright Eyes: The Story of Susette La Flesche, an Omaha Indian.* New York: McGraw-Hill, 1974.

Wishart, David. *An Unspeakable Sadness: The Dispossession of the Nebraska Indians.* Lincoln: University of Nebraska Press, 1994.

Zanjani, Sally. *Sarah Winnemucca.* Lincoln: University of Nebraska Press, 2001.

Zhu, Liping. "'A Chinaman's Chance' on the Rocky Mountain Mining Frontier." *Montana: The Magazine of Western History* 45, no. 4 (Autumn/Winter 1995): 36–51.

Zimmerman, Charles Leroy. *White Eagle: Chief of the Poncas.* Harrisburg, Pa.: Telegraph Press, 1941.

INDEX

Northern Ponca Indians (Standing Bear and followers on old Niobrara Reservation), 96, 119, 136–38, 141, 150, 155–56, 165–66, 177, 181–84

Omaha, Nebraska, 1, 30, 32, 52, 56, 71, 83, 89, 122, 141, 169, 183, 187
Omaha Daily Herald, 51, 54, 65, 72, 74, 175, 187
Omaha Indians, 13, 37, 53, 58, 63, 65, 72–73, 84, 93, 183, 188, 190; Omaha Reservation and Agency, 51–53, 57–58, 67–68, 72, 121, 175; Poncas to move in with, 16–18, 23, 57, 120–21, 123; sell Ponca land, 14; Standing Bear and followers seek refuge with, 48–49, 64, 67–68, 175
Omaha Ponca Relief Committee (Ponca Relief Committee), 5, 11, 53, 56, 73–74, 83, 85–86, 89, 96, 125, 127, 132–33, 145, 169, 176, 190
Osage Indians, 13, 21, 27; Osage Agency and Reservation, 120; Osage mission, 35; Poncas to live with, 19, 39
Otoe Reservation, 22–23, 35, 37, 55; Otoe agent, 23

Paddock, Algernon S., 31, 157
Parkman, Francis, 164
Pawnee Indians, 27n, 30, 50, 62n, 189
Peace Commission, 10
Phillips, Wendell, 75–76, 81n, 97
Plessy v. Ferguson, 169
Ploughed Under (novel), 168, 190
Plumb, Preston B., 120
Pollock, William J., 125–26, 182
The Ponca Chiefs: An Indian's Attempt to Appeal from the Tomahawk to the Courts, 187; reviewed by Helen Hunt Jackson, 93
Ponca City, Oklahoma, 1
Ponca Indian Committee, 75, 88, 100n
Ponca Indians, 1, 5, 9, 11–23, 29–40, 45–58, 63–77, 85, 89–94, 96–97, 109, 113–27, 131, 133–44, 149, 157, 162–69, 175–79, 181–90; agency, 15, 18, 29–30, 36, 140; delegation of chiefs to the Indian Territory, 19–22, 87, 121; eastern lecture tour of, 3, 83–98; relief bill for,

46, 119, 122–23; removed to Quapaw Reservation, 1, 3, 11, 15, 17–20, 22, 29–40, 55, 57, 64, 74, 90, 92, 97, 113–14, 117, 119–20, 123, 126, 139, 149, 152, 156–57, 176–77, 186, 188; second removal of, 39–40, 45, 115; villages of, raided by Lakotas, 13, 15–18
Ponca Relief Committee. *See* Omaha Ponca Relief Committee
Ponca Tribe of Indians v. Makh-pi-ah-lu-tah or Red Cloud, 131
Poppleton, Andrew Jackson, 4, 55, 57, 71, 74, 80n, 84, 131, 133, 168–69; brief biography of, 56; former mayor of Omaha, 4; role in Standing Bear's trial, 64–66
Prairie Flower, death of, 37, 85
Price, Hiram, 165–66, 172n, 181
Prince, Frederick Octavius, 75, 86–87, 89–90, 96
Prucha, Francis Paul, 9

Quaker Policy, 12
Quapaw Indians, 13, 20, 22, 28n, 39, 53; agency, 22, 54
Quapaw Reservation, Poncas removed to, 11, 35, 38, 40, 48, 46, 115

Red Cloud, 10, 70, 115, 83, 98n, 131, 145n
Red River War, 2, 109
Reid, Whitelaw, 91–92, 98
Riggs, Rev. Alfred L., 30, 33, 73, 140, 150, 157
Rocky Mountain News, 70–71
Roosevelt, Theodore, 1

Sand Creek Massacre, 10, 12, 102n
Santee Sioux Indians, 41n, 53, 150; agency, 33, 73, 182; mission, 20; reservation, 183
Saunders, Alvin, 53, 157, 165, 172n
Schurz, Carl, 3, 4, 30–31, 45–46, 49–50, 57, 69, 73, 76, 83, 88, 90, 92–93, 97–98, 111, 113–27, 132, 134–35, 137, 139, 141–42, 144–45, 149–51, 158, 162–67, 169, 175–78, 181–82, 184–86; annual reports of, 90, 96, 113–15, 149; appears before Senate Select Committee, 122, 132, 134–35, 141–44; brief biography of,

VALERIE SHERER MATHES is a professor of history at the City College of San Francisco. She is the editor of *The Indian Reform Letters of Helen Hunt Jackson, 1879–1885* and the author of *Helen Hunt Jackson and Her Indian Reform Legacy.*

RICHARD LOWITT is professor emeritus of history at the University of Oklahoma. He is the author of a number of books, including a three-volume biography of George W. Norris, and is the coeditor of *One Third of a Nation.*

The University of Illinois Press
is a founding member of the
Association of American University Presses.

Composed in 10/13 Sabon
by Jim Proefrock
at the University of Illinois Press
Designed by Dennis Roberts
Manufactured by Thomson-Shore, Inc.

University of Illinois Press
1325 South Oak Street
Champaign, IL 61820-6903
www.press.uillinois.edu